Oil and Gas in Trinidad and Tobago

Roger Hosein

Oil and Gas in Trinidad and Tobago

Managing the Resource Curse in a Small Petroleum-Exporting Economy

palgrave
macmillan

Roger Hosein
Department of Economics
The University of the West Indies
St Augustine, Trinidad and Tobago

ISBN 978-3-030-77668-8 ISBN 978-3-030-77669-5 (eBook)
https://doi.org/10.1007/978-3-030-77669-5

This Palgrave Macmillan imprint is published by the registered company Springer Nature Switzerland AG
The registered company address is: Gewerbestrasse 11, 6330 Cham, Switzerland

To Amartya who fought the odds, Johansen who climbed the mountain and Amreeta who played the music.

Foreword

This book by Dr. Roger Hosein, Senior Lecturer in Economics at the University of the West Indies, is well worth reading carefully.

Dr. Hosein likes to see numbers and numerical value of things; it is only then that he is comfortable enough to draw conclusions—on the basis of statistical data and established fact. This book is true to his preferred methodology and approach, and gives the reader an insight as to why Dr. Hosein is regarded as an objective public intellectual when he comments on matters of political economy in Trinidad and Tobago and the region. He is not afraid to probe hard issues in detail, and, whatever the facts and statistics tell him, he will articulate clearly, unequivocally. He speaks truth to power when he needs to and always, he provides possible solutions and recommendations.

This book is a case study on the phenomenon of Dutch Disease in the history and experience of Trinidad and Tobago, a small petroleum producing nation, where for decades the petroleum industry has been responsible for 80% of the country's exports and has contributed 45% of Trinidad and Tobago's GDP and diversification of the country's production base, export earnings and international markets has proved to be elusive, while restructuring of its industrial base to transform its output of products, has proved to be a formidable challenge.

This is the dilemma that Dr. Hosein researches, examines, outlines, analyzes and draws conclusions on. And it is on the basis of this analysis and conclusions drawn, that a way forward, out of the Dutch Disease dilemma, for Trinidad and Tobago is recommended.

No one, amongst contemporary economists has so doggedly pursued matters of the Trinidad and Tobago economy as has Dr. Hosein. Dr. Hosein has also in the recent past, written about Dutch Disease as a theoretical construct and has examined the evolution and performance of the Trinidad and Tobago economy against that background. It is for this reason that students of economics, readers with interest in Trinidad and Tobago, of Caricom countries, and those with a practical interest in the manner in which the Dutch Disease dilemma unfolds in a small economy and how successive policy decisions have had some value but failed in comprehensively addressing the challenge and those interested in engaging policy interventions that can make a decisive difference—all of these interested parties can benefit immensely from reading this book and reflecting on the research findings, analysis, thoughts and ideas contained in "Managing The Resource Curse In a Small Petroleum Exporting Economy."

The first four chapters outline the history of oil production, oil refining, production of natural gas and the development of the petrochemical sector. These alone are a source of enrichment. Chapters which follow address the Dutch Disease reality and explore ways and means of evolving successfully from the Dutch Disease trap.

The book concludes that fossil fuel represents a sunset industry and that Trinidad and Tobago must shift gears to become a renewable energy player as it embraces diversification, structural industrial shift and economic transformation to become a more competitive and resilient economy.

This book is packed with statistics and charts that establish facts and illustrate trends. These are the anchors on which the narrative is built. The narrative is focused on recounting the pertinent facts of history, making sense of the numbers, identifying the big picture problem and positing possible solutions and action interventions.

Ultimately this book is illustrating the journey that has led to this point where transformation of the economy has become an urgent necessity and it suggests ways and means of how transformation might be achieved.

In this sense it is a caring book about sustainable development solutions for a one product middle income country that needs to transform its economy to maintain its standard of living, to continue to grow and to achieve productivity and prosperity with greater equity and more inclusion.

Dr. Hosein, in this book, is very strong in theory. In looking at the past he tries to understand what theoretical models may have influenced policy action, in analyzing problems he tries to understand what theoretical models might lead to solutions and in proposing solutions he tries to rationalize them in the context of viable economic models.

For him there is a necessary link between, economic theory and policy making; good policy and bad policy, and policy results depend on execution which can bring success or failure and can determine economic progress, stagnation or regress.

This is a book of great academic strength and deep analysis but it is also a practical book on what has been done right and wrong, what can be done better and what it makes practical sense to do in the present and immediate future. Theory, policy, strategy, practice and correction converge in this very readable book. The book is easily digestible too, written as it is in short spurts of information, which build up to each coherent chapter which links with other chapters in the book to form a thesis, tell a story and make an argument.

At the heart of this book as recurrent themes are, diversification, economic restructuring and transformation of the Trinidad and Tobago economy. These are underscored by some persistent concerns: export diversification and expansion, foreign exchange earnings, labour market responsiveness, resilience and productivity and the reforms necessary for a more competitive economy in which trade and investment can flourish and development can take off and become sustainable. In this regard the role of tertiary education and the strategic value of recent Venezuelan migration become important concerns examined here.

"Managing the Resource Curse in a Small Petroleum Exporting Economy" is a timely book on the Trinidad and Tobago economy, its historical evolution, its challenges, dilemmas, the pressing need for economic restructuring and transformation, and possible avenues of solutions.

Other books have been written on the Trinidad and Tobago economy and on the Petroleum industry in Trinidad and Tobago, but Dr. Hosein's book will remain a significant contribution.

This book does not tell anyones story, it does not justify any action or cast blame on any decisions. It does not begin with a premise. It simply tells the story of Trinidad and Tobago's economic history of the Energy sector and demonstrates on the basis of facts and statistics the point to which that economic history has led the economy of the country, Trinidad and Tobago and the dilemma that this poses for sustainable development, which requires resolution and urgent, concerted action on policy, strategy and implementation.

The linking of economic theory, policy and results add to the intellectual depth of the work and grounds practical solutions advocated in sound economic thinking.

Dr. Roger Hosein has written an important book here, of great value to an understanding of the economic challenges and opportunities of a small energy dependent economy such as Trinidad and Tobago. This is a good book which provides the evidence-based context for problem identification, deep analysis and solution finding.

A good piece of work, in my view, depends on the quality of evidence presented, the meaningfulness of the analysis conducted, the fundamental questions asked, the problem or dilemma identified, the logical and/or creative solutions posited and the theoretical framework that gives validity for these. If I am correct then this book represents a valuable piece of academic work and a sound intellectual contribution on Trinidad and Tobago with practical applications value.

It is my hope that many students, policy makers, economic thinkers and sustainable development advocates and anyone interested in development issues, will read it.

Bhoendradatt Tewarie
Former Minister of Planning and Sustainable Development and
Retired Principal, UWI
St Augustine, Trinidad and Tobago

Contents

Abbreviations

ATF	Aviation Turbine Fuels
BP	British Petroleum
Bpd	Barrels per Day
BT	Booming Tradable Sector
CAB	Current Account Balance
CARICOM	Caribbean Community
CBTT	Central Bank of Trinidad and Tobago
CEPEP	Community-Based Environmental Protection and Enhancement Programme
CSO	Central Statistical Office
CSP	Community and Social Personal
CSR	Corporate Social Responsibility
CXC	Caribbean Examinations Council
DfD	Dollar for Dollar
DSE	Dynamic Shift Share
FDI	Foreign Direct Investment
FO/LO	Farm-out/Lease-out Program
GARCH	Generalized Auto Regressive Conditional Heteroscedasticity
GATE	Government Assistance for Tuition Expenses Programme
GCI	Global Competitiveness Index
GDP	Gross Domestic Product
GORTT	Government of the Republic of Trinidad and Tobago
H/O	Heckscher Ohlin Theorem
HH	Henry Hub
HHI	Hirschman-Herfindahl Index
HSF	Heritage Stabilisation Fund

ICRG	International Country Risk Guide
IDB	Inter-American Development Bank's
IDC	Industrial Development Corporation
IIP	Intra Industry Productivity
IPSC	Incremental Production Service Contract
ISCOTT	Iron and Steel Company of Trinidad and Tobago
ISRF	Interim Revenue Stabilization
LNG	Liquefied Natural Gas
LPG	Liquefied Petroleum Gas
MDGs	Millennium Development Goals
MEEA	Ministry of Energy and Energy Affairs
MIPED	Mayaro Initiative for Private Enterprises Development
MNC	Multi-National Corporation
MSEs	Micro and Small Enterprises
MSTTE	Ministry of Science, Technology and Tertiary level Education
NBT	Non-Booming Tradable Sector
NEC	National Energy Corporation
NGC	National Gas Company
NGOs	Non-Governmental Organisations
NT	Non-Tradable Sector
OECD	Organisation for Economic Co-operation and Development
OPEC	Organization of Petroleum Exporting Countries
OWTU	Oilfield and Workers Trade Union
PF	Point Fortin
RBI	Resource Based Industrialization
RCA	Revealed Comparative Advantage Index
REER	Real Effective Exchange Rate
ROTE	Review of the Economy
R^{rme}	Resource Movement Effect
S^{e}	Spending Effect
SSE	Static Shift Share
SWF	Sovereign Wealth Funds
T	Tradable Sector
T&T/ TT	Trinidad and Tobago
T&TEC	Trinidad and Tobago Electricity Commission
TCF	Trillion Cubic Feet
TIL	Trinidad Leaseholds Limited
TPM	Transition Probability Matrix
TRINTOC	Trinidad and Tobago Oil Company
TTEC	Trinidad and Tobago Electricity Commission
U.K.	United Kingdom
UBOT	United British Oilfields of Trinidad

ULSD	Ultra-Low Sulphur Diesel Plant
UN	United Nations
UNCOMTRADE	United Nations Commodity Trade Statistics Database
UNCTAD	United Nations Conference on Trade and Development
UNDP	United Nations Development Programme
URP	Unemployment Relief Programme
USA/US	United States of America
UWI	University of the West Indies
VECM	Vector Error Correcting Model
WB	World Bank
WDI	World Development Indicators
WIFA	Women in Fishing Association
WTI	West Texas Intermediate
WWII	World War II

List of Figures

List of Tables

CHAPTER 1

Introduction and Overview of Study—The Challenge of Managing Oil

This book looks at the issues around managing the boom bust cycles in a small petroleum-exporting economy. The literature on the boom bust petroleum cycle is large both empirically and theoretically. This book focuses on the empirical experience of a small exporter Trinidad and Tobago and emphasizes the economic history in the crude oil production, oil refining and natural gas sector.

1.1 Purpose of the Study

Trinidad and Tobago is a country which has lived the experience of a classic case of Dutch disease, twice. This book outlines the economic history of oil and natural gas in Trinidad and Tobago, and details Trinidad and Tobago's experience with the Dutch Disease. In the context of falling reserves and in recognition of fossil fuel energy as a sunset industry, this also makes recommendations for the improvement of the country's external competitiveness and for a restructuring and transition to economic sustainability.

The purpose of this study is to provide a rich economic history of the events that shaped the petroleum sector of the T&T economy as well as to provide detailed policy suggestions as to how the economy can escape the entrapment of the bust phase of the boom bust cycle.

R. Hosein, *Oil and Gas in Trinidad and Tobago*,
https://doi.org/10.1007/978-3-030-77669-5_1

1.2 Rationale

The T&T economy has been economically stagnant since 2009. In the past it has experienced long periods of growth followed by long periods of stagnation/contraction. This book was motivated by the absence of a long wave economic analysis of the T&T economy. The IMF and a few other authors cover short periods of time and Terrence Farrell in the book and Underachieving Society covers the period 1950–2010 but this is the first attempt to cover such an extensive period and understand the various economic contours of each period.

1.3 Objective and Layout

The book targets a range of readers but particularly post graduate students and policy makers. It provides a roadmap of guidelines that can help to reduce the symptoms of the economy away from chronic Dutch Disease problems.

The book is divided into 12 chapters. The next three chapters are devoted to the history of crude oil production, refined oil output and gas production. On this basis the origin of Dutch Disease and its impact on growth and productivity are examined theoretically and empirically in Chapters 5 and 6. The latter sets the stage for investigating the role of the state in the sector, its use of energy rents in providing employment, its management of the sovereign wealth fund and its development of human capital in Chapters 7, 8 and 9 respectively. Chapters 10 and 11 tackle the policy measures to boost the non-energy and energy sectors, respectively from a competitiveness standpoint and Chapter 12 provides a summary conclusion.

More specifically, this chapter traces the economic history of the crude oil sector from the time crude oil was discovered to the present. The discussions in this chapter cover where available, the trends and issues with regards to crude oil prices, production, number of wells drilled, employment, depth drilled, export revenues and economic output associated with the petroleum sector.

Chapter 2 outlines the economic trends in the oil refining sector with the analysis decomposed into 3 distinct periods: the period before Texaco (1910–1955), the period of Texaco (1956–1985) and the period after Texaco (1986 to the present). The planned reopening of the refinery is discussed (the refinery was closed in November 2018) and it emphasizes that if the refinery is reopened, it should not be under state ownership. Chapter 4 focuses on natural gas and its economic history in T&T.

Chapter 5 focuses on the resource curse with a specific focus on petroleum products. The chapter also discusses the theoretical outlines of the Dutch Disease and its relationship to premature deindustrialization as well as the impact of the Dutch Disease on sectoral trade performance. The chapter also assesses the long-term impact of the Dutch Disease on economic growth. Chapter 6 focuses on the relationship amongst the Dutch Disease, the Baumol Cost Disease and Labor Productivity. This chapter establishes that in the context of the Dutch Disease an asymptotic stagnancy sets into economy and the growth of the slowest growing (services) sector that compromises the overall growth of the economy. This is the Classic Baumol Cost Disease, dilemma. Chapter 6 focuses on resource-based industrialization on the context of petrochemical production. This chapter outlines the discussion associated with the state as an entrepreneur in T&T, getting the petrochemical sector ball moving. It then elaborates on the impetus of the Black Power Movement for changes in the energy sector as relates to petrochemicals. After discussing real value added in the petrochemical sector, the chapter then assesses the economic value of the country of getting into methanol blending with gasoline.

Chapter 8 looks at the available macroeconomic data and assesses the impact in the post adult suffrage era of the economy using energy rents as a starting point for the conversation. The post 1955 period is divided into the sub periods 1955–1972, 1973–1982, 1983–1993, 1994–2008 and 2009–2020. The period 1955–1972 boom is defined as pre-first boom whilst the period 1973–1982 is treated as the first petroleum. The first depression is classified as the period 1983–1993 and the second boom as the period 1994–2008. The period 2009–2020 is the current period as treated as the second depression (although the earlier part of this period was a period of stagnation).

Chapter 9 has three sections. The first section of Chapter 8 focuses on Make Work programs introduced in the T&T economy in the form of the CEPEP program. This section discusses the various Make Work programs starting from the Prime Minister's Special Work Program in the 1950s to the Development Environmental Works Program (DEWD), Labor Intensive Development Program (LIDP), Unemployment Relief Program (URP) and the Community Environmental Protection Enhancement Program (CEPEP). From the start of the CEPEP program in 2002 to the present (2020), the state dished out TT$7.4bn on this program.

Public work programs can compromise the output level of any economy in which they exist by employing workers in extremely low productive sectors. Even more if some entrepreneurs pursue rents rather than Schumpeterian innovation, this can also compromise the output level of the economy. This section frames out and calculates the welfare cost to the T&T economy imposed by CEPEP.

The second part of Chapter 9 discusses the economic merit of various modifications to the HSF program in T&T. In small capital-starved resource-rich countries, it is imperative that the government make prudent decisions regarding consumption and investment. This specific section outlines four pathways regarding the possible relationship between consumption and investment as espoused under the permanent income hypothesis, the Bird in Hand (BIH) hypothesis, the "optimal strategy" and the resource curse strategy. This section then outlines and discusses the performance of the HSF and then sets out various steps that can strengthen the mechanics of the HSF, including the adoption of a more BIH approach.

The third section of Chapter 9 addresses the deployment of the Hartwick rule in the T&T economy as relates to tertiary level education, funding. Once the boom commenced with the surge in natural gas production after 1998 and the gradual increase in the price (and production) of crude oil, the government introduced programs to support the financing of tertiary level education. These interventions whilst horizontally efficient did not respect the vertical inefficiency aspect of the situation and so some proportion of the funding was unnecessary and wasted. This chapter illustrates this vertical inefficiency and outlines an income contingent loan program to reduce some of the problems associated with the currently applied, GATE program.

Chapter 10 outlines a series of policy interventions to boost the non-energy sector, in the context of a decline in the non-energy exports from TT$48.5mn in 2013 to TT$28.5mn in 2019. The chapter focuses on several possible policy interventions, these include: (a) devaluing the currency, (b) improving the Ease of Doing Business (EODB) setting, (c) building on the Rybczynski gains from the Venezuelan immigrants, (d) deepening trading ties with the country's natural trading partner and (e) building a more private sector driven ETeCK Park arrangement. This chapter also outlines several other enabling environment changes including the need for fiscal responsibility legislation, pushing specialized economic zones, public procurement and transitioning from Central

Statistical Office to the National Statistical Institute of Trinidad and Tobago.

Chapter 11 discusses the comparative advantage, energy sector of the T&T economy and outlines several measures that could prolong the economic benefits from the sector. The chapter outlines the status of deepwater exploration and the need to continue the same. It assesses the modifications to the Supplemental Petroleum Tax (SPT) and further changes that the state should consider. It also emphasizes the need to strategically partner big producers with smaller more cost efficient and nimble producers. The importance of reopening the Petroleum refinery is emphasized. The chapter also discusses the importance of accessing cross-border gas as well as promoting a greater degree of local content activities in the sector as a whole.

Chapter 12 provides a summary of the steps that T&T or any similar small energy exporting economy should avoid, should they be blessed by an oil boom.

CHAPTER 2

Economic History of Oil Exploration and Production in T&T, 1857–2020

2.1 Introduction

In 1859, Edwin Drake found commercially usable quantities of crude oil in Titusville, Pennsylvania. Drake was employed by Seneca Oil Company when he struck oil on the 27 August 1859. Drake utilized a 'Drive Pipe' technique practiced by salt extractors to drill 3 ft. a day, until he struck oil at 69 ft. This was a defining moment in the history of crude oil production internationally and indeed came at an appropriate period of time—when sperm whale oil had begun to decline. Sperm whale oil was used principally as an illuminant in lamps and candle wax. Dvosky (2012) noted, "Back at the start of the industrial age, whale oil was used for heating, lubrication, soap, candle wax, and the processing of textiles and rope. But its true value came as a fuel source for lamps." Sperm whale oil was found to burn brighter and clearer than other whale oils without an unpleasant odor (Dolin 2007).

As the amount of sperm whales caught fell, the cost of sperm whale oil increased[1] and consequently, the cost of this illuminant was pushed beyond the reach of many consumers. In this regard, a search began for a lower priced substitute. James Young in Scotland in 1848 was the first

[1] Eaton (1866) recorded that the price of whale oil ranged from US$0.30 in 1831, US$0.63 in 1843, US$1.92 in 1866 per half gallon of oil.

R. Hosein, *Oil and Gas in Trinidad and Tobago*,
https://doi.org/10.1007/978-3-030-77669-5_2

to produce oil from bituminous shale. Young successfully distilled cannel coal at a low heat to produce bituminous shale (Scottish Engineer Hall of Fame 2014). Indeed, he noted that he could obtain several useful fluids from the slow distillation of the bituminous shale. Young was the creator of Paraffin Oil, which he later used to start a company to sell candles made from paraffin wax. By 1850, Young and his business associates, Edward Binnie, and Edward Meldrum created a business which was the first commercial oil-works in the world. This heralded the birth of the world's petrochemical industry.

As concerns Trinidad and Tobago (T&T), the 5 million hectares spanning the country including the 2000 m water depth contour is 90% made up of sedimentary rocks—the type usually associated with the presence of hydrocarbons (Tewarie and Hosein 2007; Alleyne and Stoute 2014; Boopsingh and McGuire 2014).[2] Indeed, the existence of oil was long suspected by scientists, geologists and explorers in T&T before actual exploration. Specifically, Higgins (1996, p. 1) noted that, "There is a record that huntsmen knew of the oil seeps in Guayaguayare Mayaro area and when a sample of the oil was brought to the warden in 1870 it was such a fine oil that a London chemist wrote it off as artificial."[3]

Exploration for crude oil in T&T commenced as early as 1857, when the Merrimac Oil Company of the USA drilled, what was perhaps the first successful oil well in the world, at La Brea, Trinidad. Indeed a former Chairman, of the Geological Society of Trinidad and Tobago, Dr. A.L. Down (1960) noted "The Merrimac Company, registered in 1857, made attempts to produce oil by distillation of pitch, but furthermore in the same year they drilled a well to a depth of about 280 feet, which was a much greater depth than Drake's well in Pennsylvania - and two years earlier - and produced oil therefrom. In spite of their success, the Merrimac Company went into liquidation; in all probability transportation was one of their major troubles as the discovery of oil in the United

[2] "An Assessment of the Economic Impact of Climate Change on the Energy Sector in Trinidad and Tobago".

[3] "The presence of oil and asphalt in Trinidad could not escape the observations of the visitors from Europe. San Fernando hill, the mountain of An-naparima was an obvious land fall, the approach to which, through the Boca de Serpiente, was located so close to La Brea that the early explorers could not fail to notice the pitch accumulations, which must have been of great use to those early mariners" (Penny and Lonsdale-Harris 1955).

States and the development of the shale oil industry in Scotland and elsewhere in the late 1850s resulted in the potential markets for Trinidad oil being supplied from closer sources." However, until 1906 the oil sector remained in a budding state and it was noted that "asphalt mining, or more correctly speaking asphalt digging, comprises the major portion of the mineral industry of the colony" (MEEA 1906, p. 3). (The MEEA refers to the Ministry of Energy and Energy Affairs.)

Walter Darwent played a significant role in the start-up of the oil industry in Trinidad and Tobago. Darwent was an Englishman who served in the American Civil War. Darwent came to Trinidad in 1865 to explore for oil and in 1866, he drilled a well in Aripero (South Trinidad) but abandoned it because of troublesome clays (Besson 2008a). After drilling a dry hole in San Fernando, Darwent's persistence took him back to Aripero, where he made another attempt at oil extraction and he struck oil on March 15, 1867 (Besson 2008a). He was able to get a group of local investors to pull together resources to buy drilling equipment to cut through various types of soil. He also gained funding from a local subsidiary of The West Indies Petroleum Company in the USA, The Trinidad Petroleum Company Ltd., to visit the USA to purchase materials. However, Darwent never made it to New York to purchase the much-needed new drilling equipment as he died from fever in La Brea on September 28, 1868 (Brereton 1996). When Darwent died, a shortage of entrepreneurship emerged and the industry found itself starved of vital resource inputs such as physical capital, human capital and transportation (Higgins 1996).

Two other early pioneers in the history of exploring for oil in T&T were Randolph Rust and John Lee Lum. Rust, was born in London on the 24 July 1854. In 1881, Rust came to work in Trinidad with the firm Cambell Hannays, the fore running company of Gordon Grant and Company (T&T Chamber of Industry and Commerce 2006). Before prospecting for oil in Trinidad and Tobago, Rust ventured off to British Guiana in pursuit of gold, but he contracted blackwater fever in the jungle whilst opening up the goldfields and returned to Trinidad (Trinidad and Tobago Chamber of Commerce and Industry 2006). In 1881, he met an American by the name of Henry Trowbridge, with whom he engaged in business and together they opened the firm, Rust Trowbridge and Company, which were general commission agents, merchant insurance and shipping agents, importers and exporters and wholesale dealers in provisions (Higgins 1996). In 1895, Rust visited Guayaguayare and found a 25-acre puddle of asphalt and pools of petroleum (T&T Chamber of Industry and Commerce 2006). He also stumbled upon Darwent's old well, which was flowing oil onto the forest floor in Aripero (Boopsingh and McGuire 2014).

Rust partnered with John Lee Lum, a businessman who was the owner of an adjacent property in Guayaguayare. Lee Lum provided finance for Rust's expedition and they acquired the Aripero Estate which was started by Darwent. They also obtained a concession for some 50 square miles at Mayaro/Guayaguayare (Brereton 1996). Finance was challenging and when Rust and Lee Lum's funds had dried up, they successfully pursued seed funding in Canada and the Oil Exploration Company of Canada, was so formed and began operation at Guayaguayare on May 30, 1902 (Higgins 1996). Equipment to drill in Guayaguayare was brought from Port of Spain via a coastal steamer (Besson 2008a). Jobs were obtained by the residents of Guayaguayare, a predominantly fishing and agricultural village at the time, to clear the bushes and forests for equipment and manpower. Wooden structures were set up in the Guayaguayare forests for the drillers (mainly Canadians) and by July 2, 1902, the Guayaguayare Well No. 1 struck oil. This was the dawn of a significant era. It was noted that Rust "... had fallen deeply in love with Trinidad, his adopted home and served it long and faithfully as oil pioneer, businessman, councilor, mayor of its capital city, founder of the Scout Movement, and commissioned officer of the Trinidad Light Infantry Volunteers, which he commanded during World War I" (Trinidad Guardian Newspaper 2006).[4]

This chapter provides an assessment of how the petroleum sector of the T&T economy evolved from 1857 to 2020 by tracing the evolution of several key economic activity variables including:

- the production,
- prices,

[4] In one of Rust's last public lectures, he drew attention to "the future possibilities of what now could fairly be called Trinidad's latest, but by no means least, industry—petroleum and its products." Rust went on to state "For years the pioneers of this new industry have fought an uphill battle in the face of much discouragement and many difficulties, but our faith has never failed" (cited in Randolph Rust [1854–1930], Biography).

- number of companies involved in the sector,
- number of employee,
- exports, and
- the value added by the sector (where data is available).

This chapter after a significant surveillance of the literature proceeds by dividing the discussion landscape into the following time periods: The early years until 1928, 1929 until the end of the Second World War, 1946–1972 and 1973 to the present. The early years to 1928 represents the period up to the Great Depression when the global economy including energy markets were thrown into turmoil. The period 1929–1945 represented a period of different types of turmoil motivated by the circumstances after the Great Depression and by the circumstances leading up to and during the 2nd World War. The period 1946 to 1972 is one where the global economy and energy markets progressed relatively smoothly. The period after 1972 up to the present for T&T is characterized by two boom and two bust scenarios. The first boom occurred in the period 1973–1982 followed by the first bust from 1983 to 1993. The second boom, like the first, started in 1994 with the increase in the production of natural gas and then after 1998 in the price and production of crude oil. Natural gas prices also increased until 2010. After 2010 as the production of natural gas fell the T&T economy stagnated until the present (2020).

2.2 Oil Based Economic Activity in the Period 1908 to 1928

In 1908, a paltry 37 barrels of crude oil were produced in Trinidad but by 1909, production reached 47,295 barrels. In 1917, annual production of crude oil, for the first time, crossed the 1 million marker and climbed steadily thereafter so that in 1928 production of crude oil stood at 7,684,450 barrels or 317% more than in 1919.[5] Two primal factors helped the Trinidad Oil industry grow rapidly in this era. The first was the

[5] The rapid increase in production was partly on account of TLL's successful exploitation of Forest Reserve, the conspicuous success of the drilling activity of Apex Trinidad Oilfields and Kern Trinidad Oilfields. Note though, the relatively small increase from 1917 to 1920 was on account of a shortage of drilling equipment during WWI (a similar problem also limited the growth of production during WWII).

rapid absorption by the London Stock Exchange of the shares of those oil companies operating in T&T which sold shares therein (e.g. Trinidad Oilfields Limited).

The second factor was Winston Churchill's (First Lord of the British Admirability) encouragement of the Royal Navy to turn to oil. He noted, "The ordeal of coaling ship exhausted the whole ship's company. In wartime it robbed them of their brief period of rest; it subjected everyone to extreme discomfort".

During World War I (1913–1918), the average annual production of crude oil was 1,182,536 million barrels. The rapid increase in production in the 1920s was in part due to a major block of infrastructure improvement from 1926 to 1927 in which TLL improved its refining, storage and piping capacity to benefit its refining operations.
In this early time period, the price of oil declined from US$0.72 in 1908 to US$0.61 in 1912. However, in the period 1917–1920, the price of oil averaged US$2.16, approximately 238% higher than in 1915. In 1920 the price of oil escalated to US$3.07 per barrel. However, after 1920, the price of oil declined and in 1928 stood at US$1.17 per barrel, or 62% lower than in 1920. From a simplistic perspective, a gauge of the level of economic activity in the crude oil sector can be gleaned by looking at the product of crude oil prices and crude oil production. Using these numbers, crude oil revenues in 1920 were 1005% more than in 1915 and the average revenue for the period 1917–1920, was 7 times that of 1912–1915 (see Fig. 2.1). On this basis the economy certainly had some degree of buoyancy and indeed would have experienced an "oil boom" (Higgins 1996, Boopsingh and McGuire 2014; Penny and Lonsdale-Harris 1955).

Using rudimentary and technologically deficient tools, the amount of feet drilled in the early years of the industry was trivial by modern standards and indeed from the time that data was consistently available after 1906, the depth drilled averaged less than 50,000 feet per annum before 1914 (see Fig. 2.2). For the first time in 1921, however, more than 100,000 feet were drilled. After 1921, the depth drilled continued to increase and in 1928 perched at 243,186 feet, 209% more than in 1920. In the period 1908–1918 the average depth drilled per annum was 37,711.55 feet per annum but in the next decade (1919–1928) it averaged 155,220.3 feet per annum. The increase in the depth drilled occurred in part as much more wells were being drilled on an annual basis. Thus by 1902, cumulatively 5 wells were drilled in Trinidad, increasing

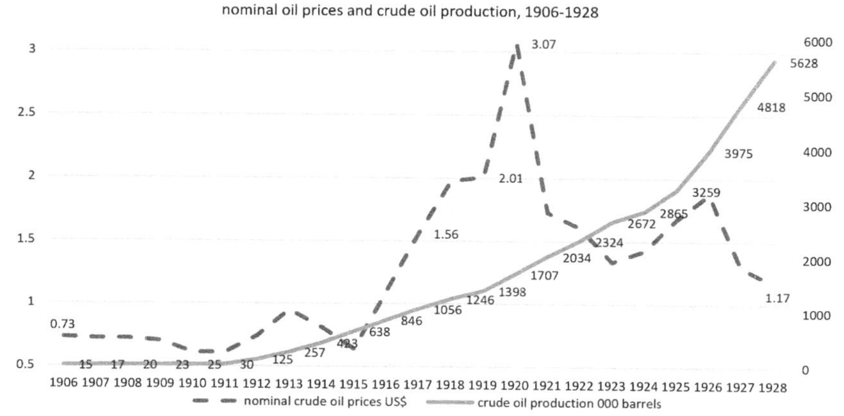

Fig. 2.1 Crude oil price and production in 1908–1928 (*Source* Mines Administration Report, 1906–1915, 1916–1926, 1927–1938)

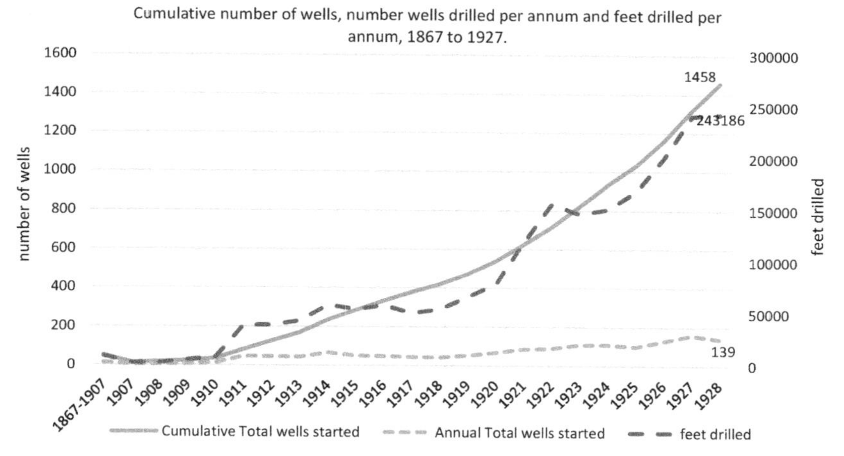

Fig. 2.2 Number of wells and feet drilled (*Source* Mines Administration Report, 1906–1915, 1916–1926, 1927–1938)

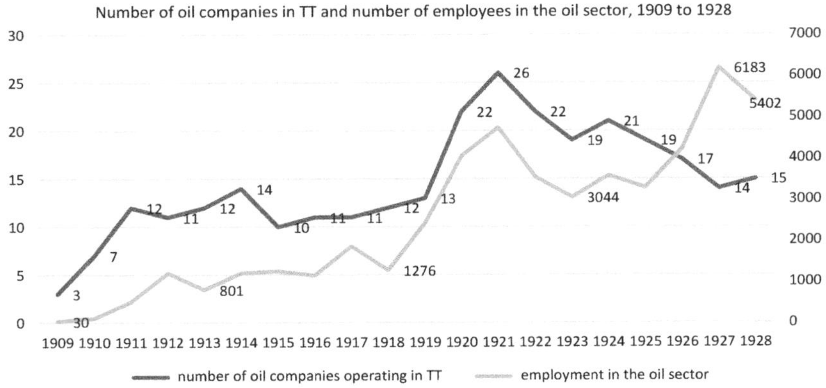

Fig. 2.3 Early Company and employment overview (*Source* Mines Administration Report, 1906–1915, 1916–1926, 1927–1938)

thereafter and to reach double digits for the first time in 1910 and subsequently escalating rapidly to over 100 wells in 1923. Cumulatively by 1928 some 1458 wells had been drilled in T&T (see Fig. 2.2).

As the news spread about the success of oil production in the T&T economy, more companies embarked upon starting businesses in Trinidad (see Fig. 2.3). Thus, the number of firms increased from 1 firm in 1902 to 2 in 1904 and to 3 firms in 1906–1909. By 1921 though, the number of firms escalated sharply to 26 in 1921, although by 1928 the number of firms declined to 15, no doubt in part because oil prices fell and the profitability of the sector declined. In addition, as the price of oil fell after 1920, some of the smaller (weaker) companies failed and fell by the way, but UBOT, TLL and Apex grew. Overall employment in this period increased from the first formally recorded value of 30 in 1909 (Government of T&T 1909) to 5402 in 1928.

2.2.1 *Exports*

From 1890 to 1923, the sectors that generated the most export earnings were cocoa, asphalt, coconuts and copra as well as sugar, molasses and rum. Cocoa exports from T&T in particular increased from $2,948,920

West Indian dollars in 1890 to $8,574,653 in 1907, an increase of 237%. This increase in 1907 was an account of cartel like behaviour by Ecuador, Brazil and the Dominican Republic and to a lesser extent, Trinidad and Tobago (de Roberts 1980). Between 1908 and 1917 cocoa exports remained moderately constant at an annual average of $6.6 million, but in 1920 increased to $15,486,619, an increase of 220% (when compared to the 1912 value) on account of the First World War. Bekele (2003) describes the period 1850–1920 as the Golden Years of cocoa production in Trinidad and Tobago. However, by 1921 the value of cocoa produced in the colony declined to $6,536,904 and remained dormant until 1925, with the average value in the period 1926–1928 being $7,348,441. (Note that around 1921 there was a switch in market demand away from the type of cocoa T&T produced. Even more by 1920, cocoa planted after 1914 came on stream, and shifted the international supply curve of cocoa, so that prices became moderately depressed, Bekele [2003].)

With regards to sugar, economic activity did not change much between 1890 and 1914. Economic activity in this sector increased between 1915 and 1925, to an average export level of $6,605,932, in comparison to $2,877,625 in the time period 1890–1914. In 1920, the export revenue from sugar was $13,138,997 which was 2.6 times than in 1919 (between September 1919 and May 1920, raw sugar prices increased from 6½ cents per pound to 22½ cents). During the First World War, the production of beet sugar in Europe declined, and so there was an increase in demand for cane sugar. As the war ended and beet sugar production revived, the world experienced an overproduction of sugar to the extent that world sugar prices fell, along with T&T's sugar export revenues which in 1927, stood at $3,767,952 or 71% less than in 1920. In 1928 export revenues from sugar slightly recovered, to $5,906,625.

Export revenues from the asphalt sector remained relatively flat between 1890 and 1900, averaging $556,415. However, asphalt exports increased per annum from $551,208 in 1900 to $973,805 in 1903, an increase of 77%. Although export revenues from the asphalt sector fell from 1903 until 1905, but it thereafter increased until 1913 to $1,106,712, 90.8% more than in 1905. By 1918 the export revenues from this sector fell to $426,360, a mere 38.4% of the 1913 level. Export revenues would show some signs of recovery thereafter and in 1927 fetched $2,229,298, 422% more than in 1918.

Between 1890 and 1900, coconut and copra exports from the T&T economy were on the decline. After 1900, however, there was an element of resurgence in coconut and copra exports and by 1920 this escalated to $1,805,225, 1911% more than the $89,766 export revenues which was fetched by this sector in 1900. The 1921 export value of coconuts and copra, however, was a mere 45% of the 1920 value. This industry experienced fluctuating export revenues between 1922 and 1928. Post 1919 the reason for the decline in exports from this sector was in part a result of drought in 1919, and both the red ring and bud-rot disease in 1921–1924. The 1928 level of exports, however, was more than twice that of 1915 mainly because of the coming into bearing, of new areas (Alleyne 2010, p. 135; Government of T&T 1916–1926).

In the period 1890–1928, petroleum product exports escalated. In 1909, petroleum products exports stood at a trivial $120 which increased to $360,006 by 1913 and even further to $11,967,792 in 1928. The export revenues gained from the export of petroleum products would move to the top of the export revenue earning list for T&T by 1924. From very early on, as the petroleum sector grew in size, there were some negative effects (real and or perceived) in other productive segments of the economy. Indeed in 1927, the then Government of T&T appointed Sir Thomas Holland to appraise the oil industry of T&T. Holland wrote, "During my stay in the colony I have received views from various sources, firstly regarding the justification for increased taxation, and secondly regarding the methods by which additional revenues from the industry might be obtained. During the discussion on this resolution, expression was given to what appears to be from the evidence that I have obtained, a prevalent impression in Trinidad, namely, that oil working displaces and in other ways injures the staple agricultural and planting industries, without contributing from its profits a sufficient compensation by way of revenues. The form of additional taxation mostly commonly proposed is export duty on oil and its products. The impressions referred to appear to have grown and without close analysis of the facts; they are however, worth critical examination, although it is beyond my province to discuss the merits of the more extreme assertions made to the effect that in displacing locally the planting industry, the development of the oilfields is economically a drawback rather than an advantage to the colony. Obviously, its adds to the stability of the community to increase its variety of industries instead of remaining dependent on one type which is seriously affected by similar varieties of the climate; but the intrusion of a new industry on any substantial scale naturally disturbs the equilibrium of the local complex, and complaints are therefore not unexpected. I assume, however, that my questions of taxation are to be considered only on the assumption that the development of oil resources is definitely accepted to the public interests, and my observations are limited therefore to the problem of obtaining for the state, a fair share of compensation for the inevitable depletion of a wasting asset, without at the same time discouraging the inflow of capital or forcing the established leaseholders to limit their activities to the high grade parts of the field" (Holland Report 1928, p. 16). Clearly then and as will be elaborated in Chapter 4, elements of the Resource Curse and the Dutch Disease had started to make their appearance in the T&T economy in various forms.

2.2.2 Royalties

In the early phase of economic activity in the petroleum sector, crown lands were leased mainly to British companies, although private lands could be leased to companies from other countries. This all British policy on crown lands was recognized by Sir Thomas Holland to have, "reduced the speculative element which necessarily accompanies the development of a promising oilfield," (Holland Report 1928, p. 5). The granting of leases in the UK by agents out of touch with the realities in T&T therefore created problems of its own.[6]

From a royalty perspective, one source noted that "compared with the terms granted in most countries there is no doubt about the leniency of the royalty rates hitherto demanded by the government of Trinidad" (Holland Report, p. 14). In later years, the former Prime Minister of T&T, Dr. Eric Williams (and a noted Caribbean scholar), in his book

[6] Thomas Holland noted, "Large areas granted under lease at reduced rates may form attractive baits to be non-critical investor, and thus, for purely company promoting purposes, they are attractive, but they do not help actual development. There may be some justification for laying out bait when a country is unknown and pioneers are shy, but that time has passed long ago for Trinidad, and the policy which misguided early days ought not to be followed now. There would have been fewer company failures and consequently less waste of money if a more conservative policy had been adopted in the early days of Trinidad oil. Every failure of the sort merely means heavier underwriting charges for all new companies, and consequently reduced ability to lay out capital and actual work. The policy indicated by the scale of dead rents quoted never did any good to Trinidad, even in the early days of oil; it would be harmful if followed again, but unfortunately, there is little lands left now ..." (Holland Report, p. 13).

Inward Hunger:The Education of a Prime Minister noted, "I paid special attention to developments in Venezuela and Alberta with particular references to oil depletion allowances and to the sale of concessions. Our predecessors had given away our valuable marine areas in the Gulf of Paria; it was freedom on our side of the boundary whilst in Venezuela, on its side, sold concessions to the highest bidder (cited on page 12 of 19th Eric Williams Memorial Lecture)."

In terms of actual data, there was an increase in Royalty and Wayleave collected by the government. Royalties in particular, increased from \$15,156 in 1915 to \$261,260 in 1928. Wayleave in turn improved from \$1781 in 1916 to \$60,523 in 1928. In the early days, the amount of royalties collected by the state was influenced by the fact that not all of the crude oil produced was on state land.

In closing of this section, this chapter draws on Brereton (1996, pp. 202–2013) who noted that, "*The first three decades of the twentieth century belonged to the hardy pioneers of the oil industry. Technology and equipment were primitive by later standards, and blow-outs, gushers and even oil field fires were frequent occurrences. Until the late 1920's, spectacular gushers were common. Accidents were frequent…Labourers were usually bare-footed, there were no helmets and in general safety was given low priority by the rugged pioneers who opened up the oil fields. These districts were extremely inaccessible, and heavy machinery and equipment had to be man handled through dense forests. Heavy equipment was heaved into place by human muscle, the forest was cleared by axe men, well sites and roads were graded by a 'Tattoo Gang' men and women who dug and moved tons of earth using forks, shovels and wooden trays carried on the women's heads. Miles of forest roads were dug, and hundreds of well sites were leveled by these forgotten Trinidadians, who deserved to be remembered as pioneers of the oil industry just as much as Rust and the other entrepreneurs involved.*"

2.3 1929 to the End of the Second World War

In the late 1920s and early 1930s huge oilfields in Oklahoma, Texas and in Russia were brought on stream.[7] The Oklahoma City Oilfield was

[7] The wells in Oklahoma were able to produce 20,000 BPD (Ordovician Basal Oil Creek Sand well), 20,000 MCFD (Wilcox sands well), and 6564 bopd (Cambro-Ordovician Arbuckle Limestone well). The oil wells spanned a total of 12 miles in length and 4.5 miles in width.

Table 2.1 Production and drilling trends in the crude oil sector, 1929–1945

Date	*Oil prices (US)*	*Crude oil production (barrels)*	*Total land production (Bbls)*	*Feet drilled*
1929	1.27	8,715,652	8,715,788	307,482
1930	1.19	9,418,907	9,418,957	372,530
1931	0.65	9,743,502	9,743,498	218,642
1932	0.87	10,126,065	10,126,121	173,207
1933	0.67	9,561,354	9,561,353	235,702
1934	1	10,894,363	10,894,363	351,783
1935	0.97	11,671,224	11,671,224	436,249
1936	1.09	13,237,030	13,237,030	594,523
1937	1.18	15,502,889	15,502,989	911,575
1938	1.13	17,737,201	17,737,201	905,940
1939	1.02	19,741,616	19,741,616	834,846
1940	1.02	22,226,876	22,226,876	1,020,901
1941	1.14	20,505,980	20,505,980	935,452
1942	1.19	22,069,000	22,069,178	623,000
1943	1.2	21,286,000	21,385,240	493,000
1944	1.21	21,543,000	21,634,965	456,000
1945	1.05	21,092,000	21,092,608	450,765

Source MEEA various years

opened on December 4, 1928. The stock market crash of October 1929 sparked an oversupply of automobiles on the global market and these two factors, combined to motivate a decrease in oil prices from US$1.27 in 1929 to US$0.67 (see Table 2.1) in 1933[8] (Higgins 1996; Boopsingh and McGuire 2014; Boyd 2008[9]).

Crude oil production from T&T continued to increase after World War 1, improving from 8.7 million barrels in 1929 to 22.23 mn barrels in 1940, a significant increase in a short space of time, but moderated to around 21.2 million barrels on average per annum between 1941 and

[8] During September and October of 1929, share prices fell due to disappointing results recorded by several firms. On October 28, 1929, the stock market crashed (Black Market) as a result of the decline in prices falling as much as 13%. By 1932, the stock market fell 89% from its September 1929 peak. Oil prices fell from US$1.27 in 1929 to $US0.65 in 1931. Fluctuations in prices were consistent with the collapse in the stock market, but production continued to rise, as new wells were being created (e.g. the Oklahoma fields).

[9] Boyd (2008), "Oklahoma: The Ultimate Oil Opportunity."

1945 partly on the account of the events around World War II.[10] (See Table 2.1 for relevant details.)

As concerns oil prices, these collapsed from US$1.27 in 1929 to US$0.65 in 1931 and until 1935 remained relatively depressed as compared to 1929. Indeed the MEEA report 1932 noted that "In common with other industries, the oil industry of the Colony during the past year has suffered from the financial conditions which are prevailing throughout the world, and prices obtainable for petroleum products in the world's markets have continued to be low…" (MEEA 1932, p. 3). For the period 1935–1945 crude oil prices averaged US$1.11 per barrel, with a standard deviation of US$0.08.

With regards to the depth drilled in 1929, 307,482 ft. were drilled, but amidst the stagnating economic climate of the day associated with the Great Depression, the depth drilled declined to 173,207 ft. in 1932, a decline of 44%. Not surprisingly though, as the price of crude oil slowly recovered in the aftermath of the Great Depression, so did the search for crude oil to help "fuel" the recovering global economy (Penny and Lonsdale-Harris 1955; FIRST 2014). Drilling improved to 1,020,901 ft. in 1940, 489% more than in 1932. Note, the advent of the Second World War led to a decline in drilling activity to 450,765 ft. in 1945, or a mere 44.15% of the level drilled in 1940 (Higgins 1996; Penny and Lonsdale-Harris 1955).

As oil prices recovered after the Great Depression, the number of companies expanded to the extent that by 1938, the number of companies in the petroleum sector of T&T increased to 24 (as compared 15 in 1929), but moderated, not surprisingly, to 15 companies in 1944, no doubt in part on account of the cumbrousness of getting material supplies.[11]

As concerns employment, Table 2.2 shows that in 1929 the petroleum sector employed 5307 workers and this increased to 13,402 workers by 1945 (14,039 in 1938), as the output from this sector increased. The

[10] By 1929, T&T had become the main producer of petroleum in the British empire. (Note that when oil production is from "flowing" wells even if prices fall, its production will not necessarily fall. In some cases, if leasing arrangements have production stipulations, then this can also influence production rates.)

[11] The MEEA report (1942, p. 1) noted that "Towards the end of this period, it became difficult to obtain delivery of equipment and materials manufactured from steel and other commodities in short supply."

Table 2.2 Company and employment overview 1929–1945

	Number of companies	*Number of persons employed in the petroleum sector*	*Employment in asphalt*	*Number of wells*	*Cumulative number of wells*
1929	15	5307	888	159	1617
1930	14	6403	828	163	1780
1931	13	4126	742	60	1840
1932	16	4836	549	61	1901
1933	15	5140	483	81	1982
1934	14	5347	557	124	2106
1935	15	6098	617	139	2245
1936	18	7680	642	171	2416
1937	21	9957	652	289	2705
1938	24	14,039	617	279	2984
1939	19	12,114	558	245	3229
1940	19	13,374	481	290	3519
1941	18	14,700	466	270	3742
1942	16	13,799	381	169	3911
1943	16	13,601	381	127	4038
1944	15	13,718	514	105	4143
1945	16	13,402	470	110	4253

Source MEEA reports, various years

decline of the asphalt mining sector continued as well into this period, and by 1945, only 470 people were employed, as compared to 888 in 1929.

In terms of the cumulative number of wells drilled, by 1945 this had increased to 4253 (see Table 2.2). This interprets that between 1929 and 1945, 2636 new wells were drilled. On an annual basis, the number of new wells drilled decreased from 159 in 1929 to 60 in 1931 amidst the Great Depression, but increased thereafter to 290 in 1940 as companies increased their output levels. However, with the advent of war, drilling declined, and the number of wells drilled in 1945 was 110 or 37.9% of the 1940 level.

The amount of wells using the flowing technique in this time period increased from 170 in 1930 to 634 in 1945,[12] whilst the number of wells using gas/air lift increased from 19 in 1930 to 121 in 1942, decreasing thereafter to 76 in 1945. As concerns pumping, the average number of wells decreased from 544 in 1930 to 443 in 1933 but by 1945 had increased to 769. The plunger lift method was introduced in 1935 (MEEA 1935, p. 9) and by 1945 there were 212 wells in operation using this technique.

2.3.1 Exports

From the Great Depression onwards, cocoa exports continued the decline which had started in 1920 and in 1945 was 84.4% less than in 1929 (see Table 2.3). A principal contributing factor to low cocoa export revenues, was low levels of production and declining world prices on account of the sharp rise in cocoa production, internationally. Specifically, cocoa prices fell from TT$23.90 per fanega (110 lbs.) in 1919–1920 to TT$9.50 in 1921 (Bekele 2004). Many types of diseases also affected the cocoa industry in Trinidad and Tobago, during this time period (Bekele 2004).

Asphalt exports (except for a spike in 1943, when it climbed to $2,256,565), declined from $2,094,008 in 1929 to TT$933,593 in 1945, a decline of 55.42%. As concerns the coconut and copra export segment of the T&T export market, this crashed from TT$1,350,934 in 1929[13] to TT$3864 in 1942, although there was an element of recovery towards the end of the data period covered in this sector, to TT$601,121 in 1945. The falloff in coconut exports after 1933 can be attributed to the hurricane in June 1933 and a greater use of the coconuts for the manufacture of edible oils (Alleyne 2010).

[12] In 1930 crude oil production in T&T was only about 22 years old and thus the economy could be considered a youthful producer at this time. During the period 1930 to 1945 the 2nd World War also took place and this would have played an important role in the amount of wells used, as T&T was a major supplier of oil to the British during this time.

[13] Coconut production was very buoyant in 1929 on account of favourable rainfall in 1928, with larger than average nuts in 1929 and so more copra per nut was extracted in 1929, (Alleyne, T.; Roache, S.; Thomas, C.; Shirley, A. The control of hypertension by use of coconut water and mauby: Two tropical food drinks. *West Indian Medical Journal*, 2005, 54, 3–8).

Table 2.3 Leading exports from T&T 1929–1945, TT$

	Cocoa exports	*Asphalt exports*	*Coconut and cocoa exports*	*Sugar, molasses and rum exports*	*Petroleum product exports*
1929	6,941,410	2,094,008	1,350,934	5,142,299	14,646,960
1930	5,433,404	1,304,306	568,616	3,040,246	13,895,336
1931	3,906,398	1,135,666	554,472	4,426,230	9,557,336
1932	2,720,016	631,923	512,573	4,262,847	9,557,384
1933	2,668,354	724,661	515,443	5,087,269	11,437,661
1934	1,678,351	987,069	426,350	4,508,800	10,819,464
1935	2,530,627	1,092,952	241,991	4,699,241	14,056,120
1936	2,340,377	999,769	324,983	4,425,533	15,940,630
1937	3,006,595	1,191,914	6,831,342	6,425,725	19,836,420
1938	2,369,238	1,131,078	235,389	513,678	23,656,561
1939	1,212,682	1,170,585	204,394	5,364,383	26,762,296
1940	2,289,605	617,897	338,198	4,537,181	33,650,695
1941	1,749,836	938,560	60,069	7,099,333	28,980,268
1942	1,187,994	727,934	3864	559,031	33,947,691
1943	971,212	2,256,565	17,000	3,774,090	27,913,004
1944	1,411,796	1,087,514	243,273	4,783,809	39,582,389
1945	1,080,047	933,593	606,121	5,829,031	43,627,559

Source CSO, Annual Statistical Digest (1956)

Sugar exports maintained some degree of stability in export revenues between the Great Depression and the end of World War II (WWII). It averaged $4,683,807 in this time period and in 1945 the export revenues earned from the sector of $5,829,031 was only 12% more than the 1929 level.[14] Significantly though, the petroleum sector continued

[14] In this period the capacity of the sugar industry expanded and helped to absorb some of the workers shed by the cocoa industry. However, any serious ambition of T&T sugar sector to increase output to accommodate more workers was stopped in part by the International Sugar Agreement, which when signed in September 1937 and which, restricted T&T's export quota to 138,000 per annum. This restriction was supported locally by the cane farming control ordinance 1939, which was established to limit uncontrollable expansion of acreage under sugar cane. Indeed from $7,099,333 in 1941 the export revenue from the sugar sector fell by 32% to $4,783,809 in 1944. The substantive reason for this was a decline in the labour force available to the sugar sector as many sugar sector workers and workers from the agriculture sector in general left to go and work on the US bases built in T&T. Brereton (1996) notes that at its peak the bases employed around 30,000 people or 15% the entire labour force. Between 1939 and 1943 there was a sharp drop in the number of people employed in the sugar sector and those who

to be the substantive revenue earner for the T&T economy, fetching TT$14,646,960 in 1929 and a significant TT$43,627,559 in 1945, an increase of 197%. Clearly, the stage had been set and the T&T economy had switched from cocoa to sugar to petroleum but remained a monocrop economy.

2.3.2 *Royalty and Wayleave*

As the petroleum sector grew, royalties improved and would have been even higher, but a considerable amount of production accrued on private lands. During this phase in the history of the energy sector, companies were keener on producing more from existing wells than on employing resources to develop and expand new fields. When the war ended in 1945, attention shifted from on shore drilling to marine drilling and this type of activity incurred no wayleave expenses.

2.4 The Second World War Up to the Dawn of the First Oil Boom, 1945–1972

The end of the Second World War saw the emergence of a New World order. The USA emerged as the dominant global economic power and up to this point, the dominant petroleum firm was Trinidad Leasehold Limited. In 1956, the company was purchased by the Texas Company (Texaco) for £63 mn. The new company rationalized existing reserves, drilled more and extracted more from proven areas and engaged exploratory drilling in areas with unemployed acreage. The company struck oil in Guayaguayare (well number 305) which produced 640 barrels of oil per day. Indeed, the Levy Report (1956) which came after Texaco's takeover of the refinery noted, "future prospects had been re-shaped by two developments - the first related to exploration in the offshore area and the promise of substantial reserves, the second concerned projected refinery expansion, which could consolidate export position in foreign markets. Together these could pave the way to a new growth dynamic." Other commentators felt the same and it was noted

remained behind were usually the older, slower workers. Also, the US bases demanded a lot of food from the local farmers, and so significant portions of sugarcane land resources were redirected to this effort. (Between 1938 and 1943 the sugar cane crop was also affected by the frog hopper pest, Brereton [1996].)

that, "in the decade after the war, Trinidad and Tobago experienced general economic growth. The oil industry, linked to the international market in which Texaco was a player, powered the economy, which in turn benefited other sectors. Trinidad increasingly became a classic petroleum economy, always dangerously dependent on oil for export earnings and for government revenues. The American bases had created thousands of jobs, absorbing almost 20 per cent of the entire labour force. There was buoyancy in the economy, coming to some extent from consumer spending that was driven by the comparatively high salaries paid out by the Americans to local workers and staff and by the spending of the American servicemen themselves" (Besson 2008a, p. 63).

Table 2.4 shows the trends in T&T crude oil production from the Second World War up to the period of the second oil boom. The production of crude oil in the post Second World War era consistently increased and by 1968 climbed to 66.9 million barrels per annum. Land production decreased fairly continuously during this period of time and by 1967 accounted for only 61.1% of total production of crude oil in T&T and by 1972 even less, at 44%. Marine production itself began in 1954 and increased quickly so that by 1972, marine production accounted for 56% (29.2 mn barrels), of T&T's total oil production.[15]

The change that overshadowed all other changes was the consultations by oil producing economies in Venezuela in 1970, where these countries met and agreed that they needed a greater proportion of the price of each barrel of oil. On this basis, the six Persian oil-producing states demanded and obtained from the oil companies operating in Venezuela (these included Esso, Shell, Texaco, Mobil, Gulf Oil, B.P. and Standard Oil of California) a substantial increase in the prices reported for tax purposes and a built in formula for an annual increase in prices for a five year period up to 1975 (T&T's Budget Speech 1972, p. 535). The result of this action by the oil-producing countries was to increase the tax take per barrel of oil.

For example, for Kuwait there was a 56% increase in their tax take per barrel of oil, with the corresponding numbers for Iran being 55%, Nigeria at 57% and Venezuela at 43%.

[15] Mostofi (1963) notes that "The discovery of major oil reserves in the Soldado field in the Gulf of Paria and the rapid development of this field since 1956 have made the most important contribution to the growth of the Trinidad's oil industry" (p. 19).

Table 2.4 Production and drilling for oil on both land and sea

Year	*Land production (mn bbls)*	*Marine production (mn bbls)*	*Total land and marine production (mn bbls)*	*Price per barrel*	*Feet drilled*	*Average depth per well (ft.)*	*Average daily production per well*
1946	20.2		20.2	1.12	543,231	4750	30
1947	20.5		20.5	1.9	643,241	4200	30
1948	20.1		20.1	1.99	643,092	4250	27
1949	20.6		20.6	1.78	628,985	4175	27
1950	20.6		20.6	1.71	66,985	4450	25
1951	20.8		20.8	1.71	664,887	4500	25
1952	21.3		21.3	1.71	736,535	4250	24
1953	22.3		22.3	1.93	917,894	4200	24
1954	23.6		23.6	1.93	911,242	4550	24
1955	24.9		24.9	1.93	987,567	4350	24
1956	28.7	0.2	28.9	1.93	1,110,745	4250	24
1957	33.6	0.5	34.1	1.9	1,322,483	4150	31
1958	35.7	1.7	37.4	2.08	1,365,129	4601	32.6
1959	36.6	4.3	40.9	2.08	1,446,586	5141	34.9
1960	34.8	7.6	42.4	1.9	1,407,952	4609	36.1
1961	34.7	11.1	45.8	1.8	1,426,002	4654	38.7
1962	34.3	14.6	48.9	1.8	1,506,187	5274	40.9
1963	31.3	17.3	48.7	1.8	1,246,248	5601	42.6
1964	30.7	19	49.7	1.8	1,056,337	5513	42.4
1965	30.8	18.1	48.9	1.8	1,058,786	4,823	41.5
1966	35.4	20.2	55.6	1.8	1,187,202	4,427	45.1
1967	40.9	24.1	65	1.8	928,210	4328	52
1968	38.8	28.1	66.9	1.8	942,686	5356	54.1
1969	29.7	27.7	57.4	1.8	690,671	5468	48.3
1970	25.4	25.7	51	1.8	663,743	4917	44.8
1971	24.2	22.9	47.1	2.24	940,013	4273	42.6
1972	21.9	29.2	51.2	2.48	835,110	4462	47.7

Source MEEA Reports from various years

These were welcomed changes and on this basis the T&T government noted that it "cannot reasonably be expected to be significantly out of line with the rest of the oil producing countries in the developing world (Budget Speech 1972, p. 536).

As concerns drilling, as the war ended, drilling activity resumed and indeed in 1962, 1,506,187ft were drilled, 155.7% more than the 450,765 ft. drilled in 1946 as seen in Table 2.4. After 1962, drilling activity decreased slightly and by 1972 fell to 835,110 ft., (however, whilst this was 153.9% of 1946 it was only 55% that of 1962).

During the Second World War, there was not a significant amount of seismic work in T&T. In 1946 though, the geophysical work resumed. The MEEA (1948, p. 2) noted that "Trinidad Northern Areas Ltd. employed the Gravimeter Exploration Company to make an extensive survey covering the whole island south of the Northern Range. The territorial waters from Claxton Bay round the Cedros Peninsula to Islote Point and an area at high seas in the Gulf of Paria were also covered by this survey. The Trinidad Petroleum Development Co. Ltd. employed the Gravimeter Exploration Company during the first half of 1947 to make a survey over 241 square miles in the south of the Island covering the area from the Erin basin eastwards to Tableland and Moruga. Observations were made at 1225 stations. During the latter part of 1948, this survey was extended to cover 270 square miles of marine area on the south coast and round the Cedros Peninsula, a further 476 stations being used. Reflection seismograph surveys were carried out by Seismic Services Ltd. (U.K.) north of the Forest Reserve field and at Barrackpore for Trinidad Leaseholds Limited, also in the Erin Basin, North Ortoire and Penal Areas for United British Oilfields of Trinidad Ltd. Apex (Trinidad) Oilfield Ltd., and Kern Trinidad Oilfields Ltd., both employed Seismic Services Ltd. (U.K.) for reflection surveys over the synclinal portion of the Apex Field and over the south flank of the Central Range respectively."

In terms of the cumulative amount of wells in the T&T economy at this stage, this increased from 4253 in 1945 to 10,009 in 1972, an increase of 135.3%, see Fig. 2.4. In 1945, just at the end of the Second World War, 110 wells were drilled. As conditions stabilized in the economy after the war, the number of wells drilled per annum continued to rise and by 1957 stood at 321, although on an annual basis it subsided thereafter to 127 by 1969, a decline of 60%. By the close of this data period the number of wells started in a calendar year improved to 191 in 1972.

In terms of techniques of production, the number of wells, using the flowing method, although dipping from 634 in 1945 to 584 in 1951, increased to 1047 in 1961, an increase of 65.79% on the 1945 level, but thereafter decreased to 525, just at the dawn of the second oil boom, as

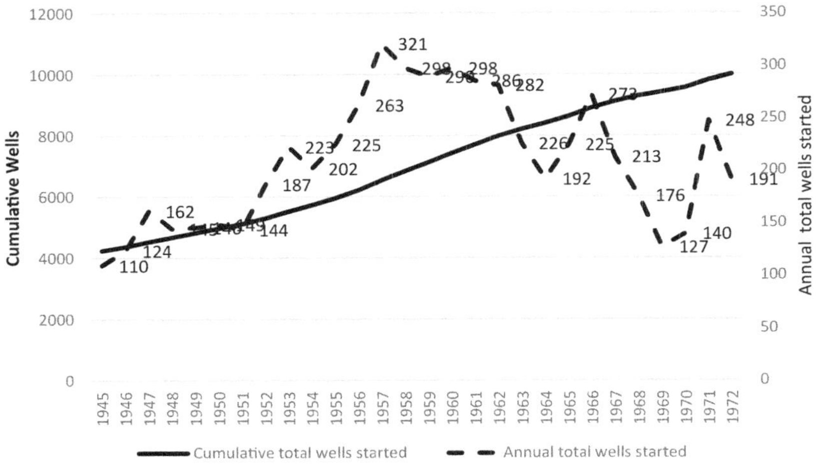

Fig. 2.4 Total and cumulative drilling activity (*Source* MEEA Reports [various years])

seen in Table 2.10 in the Appendix to this Chapter. (The decrease to 525 was due to decreased drilling and reduction in new reserve type workovers on other wells.)

In this period the gas (air) lift technique became much more popular as a method for producing crude oil, increasing rapidly from an average of 59 wells in 1946–1563 in 1970. As the number of wells using this technique increased, the associated crude oil production also increased from 680,000 barrels per annum in 1946 to 19.1 million barrels in 1968, but thereafter declined. The average number of wells operating using the plunger lift technique increased at first from 216 wells in 1946 to 309 in 1962 but thereafter declined fairly rapidly, and at the end of this period had fallen to a mere 80 wells. (The plunger lift uses the well's own energy/gas to lift fluids to the surface. Initially in the life of the reservoirs, there is typically a high gas production to support this technique. Indeed, the gas to oil ratio has to be between 300 and 500 standard cubic feet per stock tank barrel for this technique to work. As the reservoirs became more depleted little or no gas remained to support the use of the plunger lift.)

2.4.1 *Staple Exports*

After the war, cocoa production experienced a bit of a recovery and in 1954 climbed to TT$15,048,059, 1293% more than in 1946. Even so, after 1954, cocoa export revenues declined to TT$6,184,000 in 1972, a mere 41% of the level in 1954. Bekele (2004) indicated that the decline in the cocoa production in the 1920s was due to a decline in cocoa prices, the Great Depression, Witches Broom disease and competition for labour from the sugar and oil industry. There was a Rehabilitation Scheme for cocoa from 1945 to 1965 which led to increases in cocoa production (1963) but because of drought in 1957–1962 and the passage of Hurricane Flora and competition for labour from other industries cocoa exports fell. In 1971 cocoa exports were TT$4.63 mn as compared to TT$15.04 mn in 1952 (see Table 2.5).

Asphalt production in 1946 amounted to TT$3,260,141. By 1972 asphalt production reached TT$3,290,431 or 1% higher than the level of production in 1946.

Coconut production in this time period also remained stagnant and there was no sign of a recovery in this sector in this time period. Indeed by 1972, coconuts and copra production were lower than in 1945 accounting for only TT$149,400 of export revenue compared to TT$821,065 in 1946.

By 1948, after its collapse in the war years the sugar industry started to show signs of recovery. The price of sugar cane improved and with the introduction of the Commonwealth Sugar Agreement a long-term quota system was established and this helped to stabilize market conditions for T&T exporters (about two thirds) and sparked an improvement in production and acreage farmed.[16] Indeed after 1961, sugar export revenues improved and in 1972, T&T exported TT$56,901,232 of sugar (molasses and rum), 9.8 times that of 1945.

Export revenues from the petroleum sector continued to increase in this time period and went from TT$43,627,559 in 1945 to TT$831,499,600 in 1972. In the context of this rapid increase petroleum exports accounted for 79% of total exports by 1972.

[16] The Commonwealth Sugar Agreement (CSA) was signed on the 21 December, 1961. Basically, the CSA committed the UK to import sugar at a preferential tariff.

Table 2.5 Staple exports 1945–1972 (TT$mn)

	Cocoa	*Asphalt*	*Coconuts and copra*	*Sugar, molasses and rum*	*Petroleum products*
1946	1.17	3.26	0.82	7.82	41.32
1947	3.2	0	0.78	9.96	64.82
1948	8.31	0	0.05	13.39	99.23
1949	4.51	0	0.2	20.91	102.17
1950	8.36	2.66	0.33	20.08	129.18
1951	11.56	3.98	0.43	21.81	158.67
1952	15.04	0	0	20.12	173.2
1953	11.72	4.1	0.79	27.16	188.25
1954	15.04	3.76	0.61	29.34	184.89
1955	11.77	3.04	0.95	32.36	206.54
1956	10.48	2.5	0.95	27.01	256.03
1957	8.47	2.69	1.28	32.01	306.61
1958	12.74	2.83	0.56	32.08	305.78
1959	10.06	2.12	0.21	32.05	363.53
1960	8.11	2.32	0.09	37.4	392.61
1961	9.03	3.02	0.23	42.3	494.74
1962	8.79	3.02	0.15	33.5	475.25
1963	4.9	3.27	0.63	46.6	538.6
1964	4.3	4.08	0	44.7	604.9
1965	4.6	3.13	0	40.8	679
1966	4.26	3.57	0.19	35.5	580.94
1967	5.49	3.36	0.67	34.7	593.67
1968	8.13	3.2	0.46	45.5	737.4
1969	5.87	2.76	1.23	48.6	731.31
1970	9.55	3.99	0.95	42	741.81
1971	4.63	3.56	0.36	44.1	803.73
1972	6.13	3.29	0.14	56.9	831.49

Source Government of Trinidad and Tobago (various years)

2.4.2 Contribution to Output and Employment

Figure 2.5 shows the trends in the oil exploration and production GDP of T&T, hereafter called crude oil GDP. In 1966, this sector accounted for 45.9% of all the economic activity that took place in the petroleum industries subsectors of the economy. Note that just before the dawn of the second oil boom in 1972, this percentage share decreased, although not sharply to 38.6% of total value added in the petroleum sector, as shown in Fig. 2.5.

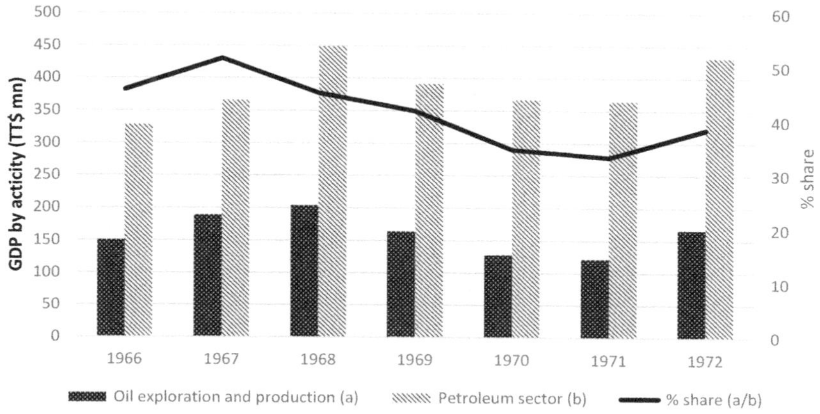

Fig. 2.5 Gross domestic product by activity—ISIC (TT$mn), current dollars (*Source* ROTE [various years])

In the period after 1968 until 1971, the T&T economy's oil sector was adversely affected by growing pressure from the USA on the imports of petroleum products with a high sulphur content and by oil produced from Alaska. Specifically, the Budget Speech (1970) stated, "The US import restriction programme has effectively reduced our opportunity for selling in that market's high value petroleum products and has forced us to concentrate on the low value and less restrictive products, such as residual petroleum oil."

In this time period (1945–1972) employment climbed from 13,587 workers in 1945 to 19,900 in 1955 as the number of wells drilled in the sector increased (see Fig. 2.6). However, basically coinciding with the decline in the number of wells drilled on an annual basis, employment in this sector declined to 11,800. As drilling improved thereafter, employment in this sector showed distinct signs of improvement and in 1972 stood at 15,670.

This period also marked a major change in T&T's participation in the energy sector of the economy. The Budget Speech 1968 (p. 408), noted that "for some time now, British Petroleum has been publishing its desire to disperse its assets in Trinidad. The government has a clear responsibility to ensure that exploitation of the limited petroleum assets, which we are fortunate to have, should bring maximum benefit to the nation."

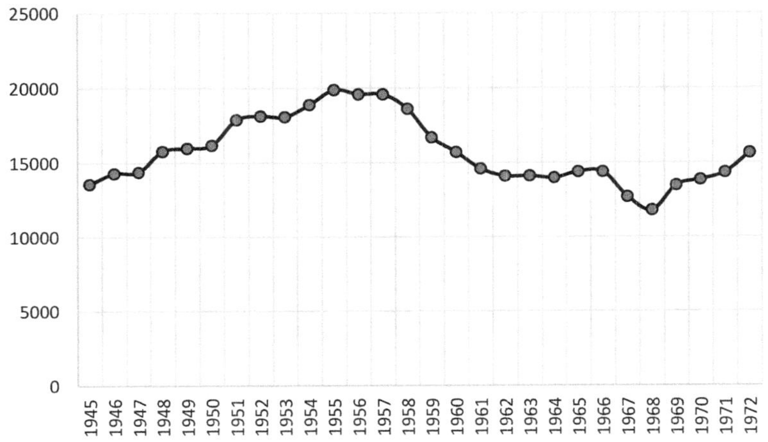

Fig. 2.6 Number of workers in the petroleum sector (*Source* CSO [various reports])

On this basis and by the next Budget Speech, it was announced that, "The government of Trinidad and Tobago has joined with Tesoro Corporation of the USA, in a joint venture which has resulted in the formation of Trinidad Tesoro Company Limited. This new company is now operating the properties formerly owned by the British Petroleum. The Government's partner, the Tesoro Corporation of the USA, is known for its high level of technical competence, especially in the field of secondary recovery" (Budget Speech 1968, p. 436). With this intervention, the stage was set for the greater participation of the TT government in the commanding heights of its economy.

2.4.3 Royalties

In the period 1955 until 1972, oil revenues averaged 43.6% of total revenues, however, the real explosion in revenues came in the very next decade and this chapter now turns to a discussion of that time period. For the present though note that in actual dollar value terms, petroleum revenues escalated from TT$39.1 mn in 1955 to TT$148.2 mn in 1972. Although nominal petroleum revenue flows increased, as a proportion of current revenues, the share of petroleum revenues fell from 48.1% in 1955 to 37.2% in 1972 (see Fig. 2.7).

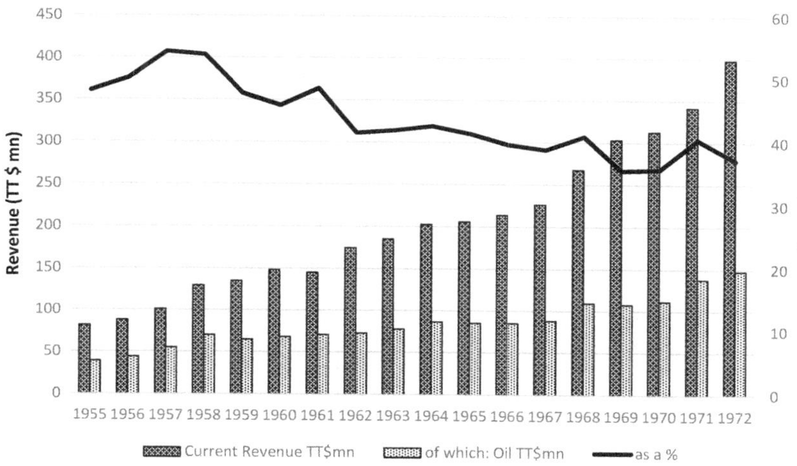

Fig. 2.7 Petroleum revenues for Trinidad and Tobago (*Source* CSO various years)

Overall, in this time period there was a clear emergence of the petroleum sector as the dominant export revenue earner and this was even before the massive surge in revenues that would occur in the next period.

2.5 1973–2020: Boom Bust Boom Bust

As shown in Table 2.6, by 1973 real economic growth in the T&T economy started to decline and as a partial consequence the unemployment rate in T&T climbed to 15.3%, as compared to 6.5% in 1955. The inflation rate increased from 3.2% in 1955 to 14.8% in 1973 and the current account balance remained persistently in deficit for this time period. At this stage the economy was certainly in need of structural reform, however, the changes in the price and production of crude oil during the 1970s perhaps motivated the government to overlook this course of action.

Significantly in the 1960s, a group of returning scholars challenged the way Caribbean economies were being run and advocated in favour of taking over the commanding heights of the economy. These economists included Best (1968), Bruce (1972), Thomas (1965) and Brewster

Table 2.6 Basic macroeconomic indicators for T&T, 1955–1973

	Economic rent US$ mn	*Real growth rate %*	*Inflation rate %*	*REER*	*Unemployment rate %*	*Current account balance (% GDP)*
1955	33.2	15.40	3.2	77.3	6.5	−11.4
1960	54.7	9.40	2.1	77.9	10	−19.7
1965	54.9	0.7	1.7	86.3	13.7	−12.4
1966	60.9	4.1	4.1	88.1	13.9	−8.7
1967	70.2	2	2.1	86	16.7	−4.8
1968	68.3	5.2	8.2	77.8	14.9	−6.8
1969	57.5	2.7	2.5	75.6	13.1	−6.8
1970	50.1	3.5	2.5	73.6	12.8	−7.1
1971	65.7	1	3.5	74.5	12.6	−13.1
1972	79.6	5.8	9.3	80.5	14	−13.6
1973	135.1	1.7	14.8	85.2	15.4	−1.9

Source CSO Reports (various years)

(1968). The government of Trinidad and Tobago, partly building on the momentum from the utterances of these returning scholars and with its appetite whet with the takeover of BP's asset in Trinidad, proceeded to note that: "Nevertheless, it is apparent that increases in the international market value of crude oil, the production of which results in the depletion of the national patrimony, cannot continue to accrue to any single enterprise, whether state owned or otherwise which is in the fortunate position of being charged with the operation of the industry, but rather should accrue to the state, the legitimate guardian of the people of Trinidad and Tobago" (Budget Speech 1978, p. 865).

In 1974, the T&T government, bought out the local operations of Shell Trinidad Limited in 1974 and rebranded the company with a more "nationalistic" name on 31 August of the same year[17] as Trinidad and Tobago Oil Company (Trintoc).

[17] A comment from Prime Minister Eric Williams on the day of the takeover of Shell is worthy of repeating here "As we proceed to lower the flag of yesterday (the honor falls to the worker with the longest service in Shell, 42 years exactly today) and hoist the flag of today and tomorrow, the flag of the nation as against the flag of an external corporation, as we see the flag, our flag, flying high and rising proud in the breeze, symbolizing the ascent of the nation and the higher destiny of the citizens of Point Fortin, let us say, with pride but with humility, we are going well and may God bless our nation."

Table 2.7 shows that in the period 1973–1993 total crude oil production increased from 51.21 million in 1973 to 83.78 million in 1978, but by 1991 declined to 41.4 mn barrels. There was a brief recovery to 52.7 mn barrels in 2005 but thereafter production fell continuously and in 2020 stood at 20.6 mn. Land-based production of crude oil fell fairly sharply from 20.2 million in 1973 to 6.7 million in 2020. In this same interval of time, marine production, although increasing from 29.98 mn in 1973 to 67.29 million in 1978 fell away to 13.9 million in 2020.

Table 2.7 Oil production 1972–2020

	Land production, mn of barrels	*Marine production, mn of barrels RHS*	*Total production, mn of barrels*	*Price per barrel of crude oil WTI, US$*	*FT. DRILLED*	*Petroleum revenues TT$mn*
1972	21.93	29.28	51.21	1.9	841,742	148.2
1975	15.1	63.5	78.6	10.7	841,384	1254.8
1980	17.1	60.5	77.6	36.0	674,187	4136.5
1985	14.4	49.8	64.3	28.0	654,209	2457.1
1990	13.4	41.7	55.0	24.5	503,602	2317.5
1995	10.8	36.8	47.6	18.4	491,931	2535.9
2000	9.7	33.9	43.6	30.3	468,786	4475.6
2005	8.8	43.9	52.7	56.4	386,345	15,851.8
2006	8.6	43.8	52.4	66.1	537,666	21,111.5
2007	8.5	35.8	44.3	72.3	583,564	19,365.4
2008	8.7	33.1	41.8	99.6	497,475	31,100.5
2009	8.4	30.5	39.0	61.7	145,615	14,825.5
2010	8.0	27.8	35.8	79.4	185,238	19,216.4
2011	7.9	25.7	33.6	95.1	370,437	23,471.0
2012	8.2	21.7	29.9	94.2	381,164	17,349.2
2013	8.4	21.1	29.5	97.9	355,605	20,837.8
2014	8.4	21.0	29.4	93.1	357,125	21,025.6
2015	7.7	18.7	26.4	48.7	461,362	10,530.5
2016	8.1	18.2	26.3	43.2	414,537	3263.5
2017	7.9	16.6	24.4	50.9	454,476	4936.3
2018	7.9	17.0	24.9	64.8	325,708	6685.7
2019	7.3	15.3	21.4	57	301,452	11,131.9
2020p	6.7	13.9	20.6	36.7	200,000	12,314.2

Source CBTT

The price level of crude oil climbed upward in this time period, as the Organization of Petroleum-Exporting Countries (OPEC) strengthened. Specifically, the Yom Kippur war of 1973 helped to trigger an increase in the price of crude oil from US$2.7 in 1973 to US$39.6 in 1981. Thereafter though, the price of crude oil dipped and by 1998 stood at US$14.4 per barrel thereafter reversing sharply to US$99.6 in 2008 and averaged US$95.1 per barrel in the period 2011 to 2014. After 2014, oil prices collapsed and in 2016, stood at 46.1% of the value in 2014. In 2020, oil prices stood at US$36.7 per barrel.

Note the period 1973–1982 when both oil prices and oil production were very buoyant represented a massive surge in petroleum revenues for the T&T economy. Specifically, petroleum revenues escalated from TT$197.3 in 1973 to TT$4253.1 mn in 1981 and decreasing thereafter to TT$1538.3 mn in 1988. Petroleum revenues averaged TT$2133.3 mn for the period 1988–1998 but surged quickly thereafter TT$31.1bn in 2008 although by 2019 it has tapered off at TT$11.1bn. As concerns drilling, between 1973 and 1992 there was an almost continuous decline in the amount of depth drilled in T&T. Specifically in 1973, 955,185 feet was drilled in the petroleum sector and until 1982, when production was still fairly buoyant, the average annual amount of feet drilled was 829,843 feet. Thereafter, however, as production fell, so did drilling and in 1993 this collapsed to 226,214 or a mere 24% of the 1973 drilling depth. Between 1993 and 2001 there was a degree of resurgence in drilling, with the depth drilled in 2007 standing at 583,564 feet. After 2007 though drilling in Trinidad and Tobago generally declined and in 2020 stood at 200,000 or 20.9% of the level in 1973 and basically back to the level of 1934. (Note that in 2009 the number of feet drilled declined to 145,615 ft., the lowest for the time period 1973–2020.) In the past there has been the emergent pattern that the fall in production was linked to the decline in drilling.

The amount of oil produced by the flowing technique fell from 37.7 million in 1973 to 11 million in 2013, with fluctuating output levels in between. The actual number of wells using the flowing method decreased from 506 in 1973 to 192 in 2013. Note that the decline in flowing production as illustrated in Table 2.10 in the Appendix to this chapter, after 1973 is reflective of the maturing of land-based fields.

The average number of wells using the gas lift technique fell from 784 in 1973 to 330 in 2013, a decline of 57.9%. Production from this technique climbed to 32 mn in 1984, the highest for this technique throughout its use in T&T, but thereafter as with the overall trend in crude oil production in TT, declined to 9.05 mn barrels in 2013. Pumping was in 1973, the dominant method of producing crude oil in TT and the number of wells basically doubled by the end of the data period (from 1551 in 1973 to 2968 in 2013). Even so, production levels from this technique declined, no doubt reflecting the maturity of the associated wells.

2.5.1 Petroleum Sector GDP and Crude Oil Value Added in Particular

In 1973, the crude oil exploration and production segment of the T&T economy accounted for TT$421.8 mn (see Table 2.8) of a total of TT$709.4 mn in the petroleum sector i.e. 59.46%. As crude oil production increased, this escalated to TT$5739.1 mn or 95.76% of the total amount of value added in the petroleum sector by 1981.[18] After 1981, economic activity in this sector fell, and by 1988 declined to TT$2673.2 mn or 64% of the 1988 total value added. By 2020, output in this sector escalated to TT$41,756 mn, accounting for 54.5% of economic activity in this sector.

2.5.2 Employment in Crude Oil exploration and production

Figure 2.8 provides data on the employment trends in the petroleum sector from 1973 to 2012. From an employment perspective, the number of people employed in the crude oil exploration segment of the T&T economy increased from 4444 people in 1973 to 5714 people in 1980. After 1980 this number declined and indeed by 1995 decreased to 2556 or 20.68% of the number of people in 1980. After 1995, the employment in this sector increased and by the close of the data period was at 5042 (Data is only available until 2012).

[18] The oil refining sector at this point was under heavy restrictions from the USA.

Table 2.8 Gross domestic product by kind of activity—ISIC (TT$ mn), current dollars

	Oil exploration and production	*Petroleum*	%
1973	421.8	709.4	59.5
1975	1854.9	2299.4	80.7
1976	2018.5	2569.2	78.6
1977	2488.1	3100.5	80.3
1978	2330.3	2977.1	78.3
1979	3207.2	4261.1	75.3
1980	5876.4	6412.5	91.6
1981	5739.1	5993.5	95.8
1982	4683.4	5103.4	91.8
1983	3846	4541.3	84.7
1984	3975.1	5065.9	78.5
1985	3940.3	4814.7	81.8
1986	3006.8	3920.8	76.7
1987	3393	4353.4	77.9
1988	2673.2	4173.9	64.1
1989	3538.9	4999.4	70.8
1990	4540.8	6368.8	71.3
1991	3818.4	5903.2	64.7
1992	3509.9	5464.1	64.2
1993	3457.3	5696.7	60.7
1994	4500	8418	53.5
1995	4463.8	8325.5	53.6
1996	4863.5	10,059.8	48.4
1997	4732.7	9130.8	51.8
1998	3350	7027.5	47.7
1999	5217	9635.3	54.1
2000	8959.4	16,073.2	55.7
2001	8686.4	15,558.8	55.8
2002	7950.7	14,765	53.9
2003	14,888.7	25,610.7	58.1
2004	18,147.6	32,302.2	56.2
2005	24,223.3	46,188.4	52.4
2006	32,249	54,517.4	59.2
2007	32,962.3	61,634.1	53.5
2008	51,236.3	89,100	57.5
2009	22,867.6	41,465	55.2
2010	31,279.4	56,298.6	55.6

(continued)

Table 2.8 (continued)

	Oil exploration and production	*Petroleum*	%
2011	36,867	71,280.2	51.7
2012	35,566.6	65,184.1	50.8
2013	39,208.2	76,254.9	52.3
2014	37,872.6	62,309	54.5
2015	21,985.3	38,266	57.5
2016	14,388.9	29,347	49.0
2017	18,053.1	35,913	50.3
2018	24,444.4	41,756	58.5

Source Handbook of Key Economic Indicators and Annual Economic Survey of the T&T Economy (various years)

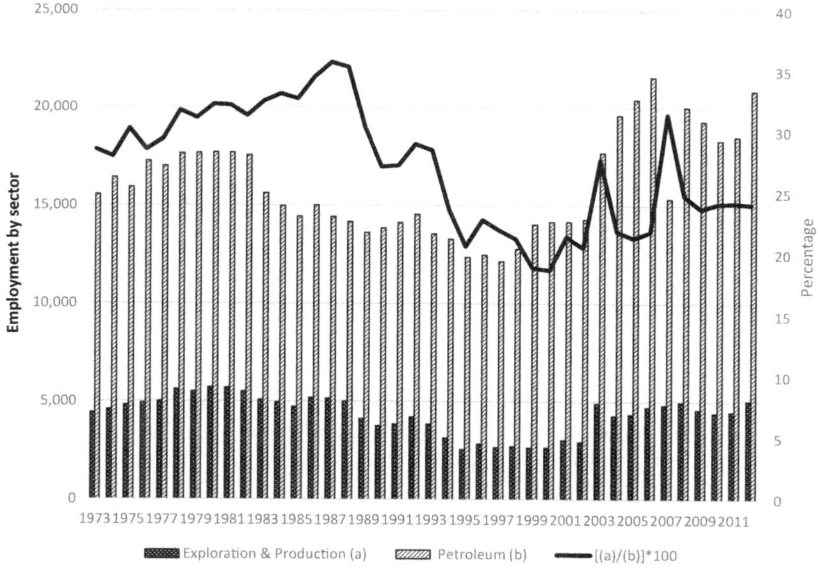

Fig. 2.8 Employment trends in the petroleum sector (*Source* MEEA and CSO Reports [various years])

2.5.3 *Exports*

In 1973, T&T exported US$0.69 bn of which 16.1% were from crude oil exports (see Table 2.9). As both the price and production of crude oil improved, total export revenues increased to 1983, of which 46.7% came from crude oil export revenues. After 1983 the export portfolio of the T&T economy widened and in 2001 crude oil export revenues declined to 9.3% of total exports revenues, as both oil prices and oil production declined. The recovery of oil prices thereafter to unprecedented nominal levels resulted in an improvement in crude petroleum export revenues to 13.7% of total export revenues in 2010, even though the actual production of crude oil in 2013 was 35% of the 1978 level.

2.6 The Oil Industry and Global Warming

Amongst greenhouse gases, carbon dioxide is the most significant contributor to global warming and in many regards, the global climate crisis is a major challenge for facing governments.

One study noted that the extraction, transport and refining of crude oil account for between 15 and 40% of total greenhouse gas emissions associated with transportation fuels such as gasoline and diesel. Different types of crude oil tend to have quite different properties, but the major impact comes from the amount of methane burned or released in large quantities in the extraction process via flaring, venting and fugitive gas emissions.

1. In this regard, many oil companies are slowly tilting their production towards renewables and global oil production is set to decline after 2025. BP amidst the decrease in demand from Covid 19 as well as the generalized thrust towards renewable energy indicated in August 2020 that it would reshape itself from an international oil company to an international energy company. Shell also announced similar cuts in September 2020 as it stated its intentions to make a greater shift to low carbon energy. In its policy guidelines the government of T&T would do well to maximize the rents from the oil sector now, whilst charting a way forward, independent of oil rents.

Table 2.9 T&T's exports in 000s US$

	Total	*Coconuts, Cashew Nuts, Fresh/Dried*	*Raw Sugar,*	*Refined Sugar*	*Molasses*	*Cocoa Beans Raw/Roasted*	*Distilled Alcoholic Beverages*	*Natural Asphalt and Natural Bitumen*	*Crude Petroleum*
1973	695,742.7	1.3	22,419.4	26.6	2971.1	2917.1	3413.2	1961.2	111,779.2
1974	2,037,663	1	52,321.3	55.1	2670.1	4757.9	5062.7	2293.6	520,050.3
1975	1,772,725	0.6	75,860	153.3	1069.6	6258.2	5451.3	1938.5	574,002.2
1976	2,219,265	0.6	47,889.8	101.1	3255.5	4131.8	4347.4	1819.3	602,495.2
1977	2,179,811	42.3	34,660.6	91.7	1984.6	8673.9	4948.1	1272.9	728,231.4
1978	2,042,711	9.7	22,280.4	80.5	1910.3	11,125.1	5896.5	150.7	764,506.6
1979	2,610,434	2	35,060.4	90.7	2173.1	9123.3	7707.6	1398	985,307.8
1980	4,077,015	10.6	27,912	92.4	1641.5	7365	7029.3	1355.7	1,635,292
1981	3,760,819	1.7	26,973.1	95.4	1864.6	7333.7	6565.7	472.6	1,612,356
1982	3,085,451	0.5	21,760.6	104.3	1029.8	4468.2	7364.4	2825.7	1,116,363
1983	2,352,662	41.3	25,086.8	133.5	603.1	2916.3	5521.8	2807	1,099,437
1984	2,173,417	0.5	25,133.1	123	715.8	3181.4	6604.6	4637.6	955,433.7
1985	2,160,912	23.5	20,843.9	21.7	608.2	2999	7247.5	6491.6	998,818.2
1986	1,385,677	30.8	23,318.9	12	1956.8	3128.4	8741.7	6074	551,809
1987	1,462,398	56.8	21,047.6	47	4108.1	3354.9	5502.5	6756.1	519,822.5
1988	1,411,983	94.8	23,601.3	19.2	1787.4	3421.6	6568.4	6339.6	420,886.8
1989	1,578,095	160	29,823.3	20.5	875.1	2991.5	7353.1	8691.8	501,894.8
1990	2,080,422	83.6	30,439.3	25.8	39.4	5569.3	9872.4	5896.7	757,578.8
1991	1,959,603	76.6	31,076.9	54.1	1215.8	4996.5	9466.2	120.9	609,431.9
1992	1,834,781	1.6	32,898.3	81.8	13.4	2698.4	10,755.1	33.6	441,179.3
1993	1,662,103	2.6	26,693.8	277.5	3.1	3852	9944.7	103.2	354,834.6
1994	1,954,277	41.7	28,013.7	2585.5	2.7	3325.1	11,176.6	8.8	352,794.2
1995	2,466,978	123.3	41,782.5	562.9	3114.9	3542.1	7708.4	146.5	391,347.7

(continued)

Table 2.9 (continued)

	Total	*Coconuts, Cashew Nuts, Fresh/Dried*	*Raw Sugar,*	*Refined Sugar*	*Molasses*	*Cocoa Beans Raw/Roasted*	*Distilled Alcoholic Beverages*	*Natural Asphalt and Natural Bitumen*	*Crude Petroleum*
1996	2,456,435	84.5	27,519.2	221.1	385.7	2752.8	16,560.6	514.9	439,512.3
1997	2,452,562	92.1	39,035.4	4698.1	15.9	2559.3	24,649.7	162.3	447,404.5
1998	2,263,756	98.6	31,436.7	437.6	8.5	2167.8	25,519	868.2	253,100.6
1999	2,805,662	102	33,235.9	462.1	26.7	2673.6	19,307.6	920	365,075
2000	4,273,440	141.3	36,112.5	390.6	73.5	2663.1	24,765	384.1	571,364.7
2001	5,113,372	117.8	26,032.7	291.5	119	1636.7	26,257	1735.4	477,351.8
2002	3,853,319	140.4	24,662.1	208	50.5	3103.9	26,557.9	3986.3	598,207.4
2003	5,117,971	52.3	12,878.3	376.7	14.7	2558.5	19,156	5241.8	446,037.7
2004	6,517,183	69.1	29,060.1	116.5	23.7	2325.6	15,970.7	1902.3	818,030.9
2005	9,611,439	88.6	26,585.8	183.9	21	2350.3	30,970.6	4984.2	1,450,597
2006	14,018,696	113.3	37,229.8	228.5	41.4	2982.6	29,730.2	8018.9	2,103,106
2007	13,375,141	81.3	20,484.5	156.8	61.7	3317.9	40,329.6	13,179.6	1,711,822
2008	18,629,838	117.4	3143.5	1801.2	36.4	2665.8	26,178.7	7331.8	2,067,621
2009	8,755,726	2.4	1882.5	324.7	57.9	1972.7	20,969.9	18,070.5	1,101,542
2010	9,991,811	3.6	199.6	173.9	45.3	2263.8	21,948.7	3208.4	1,367,494

Source Synthesized data sources

Table 2.10 Crude oil production by technique

	Flowing average number of wells	*Flowing production 000 bbls*	*Gas air lift average number of wells*	*Gas air lift production 000 bbls*	*Pumping average number of wells*	*Pumping production 000 bbls*	*Plunger lift average number of wells*	*Production plunger lift 000 bbls*
1946	615	12,346	59	680	882	5910	216	1189
1947	625	12,366	55	709	924	6149	224	1197
1948	629	11,666	56	700	1051	6549	225	1161
1949	616	11,671	70	897	1130	6871	218	1161
1950	594	10,892	101	1266	1225	7299	225	1159
1951	584	10,332	91	1347	1322	8080	222	1064
1952	594	10,296	102	1290	1420	8407	229	1239
1953	639	11,619	133	1319	1477	8128	240	1240
1954	692	12,887	154	1286	1533	8166	254	1275
1955	719	14,472	151	1256	1565	7801	269	1356
1956	795	17,696	188	1849	1592	8191	246	1184
1957	882	22,215	221	2385	1676	8316	248	1141
1958	922	24,770	266	3150	1664	8125	272	1301
1959	951	27,853	321	3928	1662	7738	264	1393
1960	969	29,743	362	4549	1586	6646	268	1400
1961	1047	32,790	403	4541	1510	6925	273	1479
1962	1026	35,006	450	5397	1486	6891	309	1582
1963	1007	34,383	460	6206	1412	6812	248	1277
1964	1012	34,105	543	7450	1386	6864	266	1312
1965	919	29,814	679	10,502	1385	7332	243	1210
1966	934	32,836	841	14,310	1398	7406	231	1051
1967	891	38,250	971	18,687	1364	7142	200	915
1968	795	39,958	1113	19,171	1302	7005	171	770
1969	708	32,358	1108	17,458	1308	6875	138	727
1970	929	27,388	1563	15,884	2008	7180	248	594
1971	559	23,334	988	13,843	1373	9467	109	505
1972	525	28,212	883	11,758	1440	10,782	80	459
1973	506	37,753	784	10,545	1551	12,070	53	301
1974	500	45,084	743	10,313	1669	12,588	36	160
1975	430	57,563	667	9812	1646	11,372	24	83
1976	438	52,668	702	11,527	1852	13,475	4	2
1977	430	52,450	697	17,526	2017	13,641	4	1
1978	506	50,216	619	19,515	2146	14,045		
1979	516	40,577	599	23,231	2281	14,442		
1980	396	36,165	632	26,564	2320	14,883		
1981	392	26,013	630	29,093	2838	14,009		

(continued)

Table 2.10 (continued)

	Flowing average number of wells	*Flowing production 000 bbls*	*Gas air lift average number of wells*	*Gas air lift production 000 bbls*	*Pumping average number of wells*	*Pumping production 000 bbls*	*Plunger lift average number of wells*	*Production plunger lift 000 bbls*
1982	392	21,354	552	29,383	2420	13,878	9	3
1983	344	15,237	496	30,127	2292	12,979	7	2
1984	319	16,303	464	32,009	2351	13,727	7	2
1985	325	16,576	463	32,838	2372	13,839	5	4
1986	352	17,952	485	30,450	2357	13,220	1	7
1987	320	13,371	529	30,117	2392	13,147	1	3
1988	331	13,952	547	28,386	2364	12,865	-	-
1989	364	14,459	554	28,229	2266	11,812		3
1990	371	17,597	567	25,966	2216	11,437	2	32
1991	368	13,927	614	26,983	2229	11,480	2	23
1992	333	12,329	627	25,595	2321	11,238	2	22
1993	326	10,439	596	23,194	2396	10,979	1	13
1994	286	11,107	608	25,443	2420	10,658	1	17
1995	265	13,251	582	23,944	2490	10,095	-	-
1996	294	12,777	556	23,688	3063	10,657	-	-
1997	354	12,452	541	21,760	3159	10,944	-	-
1998	398	12,208	539	22,164	3158	10,380	-	-
1999	395	16,033	479	20,040	2996	9538	-	-
2000	426	14,081	464	19,961	2980	9427	-	-
2001	356	12,328	470	19,739	2823	9105	-	-
2002	308	19,898	467	18,525	2674	9061	-	
2003	308	21,336	459	17,876	2822	9723	-	-
2004	311	17,010	437	15,564	2901	12,120	-	-
2005	289	26,253	439	14,133	2931	12,115	-	-
2006	259	26,609	454	13,840	2877	11,382	-	-
2007	265	22,081	416	11,225	2975	10,745	-	-
2008	271	20,961	397	10,359	3065	10,390	-	-
2009	264	18,650	367	10,280	3014	10,060	-	-
2010	251	16,027	364	10,096	3068	9574	-	-
2011	226	14,821	350	9139	3049	9453	-	-
2012	206	11,144	340	9057	3015	9580	-	-
2013	192	11,000	330	9050	2968	9450	-	-

2.7 Conclusion

This chapter reviewed the economic history of oil production and exploration in T&T. By 2020, 3.71 billion barrels of crude oil were produced, although in recent times production has slowed. From the time T&T commenced crude oil production, the staple export base migrated from agricultural goods to crude oil, from land production to marine production and the economy is now in a phase dominated by natural gas production. In total 1.629 bn barrels of crude oil was produced on land and 2.077 bn barrels offshore. Indeed in 2020, crude oil production as a percentage of total oil and gas production was 8.5% as compared to 76.6% in 1975. Reserves of crude oil though have fallen sharply over time and in 2018 stood at 243 mn barrels as compared to 1.125bn barrels in 2002 or 510 mn barrels in 1964.

In the early stages, royalties were not aggressively collected, because of all British land lease policies. However, this changed with time. As production increased and the easy oil was found, the depth drilled increased. In total since 1897, a total of 63.4 mn feet has been drilled in search of oil and gas.

Not surprisingly, given the importance of this sector and the high value added, its contribution to GDP increased over time, this created problems of its own. However, the high capital density of the sector also meant that it never employed significantly more than twenty thousand odd workers.

The global environment is changing and our understanding of the impact of increasing amounts of carbon dioxide on global warming has improved. T&T will have to keep this uppermost in its mind as it navigates the extraction of its remaining oil in the twenty-first century.

References

Alleyne, Doddridge. (2010). "Export/Import Trends and Economic Development in Trinidad, 1919–1939." IL: Canoe Press.

Alleyne, N.A., and Stoute, V. (2014). Options for Monetising Deep Water Gas in Trinidad and Tobago. SPE Energy Resources Conference. Society of Petroleum Engineers.

Bekele, L. Francis. (2003). "The History of Cocoa Production in Trinidad and Tobago." In Re-vitalisation of the Trinidad & Tobago Cocoa Industry: Proceedings of the APASTT Seminar, Trinidad and Tobago: Association of Professional Agricultural Scientists of Trinidad and Tobago.

Bekele, F.L. (2004). "The History of Cocoa Production in Trinidad and Tobago." In Proceedings of the APASTT Seminar – Exhibition entitled Re-vitalisation of the Trinidad & Tobago Cocoa Industry (pp. 4–12), 20 September 2003, St. Augustine, Trinidad.
Besson, A. Gerard. (2008a). "Black Gold, Part 2: War and Peace." First Magazine Ltd.
Besson, A. Gerard. (2008b). "Black Gold, the Real El Dorado." First Magazine Ltd.
Besson, A. Gerard. (2008c). "Black Gold Part 3: The Road to Independence." First Magazine Ltd.
Besson, A. Gerard. (2008d). "History of Oil Part 2." The Caribbean History Archives. Paria Publishing Co LTD.
Best, Lloyd. (1968). "A Model of Pure Plantation Economy." Social and Economic Studies 17 (3): 283–326.
Boopsingh, T., and McGuire, G. (2014). From Oil to Gas and Beyond: A Review of the Trinidad and Tobago Model and Analysis of Future Challenges. University Press of America.
Boyd, D.T. (2008). Stratigraphic Guide to Oil and Gas Reservoirs: Oklahoma Geological Survey SP2008–1.
Brereton, Bridget. (1996). "An Introduction to the History of Trinidad and Tobago 1783–1962." Oxford: Heinemann.
Brewster, H.R. (1968). Exports, Employment and Wages in Trinidad and Tobago and Mr. Seers' Model of the Open Economy. CSO Research Paper (5).
Bruce, C.J. (1972). The Open Petroleum Economy: A Comparison of Keynesian and Alternative Formulations. Social and Economic Studies 24 (2).
de Roberts, L.C. (1980). "El Ecuador en la época cacaotera." Quito: Editorial Universitaria.
Dolin, E.J. (2007). "Leviathan: The History of Whaling in America." New York: W. W. Norton.
Down, A.L. (1960). History of Trinidad's Oil. Geological Society of Trinidad and Tobago.
Dvosky, George. (2012). "1846: The Year We Hit Peak Sperm Whale Oil." http://io9.com/5930414/1846-the-year-we-hit-peak-spearm-whale-oil.
Eaton, S.J.M. (1866). "Petroleum: A History of the Oil Region of Venago County, Pennsylvania." Philadelphia: J.P. Skelly & Co., 299 pp.
Government of Trinidad and Tobago. (1906). "Annual Administrative Report." Ministry of Energy and Energy Affairs Trinidad and Tobago.
Government of Trinidad and Tobago. (1932). "Annual Administrative Report." Ministry of Energy and Energy Affairs Trinidad and Tobago.
Government of Trinidad and Tobago. (1935). "Annual Administrative Report." Ministry of Energy and Energy Affairs Trinidad and Tobago.

Government of Trinidad and Tobago. (1948). "Annual Administrative Report." Ministry of Energy and Energy Affairs Trinidad and Tobago.
Higgins, E. George. (1996). "A History of Trinidad Oil." Trinidad Express Limited (Port of Spain). Express Production House.
Holland., T (1928). "Oil Industry in Trinidad." Council Paper No. s6, 128.
Penny, W.F., and Lonsdale-Harris, J. (1955). "A History of Trinidad Oil."
Scottish Engineering Hall of Fame. Org, 2014.
Thomas, C.Y. (1965). "Monetary and Financial Arrangements in a Dependent Monetary Economy." Mona: ISER.
T&T Chamber of Industry and Commerce. (2006). "Randolph Rust a Man of Unfaltering Faith." Trinidad Guardian Newspaper.
Tewarie, B., and Hosein, R. (2007). "Trade Investment and Development in the Contemporary Caribbean." Ian Randle.
Trinidad Guardian Newspaper. (2006). Scouting, Cadets and Boys Brigade.

CHAPTER 3

History of Oil Refining in T&T

3.1 Introduction

This chapter traces out the economic history of the oil refining subsector in the T&T economy.

The refining of hydrocarbons in T&T may be argued by some to have started even before commercial production of oil in T&T. Indeed, the Merrimac Oil Company in 1857, set up a plant mining the asphalt from the Pitch Lake, to manufacture illuminating oil. Furthermore Arthur Beeby Thompson in 1907 constructed a small still and condenser at Guapo and in so doing formed, what to the best of this research inquest, represents the first proper attempt to produce refined products from crude oil (Beaubrun 2008).

The first real refinery was established in 1911, by Trinidad Oilfields Limited in Point Fortin (MEEA 1911). In 1913, two small refineries were setup, one in Tabaquite by Trinidad Oilfields Limited, and the other in the Perseverance Estate in Point Fortin. The Trinidad Central Oilfields also constructed a larger refinery to treat crude oil (MEEA 1913–1914).

The push to get refineries going from early was central to the British cause. Indeed, one of the primary motives of one of the earliest pioneers of Trinidad oil, Randolph Rust, was to create a stable source of fuel supply for the British navy. In this regard, in a speech to the Victorian Institute, Randolph Rust noted, "*it has also been manifest that Great Britain, before adopting Oil as fuel for her Navy, must be sure of a source of supply which*

R. Hosein, *Oil and Gas in Trinidad and Tobago*,
https://doi.org/10.1007/978-3-030-77669-5_3

the outbreak of war will not cut off, and that it is therefore important that sources of supply should, if possible, be found on British territory..........In the light of my discoveries, I felt Trinidad, England's most valuable possession in the West Indies, being as it is one of the keys to the Panama Canal, now rapidly approaching completion, might herself one day be one of the chief sources of supply of oil fuels, and thanks to that and her unique position, might become one of our very most important naval bases...".[1]

In the same vein, "*Winston Churchill, while serving the British Government as First Lord of the Admiralty, had listened to the advice coming from Admiral Fisher, ... with regard to the availability of oil in Trinidad, had decided to change the Royal Navy from burning coal to using oil to fire its furnaces. Trinidad became for all intents and purposes, a gas station in the South Atlantic*" Besson (2008b, p. 3). Thus, one of the early factors influencing the refinery sector in T&T was some degree of imperial preference by the British.

This chapter, after surveilling the available literature, divides the discussion of oil refining activity in T&T into three periods, before Texaco, after Texaco up until state takeover (of Texaco) in 1985 and state takeover of the Texaco refinery up to its closure in November 2018.

3.2 Before Texaco: The Period Before 1956

From the start of commercial oil exploration activity in T&T, several oil refineries were built. This chapter focuses on the Petrotrin[2] (previously Texaco) oil refinery located in Pointe-a-Pierre on the south-west coast of Trinidad, as it is the only refinery that has withstood the multiplicity of challenges for, roughly one hundred years of existence. Specifically, the refinery at Pointe-a-Pierre started as a Distillation Unit setup in 1917 by Trinidad Leaseholds Limited (TLL),[3] from which it exported, refined products. This initial plant cost the company £42,000, which processed 1200 barrels per day and remained in use until 1928.

[1] Cited in Julien (2005) "The emergence of the National energy Sector," 19th Eric Williams Memorial lectures.

[2] Note that Petrotrin was closed on the 30 November 2018. A tender to restart the refinery has since been posted.

[3] Higgins (1996, p. 195) notes that "*Trinidad Leaseholds Limited was undoubtedly the most important company in the development of Trinidad's oilindustry.*"

TLL pumped oil to its refinery at Pointe-a-Pierre via 6-inch pipelines from its various fields.[4] The company had wells in Fyzabad, Barackpore and Guayaguayare. By the 1920s the refinery was also refining crude oil from other companies such as: Apex Oilfields Limited, Trinidad Oil Producing and Refining Company Ltd, Oropuche Oilfields Limited, Palo Seco Oilfields Limited, New Dome Oilfields and the Siparia Trinidad Oilfields Limited. After October 1919, TLL exported refined petroleum products.

By 1912, 37,842 barrels of crude oil were cumulatively refined in the colony and in 1917, 505,002 barrels of crude oil were refined in the colony (see Table 3.1). Annual throughput by 1918 increased to 2,106,369 barrels. This increase was partly orchestrated by the decision to switch the Royal Navy Ships from coal steamers to fuel engines in 1915. Indeed, an increased volume of crude had to be refined to supply these ships, and demand increased further when World War I started in 1914. Between 1923 and 1925 the volume of crude oil refined increased from 2,360,279 barrels to 3,433,902 barrels, an increase of 45.49%. This was in part because the British Military had established a base in Trinidad to secure fuel supply for its fleets. The amount of crude oil refined continued to increase and in 1927 stood at 4,796,223 barrels increasing further by approximately 2 million[5] barrels to 6,725,383 barrels in 1928. By 1930 output levels of refined crude oil increased to 7,989,679 barrels but by 1932 declined to 6,899,144 (on account of the Global Recession).[6]

The refinery at Pointe-a-Pierre was further advanced in 1938 when additional installations were made at the No. 5 Dubbs and hydrogen and isooctane plants. By 1939, the economy was refining and exporting 17

[4] TLL constructed roads to their Morne L'Enfer estate, erected bungalows, and storage tanks to store oil. They later laid pipelines from their oil fields to the refinery at Point-a-Pierre.

[5] Specifically, the MEEA report (1927, p. 24) noted that, "*considerable extensions to the refining and shipping depot at Point-a-Pierre were in progress during the year. However, by the end of 1927 the rapid increase in the refinery process technologies globally challenged the company to upgrade its refinery. In August 1928 and December 1929 the company brought on stream two topping plants. They also introduced a new steam turbine driven power station. The company also introduced a Edeleaneau testing plant to reduce aromatic hydrocarbonsfrom the process of producing kerosene. This was on account of changes at TLL*".

[6] With the passing of time and the injection of significant amounts of foreign capital, one source noted, "*This company continues to be the most important one in the colony from the refining and marketing view point*" (MEEA 1931, p. 6).

Table 3.1 Comparative statement of oil refined in the colony

Year	*Barrels*
Cumulative to 1912	37,842
1913	9484
1914	35,061
1915	58,437
1916	107,822
1917	505,002
1918	2,106,369
1919	1,149,943
1920	1,391,373
1921	1,495,487
1922	1,806,016
1923	1,820,018
1924	2,360,279
1925	3,433,902
1926	3,890,343
1927	3,786,876
1928	4,796,223
1929	6,725,383
1930	7,642,726
1931	7,989,379
1932	6,899,144
1933	7,635,296
1934	9,029,810
1935	10,846,584
1936	11,848,285
1937	13,028,161
1938	15,111,046
1939	17,596,932
1940	19,414,920
1941	22,060,110
1942	20,812,467
1943	21,914,247
1944	22,498,439
1945	23,170,211

Source MEEA, various years

times more than its 1920 output level per annum, and 4.41 times the level of output in 1926.

With the start of the second world war the MEEA (1940, p. 1) noted, "… *the operations of the industry have been primarily determined by Government requirements for War purposes and it is satisfactory to record that the petroleum resources of the Colony have been able to fulfil, without difficulty and without departing from normal production methods, all demands made upon them.*" During the war itself, a project code named Project 1234 was built in a 14-month period. In this regard, the Petrotrin publication labelled, "Down Memory Lane: The Evolution of Petrotrin" (2013, p. 13) noted that: "*Project 1234 began at Pointe a Pierre and was completed in 14 months. The completion of this project resulted essentially in a new refinery at Point-a-Pierre. Project 1234 involved a two stage reforming unit to produce butane – butylene, a sulphuric acid alkylation unit for reacting with iso-butane to make alkylate, an isomerization unit to convert normal butane into iso butane, a crude oil topping unit and a gasoline re-run unit to produce spirit for blending with alkylate.*"

3.2.1 Refinery Output

The Table 3.2 shows that, prior to the take-over by Texaco, the main refinery output was fuels/oil flux[7]; followed by gas/diesel oil, Liquefied Petroleum Gas (LPG) and Aviation Turbine Fuels (ATF) produced by Trinidad Leasehold Limited (TLL). The petroleum products from T&T were very important and indeed just after the WWII it was noted that, "*no company in the world, certainly no British Company did so much for the War effort in relation to its size as Trinidad Leasehold Limited*" (Besson 2008b, p. 50).

Just prior to the takeover by Texaco, several pieces of legislation were passed to facilitate the importation of crude oil. The first of these was the Government's Duty Exemption Laws of 1948 which prompted the enhanced growth of the refinery sector. The 1948 laws allowed TLL to import both crude oil and blending stock duty free. In order to protect and encourage the production of local crude oil, Trinidad Customs imposed duties, on imported crude and refined petroleum products, but permitted imports of crude oil and charging stocks, free of duty. Indeed, it had become clear that by the end of the war that refining capacity in Trinidad was considerably in excess of that required to process indigenous production. Consequently, Government granted several applications to Trinidad Leaseholds Limited to import crude oil free of duty, and on 31 December 1948, these permits altogether covered an average volume

[7] Flux oil is a petroleum distillate used to produce a long-term reduction in the viscosity of bitumen.

Table 3.2 Refinery output and capacity utilization (1956–1986)

Year	*Crude oil production 000 barrels*	*Refinery throughput 000 barrels per annum*	*Refinery throughput less crude oil production 000 barrels per annum*	*Refinery capacity utilization ratio %*
1956	28,929	44,882	15,953	90.8
1957	34,064	50,467	16,403	97.4
1958	37,355	60,256	22,901	102
1959	40,919	68,061	27,142	105.4
1960	42,357	65,734	23,377	61.9
1961	45,768	103,755	57,987	94.8
1962	48,867	109,256	60,389	99.8
1963	48,678	120,000	71,322	96.7
1964	49,731	127,550	77,819	89.4
1965	48,859	137,165	88,306	96.4
1966	55,603	144,193	88,590	101.3
1967	64,995	138,925	73,930	95.2
1968	66,904	151,282	84,378	99.4
1969	57,429	154,077	96,648	96.8
1970	51,043	154,850	103,807	97.3
1971	47,144	145,539	98,395	91.4
1972	51,211	143,872	92,661	86.2
1973	60,670	141,675	81,005	85.1
1974	68,136	130,811	62,675	78.6
1975	78,621	85,649	21,379	51.5
1976	77,673	117,104	39,431	70.2
1977	83,609	99,511	15,902	59.8
1978	83,809	85,809	2000	51.6
1979	78,209	82,909	4700	49.8
1980	77,608	84,609	7001	50.7
1981	69,109	63,347	−5762	46.3
1982	64,621	51,099	−13,522	40.3
1983	58,340	27,179	−31,161	23.3
1984	61,897	28,149	−33,748	24
1985	64,361	28,930	−35,431	26
1986	61,652	30,232	−31,420	26.9

Source Handbook of key economic Indicators

of 1,100,000 barrels of imports per month. On this basis, the state noted that, "*The importation of paraffinic-based crudes is essential for the local manufacture of kerosene, diesel oils and a base for lubricating oils. The company was therefore granted a permit to import duty free, for a period of*

25 years commencing on the 1st January, 1949, crude oil and/or charging stocks and/or blending stocks for its own account or for processing and re-exportation in such quantities as will at any particular time be necessary to maintain the companies refineries, at full operating capacity" (MEEA 1948, p. 6).

3.3 Texaco and the Years Ahead

The Second World War led to a change in the dominant economic power in the world away from the UK towards the USA. This shift was felt in T&T, as in 1956, Trinidad Leaseholds Limited was taken over by the Texas Company, of the USA. The Texas Company previously had a small part to play in the T&T economy in 1912 when it was involved in marketing kerosene. In 1938 it was also involved in the Antilles fields with Mc Coll Frontenac's Antilles venture (Higgins 1996). In 1940, Texaco (as the Texas Company came to be called) also entered a processing agreement with TLL to refine their imported crude oil. Texaco, in realization that refined crude was of greater demand, value and importance during the war, struck a deal with TLL's refinery in order to refine their raw crude and obtain higher returns (Higgins 1996). In 1949, this company also purchased the Brighton Terminal, Limited, a 5000 bpd refinery from a company in New York (the Barber Oil Company) and with this came the rights to utilize part of the Brighton jetty. At this stage, Tony Bearburn, a retired Texaco engineer noted, "*The original reason why Texaco decided to buy the Leaseholds properties was because the then Chairman of Texaco had been a major figure in the oil supply chain for the European World War II effort. He recognised the value of the Pointe-a-Pierre refinery in supplying both Europe and West Africa*" (Higgins 1996, p. 248). At the time of the takeover, the refinery consisted of the following major units: Crude Distillation, Vacuum Distillation, Visbreaking, FCCU and Alkylation Unit.

3.3.1 Crude Oil Imports

To facilitate the optimal functioning of the refinery, T&T's imported crude oil came mainly from Venezuela, Saudi Arabia, Libya, Indonesia and Nigeria. Saudi Arabia would become the biggest source for crude oil imports by T&T in 1975, although Indonesia and Venezuela were still important sources. In 1980, Saudi Arabia and Indonesia were still amongst the top five main sources of crude oil imports in T&T but Panama, Angola and Libya also joined the ranks of the most important sources of crude oil imports for the refinery in T&T, in later years.

A significant development in 1961 i.e. just after Texaco's takeover of the TLL refinery was that five economies formed the Organization of Petroleum Exporting Countries (OPEC) in 1961 namely, Saudi Arabia, Iran, Iraq, Venezuela and Kuwait. Up until the formation of OPEC, oil companies significantly controlled the oil market. The formation of OPEC, however, changed this dynamic and they became a powerful group. On October 6, 1973, the Yom Kippur War started as Egypt and Syria invaded Israel. OPEC's reactions resulted in increased oil prices from US$3.29 in 1973 per barrel to US$11.58 on January 1, 1974. As world oil prices increased, many refineries had to trim output as demand fell. Even so, Texaco proceeded to undertake ambitious and expensive refinery upgrades.

In particular, one of the main concerns of the USA regarding fuel oil imported from Texaco was the degree of sulphur which it contained. The company commenced addressing this concern by building a desulphurization plant (New York Times 1971). However, administrative obstacles related to the Ease of Doing Business in a fledgling independent state started to rear their head. Specifically, after the desulphurization plant was built at a cost of US$90 mn in 1972 (in 2018 dollars using Trinidad and Tobago's inflation rate this would amount to US$3.7 bn), it was affected by power outages as related to electricity supply. When a gas turbine driven generator was sourced and import plans to bring it into the economy were made, the company could not obtain import authorization as the Trinidad and Tobago Electricity Commission (T&TEC) had a monopoly on power generation (Higgins 1996).

The Petroleum Taxes Act of 1974 struck another blow to the company and the oil refining sector.[8] The main characteristic of this Act was the imposition of the Petroleum Profits Corporation Tax on the producing and marketing operation of companies, at the rate of 47.5% and by

[8] One of the key objective of the recommendations made by the Mostofi Commission was to "*safeguard the interest of the nation by providing certain changes in the existing tax system and other fiscal borders, and their mode of applications so as to ensure the oilindustry in Trinidad contributes in every way possible within its means, to the national income and government reserves*" (p. 35).

1975, 50%. Marketing, refining and producing were treated as independent activities so that losses in one sector could not affect losses in other sectors. These taxes adversely affected the company.[9] Trinidad oil was processed but crude imports were cut back.

Further crude prices rose but refined petroleum product prices didn't increase in tandem.[10] For example, between 1972 and 1979 oil prices increased by 1169% whilst the price of leaded gasoline increased by 137%.

3.3.2 Refinery Output and Capacity Utilization

At the point of takeover by Texaco, the T&T economy produced 28.9 million barrels of oil and refined 44.8 million barrels of crude oil with an overall refinery capacity utilization of 90.8% (see Table 3.2). With the various refinery upgrades that Texaco undertook, refinery throughput climbed to 154.8 million barrels per annum in 1970, with an associated refinery capacity utilization of 97.3%.[11] For the time in which Texaco controlled the refinery, the average utilization of the refinery per annum was 73.75% and the refinery throughput averaged 96.49 million, per annum. For the period up to the implementation of the Petroleum Taxes Act in 1974, Texaco engaged a refinery utilization rate of 98.1% and a throughput rate of 115.3 million barrels per annum. Indeed, Besson (2008b, p. 80) noted that, "*Texaco's Pointe-a-Pierre refinery was undoubtedly in the front rank of the world's largest and most highly integrated refineries. This huge industrial and residential complex stood on what once were six coconut estates with pretty French names: Bon Accord, La Carriere, Concord, Bonne Aventure, Plein Palais and Plaisance. As such, in its first 50 years, the refinery grew from a small batch distillation plant, perched on a*

[9] Levy (1958) sounded a warning bell much earlier to this effect in noting that, "*the framework of petroleumlegislation and tax practice embracing oiloperations can act either as a stimulus or a deterrent to the validity of the oil economy*" (p. 127).

[10] A factor that challenged investment decisions was the change in government's take on the petroleum sector following the Black Power rumblings of 1970s. Indeed by 1972 the then Finance Minister George Chambers noted, "*we cannot reasonably be expected to be significantly out of line with the rest of the oilproducing countries in the developing world*" (Budget Speech 1972, p. 536).

[11] Refinery capacity utilization exceeds 100% when refinery creep occurs. This is when there is an increase in capacity that is unaccounted for, and so the data can reflect a utilization rate in excess of 100%.

hillside near a vulnerable pipeline viaduct, to a huge petroleum and petrochemical complex with its attendant tank farm, reservoirs, and shipping port…".

3.3.3 Employment

From an employment perspective, the oil refining sector absorbed 6,808 employees in 1973, but by 1985 in tandem with the decline in the amount of economic activity in this sector, the employment level tumbled and in 1985, employment levels in the refinery sector stood at 3807 workers (see Fig. 3.1) a decline of 44.08%.

Significantly, refining activity in T&T was influenced by the trade union movement. Trade unionization began in T&T in 1897 with the formation of the Working Men's Reform Club formulated by Charles Phillips but took more form and action with Tubal Uriah Buzz Butler. Butler was a Grenadian born, preacher and labour leader in Trinidad and Tobago. Butler became involved in the labour movement in Trinidad in 1935 as he led a hunger march and was pivotal in protests against unfair treatment

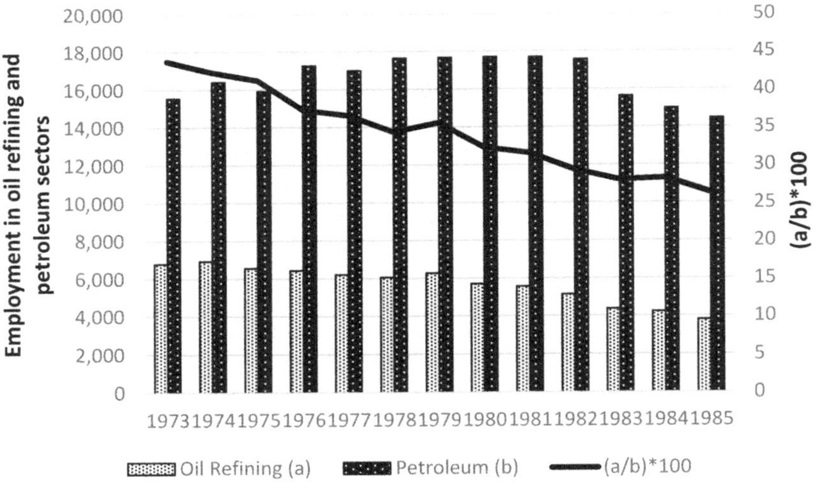

Fig. 3.1 Employment trends (level and share) in the Petroleum sector, 1973–2002 (*Source* MEEA and CSO Reports [various years])

Table 3.3 Industrial disputes involving Stoppages of work by Industry, 1956–65

	All industries	*Agriculture*		*Building*	*Mining and refining (oil)*	*Manufacturing*	*Transport and communication*
		Total	*Sugar*				
1956	7	4	2			2	1
1957	6	1					2
1958	12			1	1	3	2
1959	69	9	1	6	18	3	8
1960	31	7	2	1	6	2	4
1961	35	6	2	7		2	8
1962	75	7	5	16	29	3	4
1963	48	10	4	12	8	6	2
1964	44	5		3	12	10	4
1965	4	2	2	1		1	
Sum	331	51	18	47	74	32	35

of petroleum workers in South Trinidad and had a strong presence in the Oilfield Workers Trade Union (OWTU).[12]

In 1932 the Trade Union Ordinance was introduced, which allowed the formation and recognition of trade unions. In 1938 the Trade Disputes Ordinances permitted the formation of a Board of Inquiry and Arbitration Tribunal. The Trade Dispute Ordinance would come to hold an important place as strike activity in T&T increased considerably after 1937. The OWTU was formed on July 25, 1937 and led strike activity in the petroleum sector in T&T. Specifically, as concerns all industries between 1956 and 1965 there were 331 stoppages, of which 74 were in mining and refining with 51 in agriculture and 35 in the transport and communication sector. Table 3.3 shows the industrial disputes in each sector. Certainly, in terms of the number of incidents, the mining and refining sector witnessed more strike activity in the period 1956–1965.

The form in which data on strikes was collected and reported changed after 1965 and restarted in 1973. Consistent data is available from 1983 and in this regard note that for the period 1983–2015 there were 51 major strikes in the BT sector, 94 in the NBT sector and 77 in the NT

[12] natt.gov.tt.

Table 3.4 Average number of man days lost per worker by sector on account of major strike activity by sector

	BT	*NBT*	*NT*
1983–1993	1.18	0.64	0.04
1994–2008	1.12	0.35	0.08
2009–2015	0.7	0.12	0

Source Own derivation

sector. It is possible to develop a metric of "intensity of union militancy" by evaluating the average amount of man days lost per sector by each worker. This is illustrated in the Table 3.4 and shows that in all the listed time periods the amount of man days lost was higher in the BT sector as compared to the NBT and the NT sector. Just as disturbingly is that the amount of man days lost in the NBT sector is on average more than the NT sector. Of significance though is that in the BT and the NBT tradable sectors, there is a downward trend in the average number of man days lost per worker by sector. It is possible that the wage demands of the union in the BT sector may have played a role in the demise of the refinery as wages grew to in excess of 50% of total expenses.

3.3.4 *Gross Domestic Product*

Refining value added in T&T climbed to a peak of TT$441.1 million in 1979 (from TT$69.3 mn in 1966) but thereafter declined to TT$34.6 million in 1985, a sharp decline by most standards. In this time period, the share of the oil refining sector in total economic activity declined from 9.6% in 1966 to 0.33% in 1985, as shown in Table 3.5.

This reflects that by the time the OWTU took over the refinery its share of GDP in T&T had collapsed from 0.33 to 11.4% in 1968.

3.3.5 *Production of Refined Petroleum Products*

In terms of the production of refined petroleum products, observe that most of the products experienced an increased level of output from 1956 to 1977 but thereafter, with the exception of LPG, declined.

Table 3.5 Gross domestic product by kind of activity—ISIC (US$ mn)

	Oil refineries	*GDP*	*Share refinery in total GDP*
1966	69.8	723.7	9.64
1967	65.5	772.6	8.48
1968	101	885.4	11.41
1969	88.9	909.1	9.78
1970	96.8	958.8	10.10
1971	96.4	1033.1	9.33
1972	109.8	1214.2	9.04
1973	121.5	1495.8	8.12
1974	176.5	2445.7	7.22
1975	186.2	3091.7	6.02
1976	206.2	3552.8	5.80
1977	232.9	4394.1	5.30
1978	231.6	4987.2	4.64
1979	441.1	6443.3	6.85
1980	242.5	8730.2	2.78
1981	97.7	9789.1	1.00
1982	80.1	11,396.3	0.70
1983	123.4	10,869.3	1.14
1984	181.5	10,859.8	1.67
1985	34.6	10,541.4	0.33

Source MEEA Reports (various years)

3.3.6 *Exports Destination of Refined Products*

In terms of export destination for refined petroleum products from T&T, these were mainly the USA, Sweden, the UK, Guyana and Canada in 1968 and remained broadly the same in 1970. In 1975, the USA and some of Trinidad and Tobago's intra CARICOM market partners (Barbados and Guyana) were the main export destination for the refined petroleum products from T&T and this pattern remained relatively unchanged for 1980 and 1985. In all of the listed time periods, "bunkers" were also a main source of refined petroleum product exports. (Note that prior to 1981, UN data for the United States included that of the United States of America and Puerto Rico. From 1981 to the present, data on the United States included that of the United States, Puerto Rico and the US Virgin Islands.)

What is clear from Table 3.6 is that, just as petroleum came to dominate exports (and as well as imports, foreign direct investment and

Table 3.6 Export destination for refined petroleum products, US$

1968		*1970*		*1975*	
Partner title	*Value*	*Partner title*	*Value*	*Partner title*	*Value*
USA (before 1981)	156,345,340	USA (before 1981)	186,533,949	USA (before 1981)	530,884,540
Sweden	35,562,368	Sweden	30,915,158	Bunkers	81,292,351
Bunkers	26,062,925	Bunkers	29,001,942	Guyana	37,224,278
United Kingdom	19,097,679	United Kingdom	16,377,236	Suriname	35,439,916
Guyana	7,623,815	Guyana	8,988,884	Jamaica	28,402,356
Canada	7,440,768	Neth. Antilles and Aruba	8,967,453	United Kingdom	16,900,621
Japan	7,164,894	Suriname	8,061,466	Nigeria	15,726,197
Neth. Antilles and Aruba	6,278,223	Canada	4,433,114	US Virgin Isds	12,001,647
Caribbean, news	6,233,434	Brazil	4,138,829	Neth. Antilles and Aruba	11,539,098
Denmark	5,303,227	US Virgin Isds	4,005,714	Canada	11,296,016
Suriname	5,276,710	Côte d'Ivoire	3,155,086	Netherlands	10,742,849
1980		1985			
Partner Title	Value	Partner Title	Value		
USA (before 1981)	813,240,432	USA	158,526,915		
Netherlands	222,049,046	Italy	85,214,838		
Bunkers	181,951,960	Guyana	54,767,399		
Suriname	137,690,932	Suriname	50,034,425		
Guyana	75,857,090	Barbados	49,287,711		
Italy	64,385,482	United Kingdom	48,472,059		
Guatemala	46,188,386	Jamaica	33,461,859		
Barbados	44,055,920	French Guiana	30,384,735		
Guinea	37,455,855	Bunkers	29,893,861		
Honduras	35,281,104	Netherlands	29,325,672		
Jamaica	33,725,740	Guadeloupe	28,127,632		

Source UN-Comtrade online database

government revenues); it also locked the economy into one predominant export market, the USA. This extreme form of dependence both from a product and a market perspective reared its head in later years, when the USA brought millions of barrels of light oil on-stream, via hydraulic fracturing.

3.4 State Ownership of the Refinery to the Present

Lloyd Best pioneered the theory of the plantation economy in the Caribbean (Best 1968; Best and Levitt 1968). The plantation system brought entrepreneurs from abroad to manage the plantations within the Caribbean sphere. Best took issue with this and together with Kari Levitt, argued that: "*Dependence on imported enterprise builds into the economy an assured backwardness, vis a vis a country whose entrepreneurial dynamic is indigenous*" (Best and Levitt 1968, p. 64). On this type of backdrop, Best (1968), expressed that the islands of the Caribbean needed to take over the commanding heights of their economies. More exactly, Best advocated that in order to ensure the development of the Caribbean region, the islands must regain control over their main staple resource, new staple or quasi-staple.[13] As Best notes: "*The conclusion which emerges is that the primary planning task in both time and importance is to create a framework within which the Caribbean economy would be able to make effective decisions about development. In terms of action, this means a transformation of the character of the corporations and a drastic revision of the terms of their participation. In this connection, measures for nationalization or even expropriation cannot be arbitrarily ruled out*" (Best 1971, p. 33)

Indeed in a powerful statement in favour of taking over the commanding heights of the economy, Best and Levitt (1968, p. 63) noted that: "*To give the economy the internal dynamic necessary to create new internal linkages, it is necessary to change the pattern of tastes, to develop residential industries with lower import content and larger local purchases, to increase the degree of local processing of agricultural and mineral resources, to reallocate land resources, to halt the brain drain, to restructure financial institutions, to widen the channels of national savings and investment flows and to break down the barriers between individual*

[13] A staple is a raw material or commodity grown or produced in a country or region.

territories within the region. In conditions of plantation economy such structural transformation is not possible without breaking the traditional patterns whereby Caribbean economy is incorporated into the metropolitan economy. It is for this reason that the localization of economic decision making lies at the heart of transformation."

The drive by Best and Levitt continued the type of arguments made by Dr. Eric Williams, a noted Oxford historian and scholar who said in 1955 "*Oil where all the evidence, from the earliest times, has indicated a subordination of local interests to those of external capital*" (cited in Julien 2005, p. 18). With the work of the Mostofi Commission in hand and the push for the takeover of the commanding heights of the economy, the government of T&T (as mentioned in the chapter before) took over the assets of BP in 1969. Several other significant steps in the creation of a national energy sector took place thereafter. One of these steps included the takeover of the Texaco refinery in 1985 for US$189.2 mn. Note that the OWTU in 1982 submitted to the then government an 80-page document for the nationalization of the assets of Texaco and insisted that it not be paid when these assets were nationalized. In 1983 as the tensions escalated, Texaco and GORTT engaged in discussions for Texaco's exit. To accelerate the process, the OWTU called for a major strike in 1984.

However, unlike the purchase of the BP assets and the Shell assets, the purchase of the Texaco refinery came at a time when the economy was in the throes of an economic recession and the unemployment rate had started to climb.[14] Specifically, between 1980 and 1985, the economy had changed course and the unemployment rate moved from 9.9 to 15.7%,

[14] It also came at a time when the refinery itself was becoming redundant: One former government Minister, Barry Barnes noted, "*Texacohad expanded the refinery in Trinidad after they took it over to be all things to all men. They had basic units, they had paraffin units, they had bits and pieces of every goddamn thing under the sun, the idea being to bring in the ultra-large crude carriers (ULCCs), which could not dock at Gulf of Mexico ports at the time, into Pointe-a-Pierre, drop off crude, refine it and then ship it on to the US in smaller tankers.*" However, T&T's value to Texaco in this regard evaporated as the Louisiana offshore oil port (LOOP) which could accommodate the ULCCs came on stream. Renwick in the National Energy Flagship: A profile of Petrotrin goes on to quote Minister Barnes as saying, "*They could now get tankers directly into the US refining system, so the Trinidad refinery, along with others in the Caribbean in places like Curaçao and Aruba, became absolutely redundant. Texaco informed the government that it had no further use for the refinery here. The government was faced with the choice of it being abandoned so, very reluctantly I might say, decided it had to purchase the damned thing*" cited in the National Energy Flagship: A profile of Petrotrin.

real GDP growth moved from 10.4 to −4.1% and the current account balance migrated into deficit from 5.7% in 1980 to −12.1% in 1983 and −6% in 1984.

There were varied opinions as to whether the refinery could be profitable or not. One commentator noted that the refinery was taken over with the intention of preserving some 3000 jobs and to prevent the economy moving from an exporter of petroleum products to an importer (Jarrett et al. 2019). Indeed Ronald Jay Williams, Trinidad and Tobago's then Minister of State Enterprises noted "*…they told us they were leaving. We had no choice.*" Indeed such was the economic rhythm at that time that whilst T&T undertook this social investment another multinational, Exxon corporation, was closing its Aruba refinery and the Royal Dutch Shell Group was in heavy negotiations with the government of Curacao regarding the long-term viability of its refinery in that economy. However, one comment that rang through was that of Trevor Farrell, a university lecturer at the Department of Economics St Augustine at the time, who noted that "*It would have been cheaper to put all the workers on the dole*" Treaster (1985).[15]

One official document, The Draft Energy Policy August Volume 2 (1992, p. 11) noted *that* "*Worldwide refineries were restructured to yield large volumes of higher valued products from cheaper lower grade crudes. Those unable to effectively compete were either closed down or their operations reduced. Between 1979 and 1989 primary capacity was out by 37%, in the USA by 11% and 23% in Japan. The upgrading of refineries rendered the Caribbean offshore refining systems that were designed to provide high yield of fuel oil, obsolete and uncompetitive. Unlike those closures of refineries in Aruba and Curacao (later reopened), the operating capacity of the refinery in Trinidad and Tobago was reduced to 80,000 barrels per day, sufficient to sustain the domestic and some regional markets, though at great costs. As Trinidad and Tobago faces the nineties, it must view the future of the refinery industry against this background and in the context of certain other factors that will influence the industry in the future.*"

On this type of basis and given the position indicated above, the first major upgrade of the refinery under state leadership started in 1991 and lasted for 7 years (Petrotrin 2013). The reason for the upgrade was to assist the company in producing higher value-added products such as

[15] Trinidad to keep refinery going by Joseph B. Treaster. The New York Times, April 1985.

gasoline, diesel, and jet fuel to 63% of the barrel. This initial upgrade helped to save the refinery from being mothballed. It was done at a cost of US$353 m borrowed from the IADB (Petrotrin 2013).

A second major upgrade started in 2005 and included a gasoline optimization plant and an Ultra-low sulphur diesel plant (ULSD). The ULSD was geared towards helping the company improve the quality of its gasoline and diesel output. By 2014, Petrotrin had completed the Gasoline Optimization Programme (GOP), but at significant cost overruns whilst the ULSD project remained incomplete at the time of mothballing of the refinery. The GOP original cost was at TT$650 million dollars but expenditure increased to TT$1.48 billion dollars.[16]

3.4.1 Refinery Capacity Utilization

In 1986, at around the time when the state took over the refinery, the capacity utilization ratio was down to 26.9% and until 1996 remained at less than 50% capacity utilization. In 1997, it improved to 55.2% and averaged 85.15% between 1998 and 2003. In 2005, refinery capacity utilization increased to 94% and averaged 86.1% on average per annum between 2005 and 2014 as shown in Table 3.7. In 1989, a technical study undertaken in Petrotrin motivated the 1991 refinery upgrade programme which was completed in 1997 at a cost of US$360 mn. This upgrade positioned the company to improve on its process flexibility, to improve the yield from the inputs and of its product outputs as well as improve on the associated air emissions quality. In 1999, the refinery added a bitumen facility which had two significant aspects, a blending plant, and a loading bay. By 2000, however, given the nature of the refinery business, further investments were recommended.[17]

After 1995 refinery capacity utilization was much more buoyant and by 1998 jumped to 78.7% and by 2000 to 92.1%. For the period 2000–2014 refinery capacity utilization averaged 85.1%. As mentioned previously, the refinery was closed in November 2018.

[16] ctntworld.com.

[17] Recommendations made by A.D. Little in a consultancy exercise.

Table 3.7 Crude oil production, refinery capacity utilization and proven reserves of crude oil, 1980–2018

Year	*Crude oil production 000 barrels*	*Refinery capacity utilization ratio %*	*Proven oil reserves billion barrels*
1980	77,608	50.7	0.7
1981	69,109	46.3	0.7
1982	64,621	40.3	0.6
1983	58,340	23.3	0.58
1984	61,897	24	0.63
1985	64,361	26	0.54
1986	61,652	26.9	0.54
1987	56,383	28.1	0.61
1988	55,115	34.3	0.57
1989	54,385	31.2	0.53
1990	54,750	37.6	0.52
1991	54,385	46.3	0.54
1992	54,750	47.1	0.54
1993	45,203	42.7	0.57
1994	47,843	41.2	0.47
1995	47,690	40.1	0.49
1996	47,171	42.4	0.49
1997	45,190	55.2	0.55
1998	44,888	78.7	0.58
1999	45,689	85.7	0.53
2000	43,681	92.1	0.61
2001	41,469	87.7	0.69
2002	47,690	82	0.72
2003	48,981	84.7	0.72
2004	44,985	79.2	0.99
2005	52,740	94.1	0.99
2006	52,105	92.3	0.99
2007	43,807	93.1	0.73
2008	41,828	92	0.73
2009	39,117	92.2	0.73
2010	35,837	77.3	0.73
2011	33,550	83.1	0.73
2012	29,915	64.6	0.73
2013	29,617	80.1	0.73
2014	29,984	83.2	0.73
2015	29,660.6	75	0.73

(continued)

Table 3.7 (continued)

Year	*Crude oil production 000 barrels*	*Refinery capacity utilization ratio %*	*Proven oil reserves billion barrels*
2016	28,709.5	88	0.73
2017	26,164	78	0.73
2018	26,210.9	59	0.73
2019	23,175.6	n/a	0.73
2020p	22,321.1	n/a	0.73

Source Rhyder Scott Report (Various Years), Annual Economic Survey of T&T (various years)

3.4.2 *Exports*

The exports of motor spirits gasoline and other light oils, etc. increased from US$66.5 mn in 1986 to US$458.1 mn in 2010, an increase of 588%. The exports of lamp oil and spirits also increased from US$44.4 mn to US$109.2 mn in 1991, but thereafter decreased to US$64.6 million in 1993. After 1993, there was an increase in the exports from this sector to US$197.2 mn by 2010. Residual fuel also increased sharply from US$222.3 mn in 1986 to US$1209.9 mn in 2010 (CSO has not produced data since 2010).

3.4.3 *Oil Refinery GDP*

Table 3.8 shows trends in the oil refineries value added of the T&T economy as a proportion of total petroleum value added. By 2014, the oil refining sub segment of the petroleum sector of the economy was 7.3% of total GDP. (Changes in the level of the refinery GDP must be interpreted with an element of caution though, as the CSO lodges the activities of LNG under refineries.)

3.4.4 *Oil Refining Employment*

Employment in oil refining was poised at 3310 in 1987 but by 2002 had fallen to 2142 although it improved thereafter to 3722 in 2012 (see Fig. 3.2). As a percentage of total employment in the energy sector, refinery employment decreased from 23.3 to 17.8% in the indicated time period. The weak relationship (−0.05 correlation) between refinery employment and refinery capacity utilization may be on account of the

Table 3.8 Gross domestic product by kind of activity—ISIC (TT$mn)

	Oil refineries	*GDP*
1985	59.4	18,071.2
1986	119.4	17,259.7
1987	116	17,271.9
1988	161.5	17,284.7
1989	158.3	18,372.9
1990	562.1	21,539.3
1991	372.3	22,558.6
1992	386.5	23,117.6
1993	347.7	24,490.5
1994	666.3	28,962.2
1995	512.3	30,637.9
1996	1356	34,586.6
1997	845.7	35,870.8
1998	694.7	38,065.1
1999	1344.4	42,889.1
2000	2821	51,370.6
2001	2399.3	55,007.5
2002	2557.1	53,310.5
2003	4608.4	66,906.6
2004	5708.4	81,161.4
2005	8932.9	95,924.4
2006	8136	110,055.5
2007	10,327.8	126,209.5
2008	13,048.9	175,287.2
2009	8704.7	121,281.3
2010	9574.2	131,289.4
2011	12,848.8	150,373.2
2012	10,449.9	153,587
2013	12,850	175,608
2014	13,299	179,842

Source Central Bank online database TT

influence of the very militant trade union in the sector. One commentator, noted that, in looking at refinery costs noted "…*maybe people don't realise how over-staffed state companies are in Trinidad and Tobago. I made a little calculation when I listened to the Petrotrin presentation and it seems that the average employee is producing 30 barrels of oil a day. A profitable oil company produces 300 b/d per employee, so Petrotrin seems to be over-staffed by a factor of ten*" (stated by Pedro van Meurs at the conference

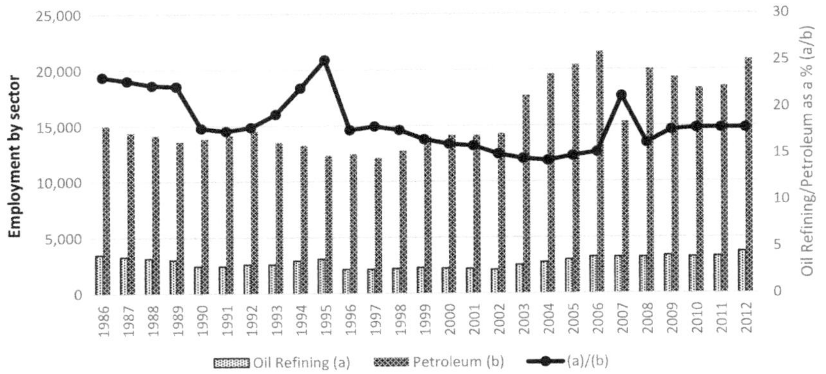

Fig. 3.2 Employment trends (level and share) in the Petroleum sector, 1986–2012 (*Source* MEEA and CSO Reports [various years])

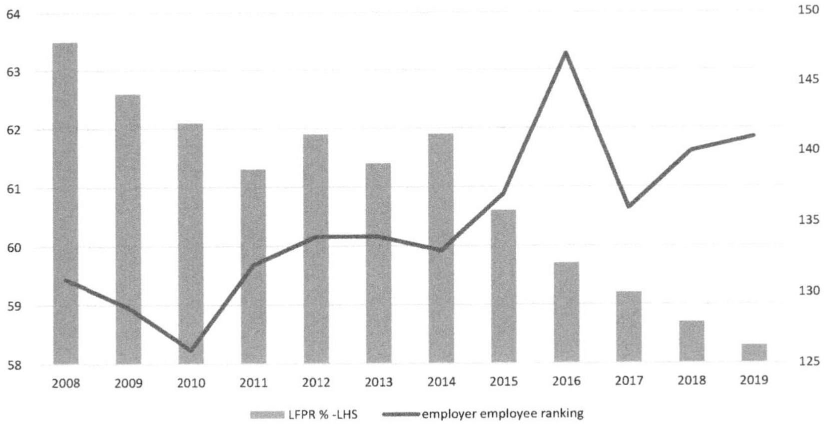

Fig. 3.3 The relationship between the labour force participation rate (%) and the employer–employee ranking from the GCI

on the "Future Development of The Energy Sector" and cited in David Renwick 2013, p. 1).

The comment below is a general comment but would no doubt have been influenced by the relationship between the OWTU and the energy sector. Specifically, in the Global Competitiveness report 2019, T&T

received the worst ranking of 141 in terms of cooperation in employer–employee relations. This would have to be addressed. Even more some element of an inverse relationship exists between the employer–employee ranking by the GCI and the labour force participation rate (Fig. 3.3).

3.5 Conclusion

This chapter provided a review of some aspects of the economic contribution of the crude oil refinery sector of the T&T economy from 1917 to 2018, when the refinery was closed. The chapter traced various economic contributions of the refinery as relates to output, employment and exports. The chapter focused on the Petrotrin refinery and traced its progress from its infancy to the period of peak performance in the 1970s. The chapter then elaborated as to how a series of factors almost at once worked together to weaken the position of the refining sector in T&T, these included the presence of rigidities in the business environment that prevented the desulphurization plant to be set up by Texaco in the early 1970s.

Additionally, the change in the petroleum tax regime increased the state's take on the refinery but in so doing reduced the firm's capacity to reinvest and adapt to the evolving global demand conditions. This helped to accelerate the demise of Texaco in T&T. The militant behaviour of the trade unions also played a role as too many man hours were lost between 1956 and 1985 and the confrontational stance of the union perhaps became an obstacle to the smooth functioning of the refinery's production function. No doubt, another determining factor was the rapid increase in oil prices in the early 1970s with a less than proportional increase in refinery product prices, the combination of which would have lowered refinery margins. The refinery was struck perhaps its most fatal blow with the development of the Louisiana Offshore Oil Port (LOOP). This changed the value of the T&T refinery, as tankers could now get directly into the refinery system of the USA. Indeed, Texaco basically announced at this point that they had no further use for the refinery in Pointe-a-Pierre.

With state takeover of the refinery several upgrades were undertaken but the refinery never recovered to full capacity utilization. Indeed this understanding is reflected in the words of the company president in March 2013 when he made a response to the demands of the Oilfield Workers Trade Union (OWTU), "*when our refinery throughput goes from*

160,000 b/d to zero and when our offshore Gulf of Paria production goes from 22,500 b/d to 7,000 b/d and when our land production goes from 14,000 b/d to 11,000 b/d, then we have to change the rules of the game. And we are going to change the rules of the game." He went on to note that "*When all these things happen twice within 12 months – because it happened in 2012 as well – we really have to take charge of things. The model changes. And the model has changed*" (Renwick 2013).

Because of massive, accumulated debt, aging infrastructure and a very militant union, the refinery was mothballed in November 2018.

Since then, the government of T&T issued a tender for the sale of the refinery and the Patriotic Energies, owned by the OWTU, won the bid. This is a major step forward, should it reopen, under private ownership that would be a major accomplishment.

References

Beaubrun, Tony. (2008). "Memories of Pointe-a-Pierre". First Magazine Ltd.

Besson, A. Gerard. (2008a). "Black Gold, Part 2: War and Peace." First Magazine Ltd.

Besson, A. Gerard. (2008b). "Black Gold, the Real El Dorado." First Magazine Ltd.

Besson, A. Gerard. (2008c). "Black Gold Part 3: The Road to Independence." First Magazine Ltd.

Besson, A. Gerard. (2008d). "History of Oil Part 2." The Caribbean History Archives. Paria Publishing Co LTD.

Best, Lloyd. (1968). "A Model of Pure Plantation Economy." Social and Economic Studies 17 (3): 283–326.

Best, Lloyd. (1971). "Independent Thought and Caribbean Freedom." In Norman Girvan and Owen Jefferson (Eds.), Readings in the Political Economy of the Caribbean. Mona: New World Group. Original in New World Quarterly, Vol. 3, No. 4, 1967.

Best, Lloyd, and Levitt, Kari. (1968). "The Mechanism of Plantation-Type Economies: Outline of a Model of Pure Plantation Economy." Social and Economic Studies 17: 283–324.

Government of Trinidad and Tobago. (1906). "Annual Administrative Report." Ministry of Energy and Energy Affairs Trinidad and Tobago.

Government of Trinidad and Tobago. (1908). "Annual Administrative Report." Ministry of Energy and Energy Affairs Trinidad and Tobago.

Government of Trinidad and Tobago. (1911). "Annual Administrative Report." Ministry of Energy and Energy Affairs Trinidad and Tobago.

Government of Trinidad and Tobago. (1913). "Annual Administrative Report." Ministry of Energy and Energy Affairs Trinidad and Tobago.

Government of Trinidad and Tobago. (1914). "Annual Administrative Report." Ministry of Energy and Energy Affairs Trinidad and Tobago.

Government of Trinidad and Tobago. (1931). "Annual Administrative Report." Ministry of Energy and Energy Affairs Trinidad and Tobago.

Government of Trinidad and Tobago. (1932). "Annual Administrative Report." Ministry of Energy and Energy Affairs Trinidad and Tobago.

Government of Trinidad and Tobago. (1935). "Annual Administrative Report." Ministry of Energy and Energy Affairs Trinidad and Tobago.

Government of Trinidad and Tobago. (1940). "Annual Administrative Report." Ministry of Energy and Energy Affairs Trinidad and Tobago.

Government of Trinidad and Tobago. (1946). "Annual Administrative Report." Ministry of Energy and Energy Affairs Trinidad and Tobago.

Government of Trinidad and Tobago. (1947). "Annual Administrative Report." Ministry of Energy and Energy Affairs Trinidad and Tobago.

Government of Trinidad and Tobago. (1948). "Annual Administrative Report." Ministry of Energy and Energy Affairs Trinidad and Tobago.

Government of Trinidad and Tobago. (1972). Budget Speech, Ministry of Finance, Port of Spain Government of T&T.

Higgins, E. George. (1996). "A History of Trinidad Oil." Trinidad Express Limited (Port of Spain). Express Production House.

Jarrett, Uchechukwu, Mohaddes, Kamiar, and Mohtadi, Hamid. (2019). "Oil Price Volatility, Financial Institutions and Economic Growth." Energy Policy, Elsevier 126 (C): 131–144.

Julien, S. Kenneth. (2005). "Eric Williams and the Emergence of the National Energy Sector." Nineteenth Dr. Eric Williams Memorial Lecture. Central Bank of Trinidad and Tobago.

Levy, W. J. (1958). The Trinidad Oil Economy: A Report Prepared for the Government of Trinidad and Tobago.

Petrotrin. (2013). "Down Memoy Lane: The Evolution of Petrotrin." Corporate Communications Department.

Renwick, David. (2013). "What's Wrong with Petrotrin's Refinery Economics?" http://www.trinidadexpress.com/business-magazine.

The Ministry of Energy and Energy Affairs Trinidad and Tobago. (1992). The Draft Energy Policy August Volume 2.

The New York Times. (1971, January 28). Desulphurization Unit Set.

Treaster, Joseph B. (1985). "Trinidad to Keep the Refinery Going." www.nytimes.com.

CHAPTER 4

Natural Gas Production

4.1 Introduction

The focus of this chapter is simple, to provide the trends in the production and utilization of natural gas in T&T and to outline the importance of LNG production on the production of natural gas.

The history of natural gas production and utilization in Trinidad and Tobago can be divided into two key periods. Pre 1968 and post 1968 (in 1968 the first commercial discovery of natural gas was made off the East Coast of T&T). Natural gas typically exists in Trinidad and Tobago in conjunction with crude oil, and in the past this natural gas was flared in the crude oil production process. In the early days, natural gas use commenced with attempts to extract the gas components from other hydrocarbons and in the T&T case this started with asphalt, sourced from the Pitch Lake. Jobity and Pantor (1995) noted that gas was extracted from the asphalt and used for lighting a "beacon placed in the tower of the Trinity church." Because of the high sulphur content of the gas at that point, the experiment was considered a failure.

Jobity and Pantor (1995) notes an American scientist was able to extract odor free gas from the asphalt but its high cost, rendered the process unprofitable. Some of the natural gas was also used for industrial activity. Example the MEEA Report 1910–1911 stated "Natural gas is used in one or two fields to fire the boilers" (p. 3). Further the MEEA report (1931) notes that the "Trinidad Petroleum Development

R. Hosein, *Oil and Gas in Trinidad and Tobago*,
https://doi.org/10.1007/978-3-030-77669-5_4

Company Limited has completed the installation of a plant for the extraction of light products from natural gas and this plant is now working satisfactorily."

The early leases in the hydrocarbon sector recognized natural gas was a useful byproduct of the oil extraction process. In 1933 gas injection techniques were introduced in the Forest Reserve area. This use of the natural gas was reflected in a rapid increase in the number of wells using the gas lift technique from 15 in 1932 to 105 in 1935. In the early 1940s in the Penal area, the first large onshore deposit of natural gas was made and in 1955 the first offshore deposit of natural gas was found. However, other commercial uses began to emerge with the passage of time and in 1953 the Trinidad and Tobago Electricity Commission started using natural gas when it established its Penal power station. Indeed, by 1963 T&TEC constructed a 16-inch pipeline from Picton to its Port-of-Spain plant. In 1958 W.R. Grace established the Federation Chemical Limited (FEDCHEM) to manufacture nitrogenous fertilizers (Grace expanded facilities in 1964 and 1966). Other industrial uses emerged in the Trinidad and Tobago economy and in 1964 the Claxton Bay cement company in south Trinidad, used natural gas at its start-up.

In 1968, a large amount of natural gas was discovered off the East coast of Trinidad by Amoco in offshore Point Radix in an exploratory well and the government began to pay more attention to the vast potential that existed in resource (gas)-based industrialization. As a result, they attempted to redirect some of the wealth that the country had accumulated from the oil sector into the formation of a few resource-based industries founded on natural gas in an industrial estate on the south-west coast of Trinidad (Point Lisas). Initially the government sought foreign partnerships to provide technology, managerial expertise, and market contacts—much along the lines of Sir Arthur Lewis' 1950 propositions.

By 1974 the use of gas in the power generation sector increased. There was also an increase in demand for more natural gas in the downstream sector. In support the government of T&T built a 16" 24-mile offshore gas pipeline project which was managed by Amoco.

By 1975, it became necessary to rationalize the natural gas sector as up to that point it was deregulated with individual companies selling gas on a case by case basis. Producing companies at this stage owned the gas transmission pipelines. At this point, the government pushed for the formation of the National Gas Company (NGC) which is discussed below.

Jobity and Pantor (1995, p. 185) noted, *"Formerly seen as a useless by-product in the search for oil, natural gas is now seen as the fuel of the future. While oil maintains the backbone of the Trinidad and Tobago economy, gas has assumed an important role over the last two decades."* In 1981 the T&T government set out in a clear manner its proposal for the development of a huge natural gas driven industrial complex. Primarily the government sought to tap into its natural gas to provide a substitute revenue inflow to compensate for declining oil revenues. The White Paper on Natural Gas (1981, p. 2) outlined that: *"Trinidad and Tobago therefore has a reasonable breathing spell of some four to five years over which period it must develop revenues other than those from oil. This breathing spell calls for a definitive national strategy and efficient immediate implementation of any of the prices or decisions which result from the adoption of such a strategy. Natural gas is the only other significant and commercially exploitable natural resource, capable of gathering revenues of the required magnitude to offset the decline in gross national revenues as forecasted."*

4.2 National Gas Company (NGC)

A major institutional change to facilitate the development of the natural gas-based sector in the T&T economy is the formation of the NGC and its subsidiary, the National Energy Corporation (NEC).

The original intent in the creation of the NGC was to administer contracts and to sell and transport gas to existing oil and gas companies in the country as the government began a new path of industrialization based on natural gas products. In NGC's Articles of Association, it is stated that, *"…. the Company was formed to be at the centre of the natural gas industry whose overall development for the benefit of the country was at stake."* In his 1975 Budget Speech, the Prime Minister of Trinidad and Tobago noted that the government would be the sole seller of gas, as a trigger of industrialization. NGC was created in August 1975 with a share capital of $45 million. The company was incorporated as a private company and by August 22, 1975 the company began its operations with its first board meeting. According to the NGC's official website the company's first year saw it servicing approximately 6 customers and had total gas sales of 370mcf for that year. Sales revenues for the first year amounted to TT$180,000 and the profits were TT$19,000.

In the 1980s NGC experienced a surge despite the overall economic decline due to the amount of construction work that had to be done to accommodate the demand for gas by new plants located in Point Lisas. A number of these projects included:

- A loop-line to the T&TEC system, a 13-mile, 20-inch-diameter pipeline between two crucial valve stations, Picton and Phoenix Park:
- A 4-mile, 24-inch-diameter line from Galeota to Beachfield.
- A 35-mile, 30-inch-diameter cross-country line from Beachfield to Phoenix Park, via Rio Claro.
- A 30-inch-diameter marine line from Cassia offshore field to Galeota station.
- A trunk line, from Mahaica to the Princess Margaret Highway, which served the distribution line connecting small consumers located in the O'Meara and Macoya estates (Vision 20/20 Operational Plan, 2009).

Today, NGC owns, maintains and operates T&T's transmission and distribution gas pipeline network of approximately 1000 km which comprises both offshore and onshore segments. The network's installed capacity is currently 4.4 billion standard cubic feet per day (bscf/d) and supplies power generation firms, global scale petrochemical plants and a wide range of light manufacturing and commercial enterprises.

An important arm of the NGC is The National Energy Corporation (NEC) of Trinidad and Tobago Ltd. It is fully owned by NGC and was incorporated in 1979 as a means of continuing the work originally started by the Coordinating Task Force which was started in 1975. The NEC was formed as part of a plan to monetize the natural gas resources of T&T along with developing and managing industrial and marine infrastructure. NEC in its early stages was also involved in the construction and operation of the first set of petrochemical plants in the country. The company also helped develop the port and marine infrastructure which is used to service all the plants at the Point Lisas Industrial Estate.

In the period 1983–1993, the economy faltered, and the NEC was absorbed by the NGC and in so doing NGC became the "prime owner in gas-based development" in T&T (Barclay 2015, p. 156). The merger of the 2 entities did bear fruit as by 2004 it had attracted investments in five methanol plants, six ammonia plants and further in two steel companies (Barclay 2015, p. 156).

In 1999, the NEC became an independent entity within the NGC Group of Companies, with a mandate to "develop and manage suitable infrastructure, in order to facilitate and promote the various activities relevant and appropriate to natural gas - related operations." In 2004, the NEC's mandate was further expanded to include the facilitation and promotion of natural gas-based development.

The NGC and NEC played pivotal roles in locating and securing investors in ammonia, methanol and urea production as well as in the eventual start-up of liquefied natural gas production in T&T. Indeed, it is possible to describe the waves of investment in the natural gas-based segment of the T&T economy into two waves; the first was led by the state sector and the second wave led by the private sector. (In this second wave, a local conglomerate (CL Financial) entered the methanol market and became one of the largest exporters in the world!)

4.3 Production and Utilization of Natural Gas in T&T

The discoveries of natural gas were milestone events in the development of T&T. The Teak field which was discovered by Amoco held about 1 tcf of gas reserves. Even more the Cassia field discovered in 1973 held more than 2 tcf of gas (Farrell 2019). The original intent in the creation of the National Gas Company of Trinidad and Tobago (NGC) was to administer contracts and to sell and transport gas to existing oil and gas companies in the country as the government began a new path of industrialization based on natural gas products (Mottley 2008).

Figure 4.1 above shows the trends in the production of natural and crude oil, both in mn of barrels. Note that after 1993 there was a clear upward movement in gas production and the economy shifted slowly away from being an oil producer, to being a gas producer. Specifically, observe that natural gas production in 1909 increased from 0.01 mn barrels of oil equivalent to 5.96 mn boe in 1952 but by 1967 increased fivefold to 26.63 mn boe. Natural gas production would continue to increase and by 1999 reached 72.1 mn boe. Beyond 1999 and with the coming onstream of several LNG trains, natural gas production would increase dramatically to 300.2 mn boe in 2010 although it declined by 25% to 228.7 mn boe in 2020.

So dramatic was the switch over from oil production to gas production that by 2020, the share of gas production in total barrel of oil equivalent

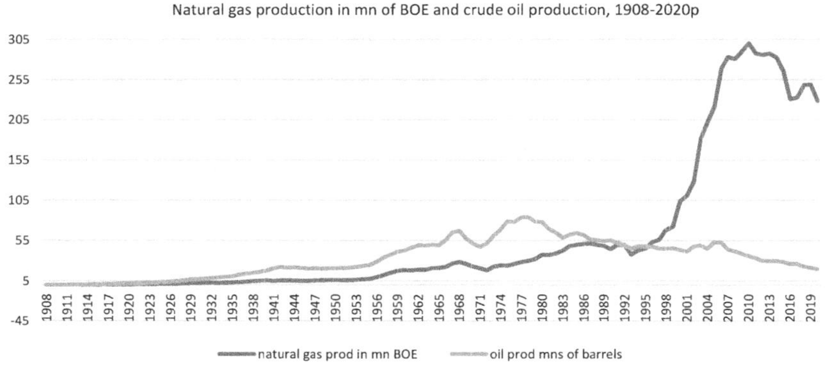

Fig. 4.1 Natural gas and crude oil production 1908–2020p

production in T&T perched at 92%, as compared to 21.9% in 1952 and 45% in 1993 (Table 4.1).

A clear outcome of the natural gas situation in T&T is that since 1999 over 90% of the produced natural gas was utilized. This is particularly good news given that for a large period in the past, this natural resource was flared.

Part of the reason for the success of the natural gas sector was geological in that some of the wells in TT were amongst the largest in the world at the time of discovery. The fact that a significant amount of gas could be produced from a few wells also helped to keep costs, manageable. At the time of discovery in the late 1960s T&T had a strong democracy with government changing hands through ballot boxes than through military intervention (e.g. Nigeria). The natural gas sector also benefitted from a long history of being a petroleum producer and the existence of a well-trained labour force that could support the industry. The NGC also developed a strong element of partnering with the MNCs and there was a pervasive sense of "we swim together or we sink together." The T&T economy also never had problems with state seizures of the assets of MNCs as occurred in countries like Venezuela.

(Chapter 5 will provide some more focus on the downstream natural gas and resource-based industrialization plants).

Table 4.1 Natural Gas production and local utilization (mmcf/d) 1985–2020

Year	*Prod*	*Util*	*% utilized*
1985	415	364	87.7
1986	417	365	87.5
1987	495	379	76.6
1988	501	422	84.2
1989	701	406	57.9
1990	643	419	65.2
1991	717	493	68.8
1992	715	529	74.0
1993	685	507	74.0
1994	745	575	77.2
1995	751	589	78.4
1996	874	674	77.1
1997	884	709	80.2
1998	996	830	83.3
1999	1281	1169	91.3
2000	1498	1364	91.1
2001	1606	1489	92.7
2002	1845	1826	99.0
2003	2544	2520	99.1
2004	2929	2850	97.3
2005	3214	3033	94.4
2006	3878	3674	94.7
2007	4057	3744	92.3
2008	4048	3699	91.4
2009	4183	3835	91.7
2010	4319	4005	92.7
2011	4149	3843	92.6
2012	4122	3823	92.7
2013	4144	3854	93.0
2014	4069	3787	93.0
2015	3833	3578	93.3
2016	3327	3104	93.3
2017	3366	3172	94.2
2018	3585	3378	94.2
2019	3588	3458	96.4
2020p	3200	3154	98.6

Source Annual Economic Survey Reports (various years)

4.4 Liquified Natural Gas (LNG) in T&T

A tremendous push in the development of the natural gas sector of T&T was the development of its LNG sector. Specifically, after the discovery of significant natural gas reserves in 1968 the first major attempt to develop an LNG plant in Trinidad was made. Negotiations between the government, AMOCO and the People's Gas of Chicago on the feasibility of such an export plant spanned two years. However, this project was subsequently abandoned because the state decided that the gas should be used for the development of local downstream industries (Sergeant et al. 2003, p. 20).

Revival of the abandoned LNG project came in the early 1980s by Tenneco. During this time period, T&T faced favourable economic conditions on account of high oil prices and subsequent large windfalls, rapid economic growth and proven gas reserves for over 80 years consumption, at the current rate. Small domestic consumption in T&T resulted in limited prospects for selling more gas and as such, Tenneco's proposal of an LNG project was entertained by the government and other major industry stakeholders. However, during the global recession of the 1980s, demand for gas from T&T's potential markets fell and failed to recover for over a decade thereafter. High projected costs by Tenneco, compounded by substantial field development and pipeline costs associated with the utilization of T&T's north coast gas reserves were the main causes for the second failure of the LNG initiative. AMOCO's inability to meet sales commitments to Puerto Rico in the early 1990s summed up the third failed attempt at the development of an LNG industry in T&T. The economic environment at this time was unsatisfactory and did not motivate LNG investors (Shepherd and Ball 2004, pp. 3–9).

Impetus for the fourth and eventually successful LNG endeavour came from the Boston-based Cabot LNG Company[1]; which at the time was the largest LNG importer in North America. With the objective of purchasing gas, Cabot approached the government of T&T. This was an opportunity that the state welcomed and so sought to reinforce through the offer of a fiscal incentive package, designed specifically for this project.

To get the trains going, a 10-year tax holiday was granted in 1999 for the establishment of Train I. Further, stakeholders for the first three

[1] Now Tractebel Inc.

Trains benefited from tax exemptions, concessions, no withholding taxes and no taxes on dividends. No incentives were granted for Train IV.

Further, Table 4.2 below details the operational aspects of the four Trains that constitute the Atlantic project. It offers a more focused perspective of the significance of each train to the overall project and to gas-based industrialization in T&T.

Table 4.2 The operational aspects of Atlantic Trains I, II, III and IV

Characteristic	*Description*
Nameplate capacity	Train I—3.3 million tonnes/year Train II/III—3.4 million tonnes/ year Train IV—5.2 million tonnes/year
Gas usage	Train I—530 MMScf/d Train II/III—560 MMScf/d Train IV—800 MMScf/d
Total project cost	Train 1—US$1 billion Train II/III—US$2.2 billion Train IV—US$1.3 billion
Main contractors	Bechtel International
Engineering process	Phillips Petroleum (optimized cascade liquefaction process)
Local input into project Target VS Actual	Train I—US$100 million VS US$175 million Train II/III—US$150 million VS US$210 million Train IV—US$175 million VS US$250 million
Start-up—Train I	April 1999
Start-up—Train II	August 2002
Start-up—Train III	April 2003
Start-up—Train IV	December 2005
Project Shareholding—Train I (liquefaction facility)	• BPTT (34%) • Shell (26%) • Repsol (20%) • Cabot (10%) • NGC (10%)
Project Shareholding—Train II and III (liquefaction facility)	• BPTT (49.25%) • Shell (28.25%) • Repsol (22.5%)
Project Shareholding—Train IV	• BPTT (37.78%) • Shell (28.89%) • Repsol (22.22%) • NGC (11.11%)

(continued)

Table 4.2 (continued)

Characteristic	*Description*
Gas supply to Trains I, II, III and IV	BPTT: 100% of Train I 50% of Train II 75% of Train III 69% of Train IV Shell: 0% of Train I 50% of Train II 25% of Train III 26% of Train IV EOG Resources Inc: 5% of Train IV
Gas transmission	Project partners- Cabot, BP AMOCO, British Gas, NGC and Repsol
Contracted Markets	Train I—Spain (60%) USA (40%) Train II/III—Spain (62%) USA (38%) Train IV—USA (100%)
Transportation of LNG	• Cabot (125,000m^3 LNG carrier Gamma) • Repsol (Methane Arctic and Methane Polar LNG tankers chartered from BP) • British Trader
Price Marker	Henry Hub: Train 1 Train II/III Train IV Fuel Oil: Train I Train II/III Spanish Electricity: Train II/III
Pricing	• Netback pricing arrangement (market prices minus shipping, regasification and distribution – Spain-Gas price linked to basket of oil prices – US-Gas price linked to gas prices in US market

Source Sergeant et al. (2003); Government of T&T (2010).

Note that the significant shareholders in the four trains are BPTT and Shell and both are also large producers of natural gas and this raises an obvious concern: as natural gas production wanes in T&T would these large upstream producers favour LNG because of their large shareholding in the various trains?

4.5 Conclusion

This chapter provided a sketch of the natural gas situation in the T&T economy. Between 1908 and 2020, T&T produced natural gas amounting to 6.613 bn barrels of oil and gas equivalent. Natural gas has grown in importance of the T&T economy in the last 25 years and after 1999 the proportion of the production that is utilized after 1999 is in excess of 90%. With the passage of time this same natural gas which was once flared or reinjected to help extract crude oil, became increasingly important and by 2020 accounted for 92.1% of the total production of oil and gas, in barrels of oil equivalent.

Natural gas remains an important source of clean fuel to the world economy and moving forward T&T would have to ensure it has an active exploration strategy to bring more gas into production.

References

Barclay, L.A. (2015). "Managing FDI for Development in Resource-Rich States: The Caribbean Experience."

Farrell, Terrance. (2019). At A Point of Inflexion: The Downstream Petrochemicals Industry in Trinidad & Tobago 2019. UTT Seminar. https://utt.edu.tt/files/cms/point_inflexion_presentation.pdf.

Jobity, Richard, and Pantor, Robert. (1995). "The Natural Gas Industry in Trinidad and Tobago." Central Bank of Trinidad and Tobago.

Mottley, W. (2008). "Trinidad and Tobago Industrial Policy 1959–2008—A Historical and Contemporary Analysis." Jamaica: Ian Randle Publishers.

Sergeant, Kelvin, Racha, Sandra, and John, Michael. (2003). "The Petroleum Sector: The Case of Trinidad and Tobago: Trends, Policies and Impact 1985–2000." Santiago de Chile: Comisi6n Econ6mica para America Latina y el Caribe (CEPAL).

Shepherd, R., and Ball, J. (2004). "Liquefied Natural Gas from Trinidad and Tobago: The Atlantic LNG Project." Geopolitics of Gas Working Paper Series.

CHAPTER 5

Resource Curse and the Dutch Disease

5.1 Introduction

This chapter discusses the resource curse and Dutch Disease. The chapter commences with a brief discussion of the importance of natural resources in general and then discusses the resource curse but with specific reference to the petroleum sector. The next section discusses the theoretical framework of the Dutch Disease after which an assessment of the impact of the Dutch Disease on premature deindustrialization will be developed.

Natural resources can provide the impetus for development via the generation of resource rents. Indeed, it can be perceived that the resources generated by the sector can be used to enable an economy's growth and development. This concept that natural resources can be positively linked to an economy's development was proposed by Smith (1776) and subsequently refined by Myint (1958 and 1965). The theory asserts that trade allows economies (especially developing economies) to bring into employment factors which would have otherwise remained unemployed or underemployed. According to Smith (1776), foreign trade, "*carries out that surplus part of the produce of their (trading countries) land and labour for which there is no demand among them, and brings back in return for it something else for which there is a demand*" (p. 342). The vent for surplus theory, as it relates to natural resources is therefore premised on the assumption that engaging international trade allows economies to monetize their excess natural resources which are not being

R. Hosein, *Oil and Gas in Trinidad and Tobago*,
https://doi.org/10.1007/978-3-030-77669-5_5

fully employed, to increase their level of exports (often a staple) and to stimulate economic growth.

The Staple Approach study of economic history lies mainly with Canada. Innis (1950) in his seminal work on the coal industries, cod-fish and fur trade, argued that with a natural resource boom, revenues are used for the advancement of the economy itself and to create industries which support the booming sector and overall this can provide the economy with widespread development. Watkins (1963) arguing in the same mould noted, "*Staple exports are the leading sector, setting the pace for economic growth and leaving their peculiar imprint on the economy and society. Foreign demand for the staple export, which is the engine driving the economic growth, lies entirely outside the new country, and many inputs of labour, capital, and materials also come from abroad, at least initially. The staple has its impact on the economy through backward, forward, and final demand linkages. These are defined as the inducements to invest in and operate industries that respectively supply inputs to the new export sector (backward linkages), to process the output of that sector (forward linkages), or to supply consumer goods to the people receiving income from that sector (final demand linkages)*," Copithorne (1979).

With the fur trade for example, a strong network of backward and forward linkages was forged as a transportation network and a trading system was also developed. In addition, for the wheat industry, strong backward linkages were required via a railroad system, with associated branch lines and support infrastructure, like grain elevators and farm machinery (Copithorne 1979). A central aspect of this staple school of thought is that it emphasizes that the greater the natural resource industry's links with other industries, the greater the benefits of producing and exporting the staple product.

Advocates of the staple theory also proposed that for resource-rich "backward" countries, another potential source for economic growth is a resource boom, which according to them would result in an influx of capital into the country allowing for reinvestment into local infrastructure and other value-adding industries, thereby producing a more diversified pattern of growth.[1]

Myint (1958) elaborated on the vent for surplus theory of Smith (1776), to emphasize the rapid expansion of exports in some sparsely

[1] Watkins (1963).

developed economies during the nineteenth and twentieth centuries. He emphasized that in these sparsely populated economies: (a) a low level of internal organization and (b) an inelastic domestic demand resulted in "surplus productive capacity." Trade, apart from motivating a reallocation of scarce resources, also served to provide a literal "vent" for the surplus productive capacity. Myint (1958) identified that from a supply perspective, two factors facilitated the expansion of exports from developing economies, these are, (a) vast tracts of unused lands and (b) underemployed labour. Caves (1968) in commenting on the vent for surplus theories, noted that these theories: "*depict the effects of trade on growth as involving the exploitation of resources, lacking in that place and at that time, any alternative uses of significant economic value. The existence of these 'surplus' resources reflects the state of economic organization in general and not a failure of the market mechanism in any narrow sense. The pace of growth and changes in the pattern of international trade associated with the absorption of such resources gives these models their distinctive stamp, in contrast to models involving resource reallocation and thus lying nearer to the core of traditional trade theory*" (Caves 1968, p. 96).

Indeed, for most economies and particularly developing economies, it is intuitively easy to identify that natural resource rents when appropriated by the state, help to relax some of the resource constraints faced by benefiting governments. Those resource constraints are especially savings, foreign exchange and fiscal constraints (UNCTAD 2012). By easing fiscal constraints in particular, a natural resource boom can help to spur domestic aggregate demand which can prompt a "big bang" effect as demand spreads to other sectors and prompts increased demand for a larger cross section of sectors (Goldberg and Pavcnik 2008). Thus for a developing economy experiencing a boom say in its petroleum sector, other things constant, one would expect an increase in demand for construction sector activity, capital goods, financial services and even agricultural products (Davis and Tilton 2008).

5.2 Resource Curse (with a Focus on Petroleum Products)

Raul Prebisch (1950) in his paper assessing the development of Latin America, formulated the hypothesis that in the long run the prices of agriculture and mineral goods dip downwards, whilst the prices of manufactured and other goods tend to move relatively upwards.[2] Hans Singer (1950) shared a similar perspective and their views came to be known as the "structuralist school." Specifically, the "structuralist school" noted that the world income elasticity of demand for primary products is inelastic; hence an increase in world income meant a less than proportional increase in demand for these goods. Prebisch (1950) concluded that specializing in primary goods in this type of setting is not the rational choice. He went on to note that developing countries should not follow the traditional theories of free trade by exploiting their comparative advantage in natural resources but instead implement protectionist policies to allow their domestic manufacturing sectors to flourish. Areski et al. (2013) tested for the existence of the Prebisch Singer hypothesis focusing on the secular trend and short-term volatility of relative commodity prices since 1650. These researchers focused on 25 series. Their test results showed that relative prices for the majority of series follow a downward trend. In another research effort, Harvey et al. examined the trend in relative prices for 25 commodities for the last four centuries. They found that 11 of the series display a significant downward trend over the entire time period or part of the time period.

Nurkse (1958) argued that international commodity markets possibly adversely affect resource abundant economies, as these markets tended to, by nature, be very unstable and that instability in these resource-related

[2] In the literature there are two diametric views on the long-term trends in commodity price. John Stuart Mill 1848, Book IV, Chapter 2 notes: "*The tendency, then, being to a perpetual increase of the productive power of labour in manufactures, while in agriculture and mining there is a conflict between two tendencies, the one towards an increase of productive power, the other towards a diminution of it, the cost of productionbeing lessened by every improvement in the processes, and augmented by every addition to population; it follows that the exchange values of manufactured articles, compared with the products of agriculture and of mines, have, as population and industry advance, a certain and decided tendency to fall.*" The second line of thought is the Prebisch Singer hypothesis (PSH). Many commentators have argued against the existence of the PSH. However, a close look at the performance of OPEC economies may prompt some to argue that there is validity in the argument.

commodities could be transmitted to the domestic economy, creating further disruptions. Nurkse (1958) went on to argue in favour of a Big Push, a wave of capital investments (Nurkse 1958, p. 13) all at once. This wave should motivate the economy out of a vicious cycle of underdevelopment to a virtuous cycle of development. Of course, resource wealth can help to produce the resources to facilitate a "Big Push."

Hirschman (1958) emphasized the limitedness of the linkages between the natural resource sector and the rest of the macro-economy. Hirschman argued that "*The grudge against what has become known as the enclave type of development is due to this ability of primary products from mines, wells, and plantations to slip out of a country without leaving much of a trace in the rest of the economy*" (Hirschman 1958, p. 110). To emphasize this Hidalgo et al. (2007) have argued that it is very difficult for production in a product space to move away from products within the product space and policies to promote these large jumps are challenging. In this type of enclosed development, the resource abundant country can be left worse off from the resource removal. It is this "worse off" that has come to have known in the literature as the "resource curse."

The actual term "resource curse," however, was first used by Auty (1993) to provide an explanation as to why mineral abundant economies were unable to use their resource wealth to boost their economies economic outcomes.

Subsequently in a detailed seminal research effort, Sachs and Warner (1997), showed that countries which are considered to be resource rich (high resource export to GDP) tended to grow slower than those considered to be resource poor over the time period 1970–1990. Sachs and Warner (1995) began with a simple regression model with growth of GDP as the dependent variable and share of primary exports (proxy for resource abundance) and log of initial GDP as the independent variables. The results of this model showed a negative relationship between growth of GDP and share of primary exports. Specifically, Sachs and Warner noted, "*A higher share of primary exports in 1970 is associated with lower growth in the next two decades……*" (p. 1). In order to show that this result was not spurious Sachs and Warner (1995) expanded the model to include other relevant variables. The other variables included were a variable for outward orientation and variables to control for capital accumulation, institutional quality and global commodity shocks. The final regression model showed that the share of primary exports remained significant and with a negative coefficient.

This is a surprising occurrence and one researcher went on to note: "*How can we reconcile the seemingly obvious fact that oil makes a country rich, with the equally undeniable fact that no countries that rely heavily on the production of oil are in any real sense developed (rich) and none even appear to be moving towards that goal? Perhaps even more puzzling is the fact that even the richest of the oil-producing countries, Saudi Arabia, is still at best a middle income country, even after decades of dominating the world oil market and in spite of owning over half of the world's proven crude oil reserves. If ever a country should be rich, Saudi Arabia, it seems, is that country. Yet the statistics tell us otherwise*" (Heal 2006, p. 167). An examination of the data shows that Saudi Arabia realized an increase in real GDP per capita of only 29.8% between 1985 and 2020, although it produced some 122 billion barrels of oil in the same time interval.

A variety of reasons have been cited in the literature for the resource curse. These include enclave effects (Humphreys et al. 2007; Gelb 2010; Wright and Czelusta 2004), income distribution effects (Lam and Wantchekon 2002; Loayza et al. 2013), a lack of transparency (Osmundsen 2010), rent seeking (Torvik 2002), educational effects (Humphreys et al. 2007), revenue volatility (Van der Ploeg and Poelhekke 2009), wasteful spending (Stevens 2015), capital intensity of the oil sector leading to higher wages (Seers 1963) and the Dutch Disease. The Dutch Disease is discussed in the next section.

5.3 Dutch Disease

A boom in a tradable natural resource such as oil, can lead to the appreciation of an economy's real exchange rate, and as a consequence it is possible that the economy's NBT sector export performance can worsen. The negative effect on the economy as a result of the resource boom is termed the "Dutch Disease." (This term was coined in 1977 by The Economist to refer to a decline in the manufacturing sector in the Netherlands after the discovery of a huge gas field in 1959.)

This section outlines a brief theoretical discussion of the Dutch Disease and sets about an assessment of the Dutch Disease on the trade structure of the Trinidad and Tobago economy using revealed comparative advantage methods. This section illustrates that the economy has lost substantive comparative advantage in a wide cross section of sectors since 1999. The point is reinforced by a reference to Balassa's revealed comparative advantage indices for the period 1999 and 2018. This section also assesses the overall real economic growth performance of the Trinidad and Tobago economy as compared to the CARICOM territories for the period 1977–2020. Finally, an auto regressive distributed lag (ARDL) framework is used to investigate the existence of the Dutch Disease in Trinidad and Tobago.

The Dutch Disease theory is based on several key assumptions, the first one being that an economy is made up of two sectors which are a tradable sector (T) and a non-tradable sector (NT). The tradable sector can be further sub divided into a booming tradable (BT) segment and non-booming tradable segment (NBT). Each segment employs a specific factor capital and one flexible factor of production, labour. Another assumption of the model is that the economy operates under conditions of full employment. In initial conditions of full employment, the employed labour force L, is assumed to be distributed as:

$$L = BT_0 + NBT_0 + NT_0 \tag{5.1}$$

Given this initial position it is now assumed that there is an increase in the price of the goods sold in the BT sector or alternatively, there is a discovery of resources, or even a favourable technological shock within the sector. Such changes will trigger an increase in the marginal productivity of labour in the BT sector, relative to the other segments of the economy. The resulting effect of this is that the labour from the other sectors (NBT and NT) will migrate towards the BT sector, a process known as the resource movement effect (R^e). With the R^e effect the distribution of employment in the economy becomes:

$$L^{re} = NBT_1 + BT_1 + NT_1 \tag{5.2}$$

The resource movement effect is illustrated in Fig. 5.1 by a rightward shift of the demand curve for BT labour (from $L^0{}_{BT}$ to $L^1{}_{BT}$), alongside a leftward shift of the labour supply curves for the NBT (from $S^0{}_{NBT}$ to $S^1{}_{NBT}$) and NT (from $S^0{}_{NT}$ to $S^1{}_{NT}$). The impact of these movements is an upward pressure on the domestic wage rate from w_0 to w_1. Note that the level of employment in the BT sector increases, whilst the level of employment in the NBT and the NT sector declines, as a consequence of the R^e.

The change in distribution of employment between the resource movement induced employment situation (L^{re}) and the initial distribution of

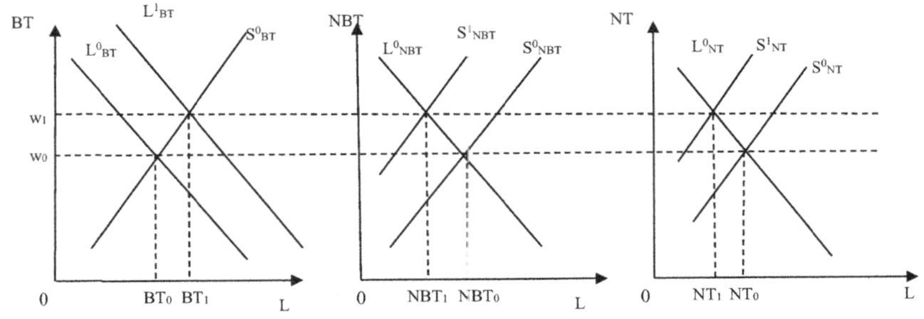

Fig. 5.1 Resource movement effect of the Dutch Disease

labour (L) can be simplistically illustrated as:

$$L^{re} - L = 0 = \Delta BT_1 + \Delta NBT_1 + \Delta NT_1 \tag{5.3}$$

$$\Delta BT_1 = -(\Delta NT_1 + \Delta NBT_1) \tag{5.4}$$

where L^{re} is the impact of the resource movement effect on the labour market. The fall in the level of employment within the NBT sector as a result of the resource movement effect is defined as direct deindustrialization. As workers in the BT sector spend their higher incomes and the government spend its higher revenues, this motivates an increase in demand for NT goods from the whole economy. This effect is called the spending effect (S^e) and results in an increase in the demand for labour in the NT sector, from NT_1 to NT_2, and a rise in the wage rate from w_1 to w_2. On the assumption of full employment, wage rates increase in the NBT and BT sector as well as illustrated in Fig. 5.2. Note there is a secondary round of contraction in the NBT sector from NBT_1 to NBT_2, this is called indirect deindustrialization.

The distribution of labour on the influence of the S^e in the economy becomes:

$$L^{se} = BT_2 + NBT_2 + NT_2 \tag{5.5}$$

So that the change in the distribution of labour between the S^e and R^e episodes can be represented as:

$$\Delta L^{se} = L^{se} - L^{re} = (BT_2 + NBT_2 + NT_2) - (BT_1 + NBT_1 + NT_1)$$

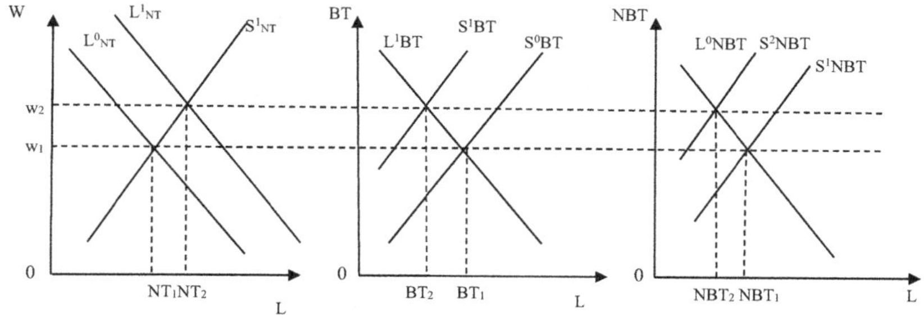

Fig. 5.2 Spending effect of the Dutch Disease

$$\Delta L^{se} = \Delta BT_2 + \Delta NBT_2 + NT_2$$

$$0 = \Delta BT_2 + \Delta NBT_2 + \Delta NT_2$$

or

$$\Delta NT_2 = -(\Delta BT_2 + \Delta NBT_2)$$

The eventual distribution of labour in the economy on account of the Dutch Disease is (L^{DD}) and can be represented as:

$$L^{DD} = L^{re} + \Delta L^{re} \text{ where } L^{re} = L + \Delta L^{re}$$

So that:

$$L^{DD} = L + \Delta L^{re} + L^{se}$$

And the total change in the distribution of labour is:

$$L^{DD} - L = \Delta L^{re} + L^{se} = (BT_2 - BT_0) + (NBT_2 - NBT_0) + (NT_2 - NT_0)$$

Given that

$$\Delta L^{re} = (BT_1 - BT_0) + (NBT_1 - NBT_0) + (NT_1 - NT_0)$$

and

$$\Delta L^{re} = (BT_2 - BT_1) + (NBT_2 - NBT_1) + (NT_2 - NT_1)$$

The overall change in the labour market on account of the Dutch Disease, given by $L^{DD} - L$, is shown in Fig. 5.3.

Given the assumption of the sector specific capital earlier, the impact of the Dutch Disease on the labour market can be stated as:

(a) Employment in the NT sector increases (from NT_0 to NT_2),
(b) Employment in the BT sector rises (but not significantly, BT_2 marginally less than BT_1 but more than BT_0) and
(c) Employment in the NBT sector falls $NBT_2 < NBT_1 < NBT_0$. These labour market changes are summarized in Table 5.1.

The combined summary effects of the R^e and S^e below are shown in the lower part of Table 5.2, depicts that the output level in the BT sector is indeterminate but likely to rise, in the NBT sector output will fall and in the NT sector likely to rise. In the BT and NBT prices are externally determined but in the NT sector prices will rise. Indeed, it is this increase in the price of the NT goods and services that triggers an appreciation of the REER in the economy.

5.3.1 *The Dutch Disease and Premature Deindustrialization*

In the natural process of economic development, economies follow a typical trajectory. In general, as an economy matures its manufacturing sector expands at first and then contracts (deindustrialization) whilst its agricultural sector persistently falls in relative size. The services sector

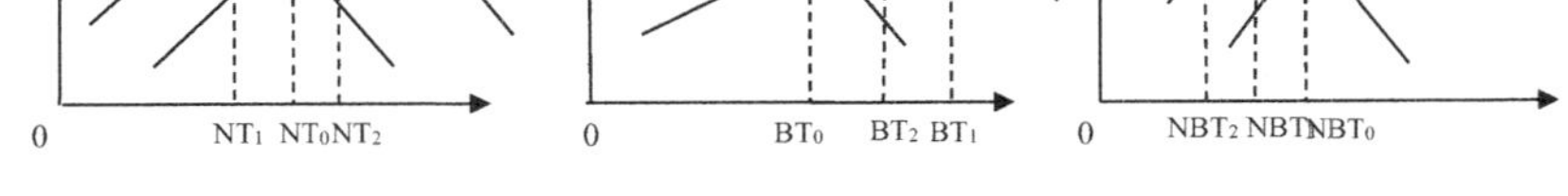

Fig. 5.3 Dutch Disease impact on the labour market

Table 5.1 Labour market changes

	L	L^{re}	L^{se}	$L^{DD} - L$	*Overall*
NBT	NBT_0	NBT_1	NBT_2	$NBT_2 - NBT_0$	–
BT	BT_0	BT_1	BT_2	$BT_2 - BT_0$	+
NT	NT_0	NT_1	NT_2	$NT_2 - NT_0$	+

Table 5.2 Summary of Dutch Disease symptoms

	Output	*Price*
R^e		
Booming Tradable (Oil Sector)	+	Given
Non-Booming Tradable (Manufacturing Sector and Export Agriculture)	–	Given
Non-tradable (Services Sector)	–	+
S^e		
Booming Tradable (Oil Sector)	–	Given
Non-Booming Tradable (Manufacturing Sector and Export Agriculture)	–	Given
Non-tradable (Services Sector)	+	+
Combined Effect = $R^e + S^e$		
Booming Tradable (Oil Sector)	Indeterminate but likely to rise	Given
Non-Booming Tradable (Manufacturing Sector and Export Agriculture)	–	Given
Non-tradable (Services Sector)	Indeterminate but likely to rise if the income elasticity of demand is greater than unity)	+

Source Author's compilation

expands continuously. In this regard, early literature on deindustrialization was germinated by Baumol (1967) but was perhaps most developed by Rowthorn and Wells (1987). Rowthorn and Ramaswammy (1999) noted that this process of deindustrialization was inevitable and need not be associated with falling levels of manufacturing output providing there is increased manufacturing sector productivity. To illustrate some of the fundamental economic attributes of deindustrialization, let A_0: share of agriculture in total output, M_0: share of manufacturing in total output, S_0: share of services in total output and let Y_L: low income, Y_M: middle income and Y_H: high income.

Prototypically, in:

> Y_L, $A_0 > [M_0, S_0]$ ... (1) i.e. in a low-income economy, the share of the agricultural sector in total output is the largest.
> Y_M, $M_0 > [A_0, S_0]$ ... (2) i.e. the share of the manufacturing sector in total output tends to be the largest.
> Y_H, $S_0 > [M_0, A_0]$ ... (3) i.e. the share of the services sector in total output tends to be the largest.

A similar relationship holds, regarding employment in the various sectors. Some researchers, such as Saeger (1997) have argued that deindustrialization is best explained by a reference to declining manufacturing employment shares in total employment and not output shares.

To provide an illustration, in the first panel of the Fig. 5.4, manufacturing output is drawn to follow the pattern indicated by Rowthorn and Ramaswammy (1999) i.e. it has an inverted U shape. As income increases the share of manufacturing output in total output increases at first (peaking at income level Y_0) and then declines. This chapter argues that in a petroleum-based economy the situation is further compounded by the fall in manufacturing employment in economies affected by the Dutch Disease, occurring simultaneously. MA_1 (the Dutch Disease induced manufacturing share of total output curve) is lower than MA_0 which occurs due to the loss of labour in manufacturing which in turn leaves the manufacturing sector with spare capacity (given that the economy is assumed to have started off at full employment, we assume that the manufacturing sector operated at full capacity prior to the resource boom).

Thus, with the resource movement and spending effect in combination, manufacturing share of output falls from λ_0 to λ_0^1 to λ_1 (read from Panel a below). The sectoral shift in the economy on account of the resource movement and spending effect sees the service sector activity proceed along S_1 instead of S_0 and the shares progress from α_0 to α_0^1 to α_1.

If we assume that at λ_0 the manufacturing sector was operating at full capacity, then the manufacturing sector shrinks as it loses labour and other

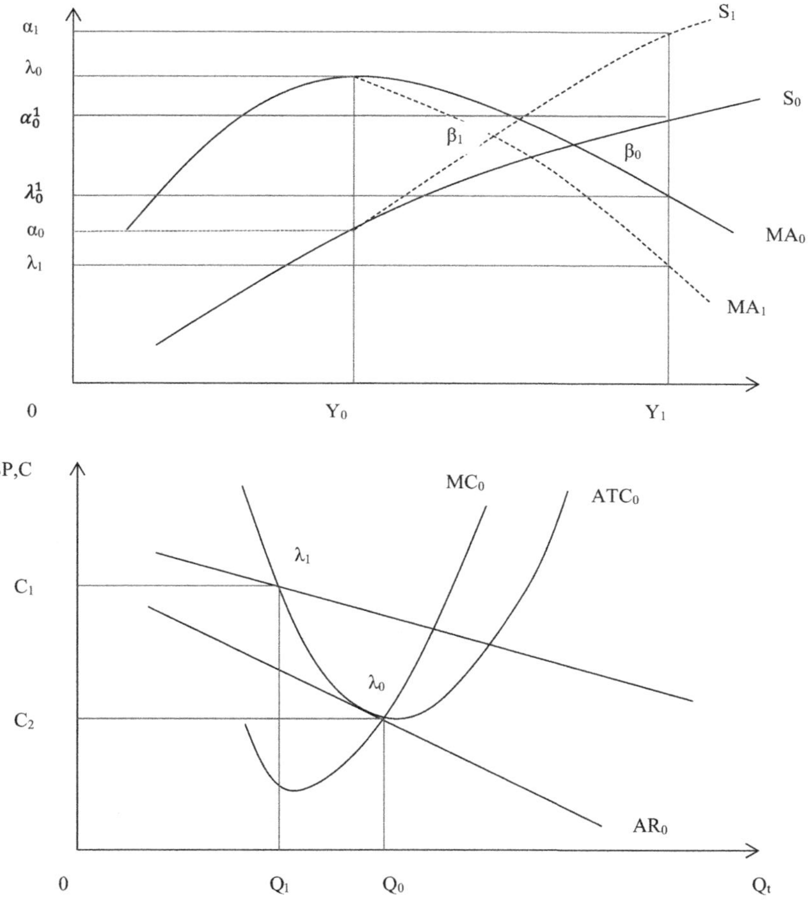

Fig. 5.4 Illustration effect of the Dutch Disease on the manufacturing sector % share

things constant, it is forced to operate with spare capacity, at income level Y_1.

The representative firm in the manufacturing sector therefore experiences a decline in output (Q_0 to Q_1) and its per unit costs rises from C_0 to C_1. In summary, with the Dutch Disease, the manufacturing sector loses workers, market share, faces higher wages and becomes less competitive externally.

In this regard Rodrik notes that "*resource booms magnify the deindustrializing consequences that trade has on countries with comparative advantage in primary products*" (Rodrik 2015, p. 22). The result for the Dutch Diseased country is a decline in manufacturing sector employment and output, as fewer investments are made into the manufacturing sector.

When de-industrialization occurs in a 'natural' format it is associated with rising living standards. This should be intuitively clear, as deindustrialization in this scenario would coincide with rising incomes per capita. Significantly, a process of continued deindustrialization will have important implications for any economy.

5.4 Dutch Disease and Sectoral Trade Performance

The Heckscher–Ohlin theorem (H/O theorem) as expressed in Ohlin's own words emphasizes, "*Commodities requiring for their production much of [abundant factors of production] and little of [scarce factors] are exported in exchange for goods that call for factors in the opposite proportions. Thus indirectly, factors in abundant supply are exported and factors in scanty supply are imported*" (Ohlin 1933, p. 92). Basically, this theory infers that countries will produce and export those commodities associated with their abundant factor of production and import those commodities which call for factors of production which are scarce. The H/O theorem also applies to the scenario where the good is a natural resource. Leamer (1984) has found that countries with a relative abundance of oil tends to export crude oil. Leamer observed the trade patterns of 60 developed and developing countries in 1958 and 1975 and found that countries abundant in labour and capital tended to export manufactures, and countries abundant in natural resources tended to export raw materials. Leamer (1984) states that the developed countries are predominately the net exporters of labour and capital-intensive manufactured goods and importers of raw materials and resource intensive manufactures, whilst the developing countries are net importers of manufactured goods and exporters of raw materials.

Kemp and Long (1985) investigate, using three alternative scenarios, the H/O model's validity. The models may be referred to as the anti-H/O model, the hybrid model and the generalized H/O model. The anti-H/O model is one where each final good is produced using only two exhaustible resources. The hybrid model is one where one of the two resources used in the production process is an exhaustible good; the other is not an exhaustible resource. In the generalized H/O Model, which is the third case, two non-exhaustible resources are combined with an exhaustible resource. Overall, what Kemp and Long (1980, 1984) find is that if a country has an abundance of an exhaustible resource it will produce and export that good or goods intensive in its use. In this regard a picture of the pattern of exports of a country can be gleaned by looking at its comparative advantage status, as outlined by Balassa (1965). Specifically, Balassa argued that the revealed comparative advantage (RCA) of a country is indicated by the country's trade performance with respect to individual industries. The RCA index is calculated based on the actual export performance of a country. More specifically:

$$RCA_i = \left(\left(\frac{T_{xi}}{T_{xt}}\right) \Big/ \left(\frac{W_{xi}}{W_{xt}}\right)\right) \times 100$$

where T_{xi} = T&T export of good *i*.
T_{xt} = T&T total export
W_{xi} = World exports of good *i*.
W_{xt} = Total world exports.
The theoretical range of the RCA is $0 < RCA_i < \infty$. A country is said to have a revealed comparative advantage in exporting a commodity, *i*, if

$$1 < RCA_i < \infty$$

To transcribe the Dutch Disease and Heckscher–Ohlin effects into sectoral trade performances, we can proceed as follows. Starting from first principles and subdividing as before the T sector into NBT and BT components, it was established that the BT sector improves on account of the R^e, in particular, and that the NBT sector contracts because of the R^e, complementing the S^e. In this regard, let F(t) show the density function of an initial index of sectoral trade performance. With the Dutch Disease, there is an emergent dichotomous pattern in the sectoral trade performance of the petroleum-exporting economy leading to a contraction in the number of sectors with RCA > 1 and an expansion in the number of sectors with comparative disadvantage (read from F(t + s)), see Fig. 5.5.

Four key changes take place in terms of the RCA structure in an economy with a pronounced boom in one of its exportable goods:

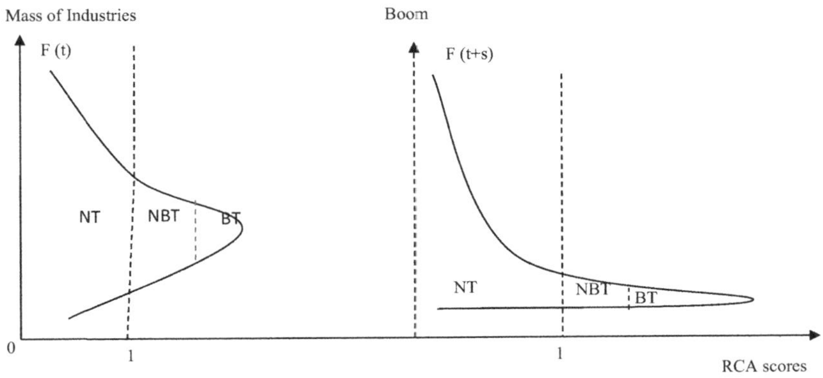

Fig. 5.5 Distribution associated with differing evolution of RCA Scores

1. Distribution becomes more bimodal as the NBT sector dissolves and two almost distinct distributions emerge, one with RCA > 1 and the other with RCA < 1.
2. Median value of RCA > 1 increases whilst the median value of RCA < 1 falls. This is intuitive as resources flow towards the BT sector on account of the resource movement sector and out of the NBT sector on account of a resource movement effect that takes place in favour of the BT sector and a spending effect that causes resources to drift to the NT sector.
3. Standard deviation of RCA > 1 scores decrease and of RCA < 1 increases.
4. Overall, the distribution becomes more skewed as there is a crowding out of the NBT sector by the NT and BT sectors.

Following Hinloopen and van Marrewijk (2001) the classification of different strengths of comparative advantage in Table 5.3 is adopted. (This classification can help to provide insights as to how the comparative advantage structure of the T&T economy changed in a "class" sense over two defined time periods.)

Based on the above, there were thirteen instances of a movement from class b to a, 1 case of a movement from class c to a and 1 case of a movement from class d to a. These class to class migrations are alarming and represent a manifest consequence of strong Dutch Disease processes at

Table 5.3 RCA classifications

Class a	0 < RCA < 1	Industries with a comparative disadvantage
Class b	1 < RCA < 2	Industries with weak comparative disadvantage
Class c	2 < RCA < 4	Medium comparative advantage
Class d	4 < RCA	Strong comparative advantage

Source Author's Computations

work. If we identify energy products i.e. section 3 (and specifically subsections 333, 334, 342, 343 and 344) and chemicals i.e. section 5 (and in particular 512, 522, 554 and 562) as the economy's BT sector in Table 5.4, then 22 of the sectors in the NBT sector would have migrated to lower states, and this is alarming.

From another dimension, consider the transition probability matrix shown in Table 5.5. (Transition probability matrices can be used when analyzing the mobility of different sectors within a specialization index.) The matrix is defined as a square array of non-negative numbers such that the rows tally to unity and represent a discrete Markov chain. Table 5.5 shows an estimated transition matrix where 1999 is the initial time period and 2019 is the new time period. The matrix shows the probability of moving from one state in the first time period to another state in the final time period.

The diagonal elements of the matrix show the probability of starting in a particular state of comparative advantage in 1999 and remaining in that state in 2019. Thus, if a sector was in a state of comparative disadvantage in 1999 there is a 0.913 probability it would remain in that state in 2019. Note the other diagonal elements are also high. Ideally policy makers would hope that the elements in the upper triangular part of the TPM will be high. Unfortunately, in the T&T case the values are low. For example, the probability of moving from a state of comparative disadvantage A to a state of weak comparative advantage B is 0.0031, this is not healthy especially in an economy where the main foreign exchange earning energy sector is maturing.

Even more, the probability of moving from a position of comparative advantage to a state of comparative disadvantage is too high in most cases. For example, the probability of moving from a state of moderate comparative advantage, C, to weak comparative advantage, A, is 0.213 and this is too high.

Table 5.4 Display of gains or losses in RCA strength by sector, 1999–2018

Master list	*Description*	*1999*	*2018*	*Change*	*Gain or loss*	*State to state*
017	Meat, edible meat offal, prepared, preserved, n.e.s	1.11	0.38	−0.73	Loss	b to a
046	Meal and flour of wheat and flour of meslin	2.24	1.27	−0.97	Loss	b to b
048	Cereal preparations, flour of fruits or vegetables	4.46	1.92	−2.54	Loss	d to b
058	Fruit, preserved and fruit preparations (no juice)	1.81	0.9	−0.9	Loss	b to a
059	Fruit and vegetable juices, unfermented, no spirit	2.66	1.9	−0.76	Loss	c to b
061	Sugar, molasses and honey	5.96	0.16	−5.8	Loss	d to b
062	Sugar confectionery	3.28	0.62	−2.66	Loss	d to b
072	Cocoa	1.04	0.26	−0.78	Loss	b to a
073	Chocolate, food preparations with cocoa, n.e.s	1.1	0.58	−0.52	Loss	b to a
075	Spices	1.11	0.37	−0.74	Loss	b to a
091	Margarine and shortening	4.27	1.93	−2.34	Loss	d to b
098	Edible products and preparations, n.e.s	1.26	0.5	−0.76	Loss	b to a
111	Non-alcoholic beverages, n.e.s	15.12	5.83	−9.29	Loss	d to d
112	Alcoholic beverages	1.81	0.87	−0.94	Loss	b to a
122	Tobacco, manufactured	1.11	2.98	1.88	Gain	b to c
333	Petroleum oils, oils from bitumin. materials, crude	3.54	1.8	−1.74	Loss	c to b
334	Petroleum oils or bituminous minerals > 70% oil	17.63	4.39	−13.24	Loss	d to d
342	Liquefied propane and butane	14.53	5.12	−9.41	Loss	d to d
343	Natural gas, whether or not liquefied	6.17	24.53	18.37	Gain	d to d

(continued)

Table 5.4 (continued)

Master list	*Description*	*1999*	*2018*	*Change*	*Gain or loss*	*State to state*
344	Petroleum gases, other gaseous hydrocarbons, n.e.s	41.9	2.38	−39.51	Loss	d to c
512	Alcohols, phenols, halogenat., sulfonat., nitrat. der	23.67	12.58	−11.08	Loss	d to d
522	Inorganic chemical elements, oxides and halogen salts	37.1	9.62	−27.48	Loss	d to d
554	Soaps, cleansing and polishing preparations	3.35	1.31	−2.04	Loss	c to b
562	Fertilizers (other than those of group 272)	6.19	3.62	−2.57	Loss	d to c
635	Wood manufacture, n.e.s	1.43	0.18	−1.24	Loss	b to a
642	Paper and paperboard, cut to shape or size, articles	3.64	1.56	−2.07	Loss	c to b
661	Lime, cement, fabrica. constr. mat. (excluding glass, clay)	3.8	0.79	−3	Loss	c to a
665	Glassware	1.89	0.48	−1.41	Loss	b to a
671	Pig iron and spiegeleisen, sponge iron, powder & granu	10.36	5.24	−5.12	Loss	d to d
676	Iron and steel bars, rods, angles, shapes & sections	14.81	1.32	−13.49	Loss	d to b
691	Structures and parts, n.e.s., of iron, steel, aluminium	1.03	0.12	−0.92	Loss	b to a
693	Wire products (excluding electrical) and fencing grills	1.24	0.24	−1	Loss	b to a
723	Civil engineering and contractors' plant and equipment	1.04	0.49	−0.55	Loss	b to a
741	Heating and cooling equipment and parts thereof, n.e.s	1.22	0.09	−1.13	Loss	b to a

Source Computed from COMTRADE data

Table 5.5 Transition probability matrix for movement amongst states, 1999–2019

From	*To*			
	A	*B*	*C*	*D*
A	0.913	0.0031	0.014	0.099
B	0.314	0.487	0.09	0.101
C	0.213	0.118	0.593	0.112
D	0.113	0.228	0.065	0.618

Source Author's Computations

Aggregately, the data shows that policy makers may need to rethink the approach to diversifying the T&T economy as it has not been yielding desired diversification results.

5.4.1 *Long-Term Impact on Growth*

To illustrate some of the long-term effects of a resource boom on an economy, consider the diagram below, which is a modified and improved version of Sachs and Warner (1995) and which assumes there are two economies, one resource rich (RR) and the other resource poor (RP). The analytics of the diagram assumes that in initial conditions both economies are growing at the same pace, to the extent that between 0 and T_0 in Fig. 5.6, the initial income in both RP and RR is the same. Assume now that at the point in time T_0, economy RR experiences a resource boom, the immediate effect of which is to displace its income upwards to point B, so that for the time interval T_0 to T_1, this economy experiences a higher level of income than economy RP, even if its growth rate falls below that of the RP economy.[3] Beyond T_1 the level of GDP in economy RR would fall below that of the RP economy. Even if at D the RR economy reverts to having the same growth rate as the RP economy, its overall level of income will be lower (Y_1) than that of the RP economy (Y_2) (Fig. 5.7).

Indeed, although between 1980 and 2020, T&T produced about eight billion barrels of oil and gas equivalent, its real GDP only increased 112.7% and even more between 2008 and 2020, real GDP declined by

[3] On account of the resource curse factors discussed in the previous chapter.

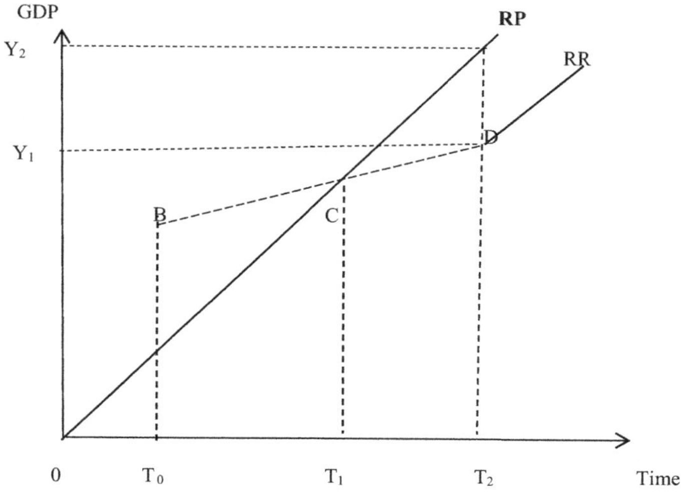

Fig. 5.6 Illustrative impact of a resource boom on the growth rate of a resource-rich economy

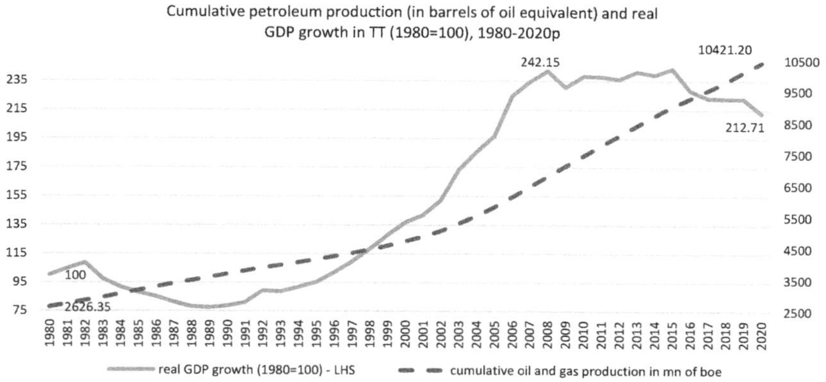

Fig. 5.7 Cumulative petroleum production

17.1%. By way of comparison in the same time period (1980–2020) the real GDP of Antigua and Barbuda grew 278% and St. Kitts grew 323.7%.

5.4.2 *Oil Prices and the Real Effective Exchange Rate—Some Econometric Evidence*

An appreciation of the real effective exchange rate is one of the channels through which the Dutch Disease works in an economy. In order to assess the impact of oil prices on the REER, data was collected for the period 1980–2018 on the real effective exchange rate for Trinidad and Tobago, real oil price level and the ratio of real GDP per capita as a measure for productivity differential, between T&T and its main trading partners. The variables used in the model was employed based on the research work of Oomes and Kalcheva (2007) and Mironov and Petronevich (2015).

The results in Table 5.6 show that the variables were either I(0) or I(1) and as a consequence ARDL model was used to test for cointegration, using the bounds test outlined by Pesaran et al. (2001). This methodology was also adopted by papers by Mustapha and Masih (2016) on Nigeria, Amin and Murshed (2017) on Bangladesh, Gasmi and Laourari (2017) on Algeria and Asmau et al. (2019) on Nigeria. The ARDL model has been acclaimed in the literature because it is simple as it has an OLS base and it can determine the existence of cointegration even if the series are I(0) or I(1). The basic model adopts the format shown below:

$$\Delta LREER_t = \propto_0 + \alpha_1 \, LREER_{t-i} + \alpha_2 \, LROP_{t-i} + \alpha_3 LDIFF_{t-i} + \sum_{i=1}^{k} a_i \Delta LREER_{t-i} + \sum_{i=1}^{k} b_i \Delta LROP_{t-i} + \sum_{i=1}^{k} c_i \, \Delta LDIFF_{t-i} + \varepsilon_t$$

The bounds test procedure as developed by Pesaran et al. (2001) to assess whether a long-run relationship amongst the variables exist is utilized herein.[4] Cointegration was confirmed at 5%. In the presence of cointegration, an ECM was deployed to distinguish between the long-run (LR) and the short-run dynamics amongst the variables. The negative and significant error correction term corroborates the existence of cointegration (see Table 5.7).

[4] The model included two dummy variables for 2004 and 2014 and we confirmed the overall significance and robustness of the model.

Table 5.6 Stationarity test results

Variable (constant specification)	*Augmented Dickey–Fuller*		*Phillips Perron*		*Kwiatkowski–Phillips–Schmidt–Shin*	
	Levels (p-value)	*1st Difference (p-value)*	*Levels (p-value)*	*1st Difference (p-value)*	*Levels (LM-Stat)*	*1st Difference (LM-Stat)*
Log (REER)	0.564	0.002*	0.74	0.003*	0.421*	0.147*
Log (ROP)	0.328	0.001*	0.315	0.000*	0.468	0.208*
Log (DIFF)	0.078	0.200	0.485	0.050*	0.301*	0.232*

*5% level of significance

Table 5.7 Estimated long-run and short-run results using the ARDL approach

	Coefficient	*p-value*
Log real oil price	0.26*	0.032
Log Productivity Differential	0.47*	0.049
Serial Correlation		*0.429*
Heteroscedasticity		*0.003*
D (Log Real Oil Price)	0.11*	0.000
D (Log Productivity Differential)	0.45*	0.003
ECT (CointEq1)	−0.93*	0.000
Serial Correlation		*0.892*
Heteroscedasticity		*0.118*

Note * and ** denotes significance at the 5% level
Source Results from Eviews10

The results in Table 5.7 indicate that oil prices has a positive and significant impact on the real effective exchange rate in the long run with a 1% increase in real oil prices, leading to a 0.26% appreciation in the REER. Note that the results also show that in both the long run and the short run, the productivity differential had a larger impact on the REER than real oil prices. Reference to the Toda-Yamamoto[5] (1995) non-causality test indicated that there existed unidirectional causality from oil prices to the REER in Trinidad and Tobago, over the 1980–2018 period.

5.5 Conclusion

This chapter focused on the Resource Curse and the Dutch Disease. The first part of the chapter outlined various influences in resource-rich economies that trigger a resource curse. The second part of the chapter focuses on the Dutch Disease. In this second part, the chapter outlined and elaborated the effect of a boom in a tradable good (BT) on the NBT and NT segments of the economy. The clear indication from the model is that whilst the boom can leave the BT sector with a marginally enhanced number of workers, the NBT sector gets both a direct and an indirect bout of deindustrialization. Collectively this double blow starves

[5] The Toda-Yamamoto causality test has been hailed in the literature for its superiority over Granger causality in the presence of non-stationary series since it avoids the potential biases and errors associated with Granger causality (see Mavrotas and Kelly 2001; Wolde-Rufael 2009).

the manufacturing sector of some of its labour and at the same time the NT sector's employment and output grows. The chapter then illustrated how these changes in the structure of production influence the dynamics of the revealed comparative advantage posture of the economy. It was found that 22 (twenty-two) of the sectors in the NBT sector migrated to a lower comparative advantage class. A reference to a transition probability matrix shows that the economy is not diversifying.

The chapter also provided some basic evidence to show that as real oil prices increase, the real effective exchange rate appreciates, for T&T. This is pivotal and the government of T&T would have to keep this in mind should oil (or gas) prices surge in the future.

An appreciated real effective exchange rate makes it difficult to diversify the economy's productive export base and thus also makes it more difficult to earn foreign exchange. With the closure of the Petrotrin refinery there is the possibility of earning more foreign exchange from blending gasoline imports with methanol and the re-exporting. This possibility is raised and examined in the next chapter.

References

Amin, Sakib, and Murshed, Muntasir. (2017). "Remittance, Exchange Rate and Dutch Disease: The Case of Bangladesh (September 2017)." International Review of Business Research Papers 13 (2). Available at SSRN: https://ssrn.com/abstract=3070057.

Arezki, R., Hadri, Kaddour, Loungani, Prakash, and Rao, Yao. (2013). "Testing the Prebisch-Singer Hypothesis Since 1650: Evidence from Panel Techniques That Allow for Multiple Breaks." IMF Working Paper 13/180, August.

Asmau, Y.J., Agility, M.S., and Amina, A.J. (2019). "Dutch Disease: Myth or Reality? An Analysis of the ARDL Model." International Journal of Business, Economics and Management 6 (3): 130–140.

Auty, R.M. (1993). "Sustaining Development in Mineral Economies: The Resource Curse Thesis." London: Routledge.

Balassa, Bela. (1965). "Trade Liberalization and Revealed Comparative Advantage." The Manchester School of Economic and Social Studies 33: 99–123.

Baumol, William J. (1967). "Macroeconomics of Unbalance Growth: The Anatomy of Urban Crisis." The American Economic Review 57 (3): 415–426.

Caves, R.E. (1968). "Vent for Surplus' Models of Trade and Growth." In James D. Theberge (Ed.), Economics of Trade and Development (pp. 211–230). New York: John Wiley and Sons.

Copithorne, L. (1979). "Natural Resources and Regional Disparities: A Skeptical View." Canadian Public Policy/Analyse de Politiques 5 (2): 181–194.

Davis, A. Graham, and Tilton, E. John. (2008). "Why the Resource Curse Is a concern." Mining Engineering 60 (4): 29–32.

Gasmi, Farid, and Laourari, Imène. (2017). "Has Algeria Suffered from the Dutch Disease? Evidence from 1960–2016 Data." Revue d'économie politique, Dalloz 127 (6): 1029–1058.

Gelb, Alan. "Economic Diversification in Resource Rich Countries." Center for Global Development (2010): 1–23.

Goldberg, K. Pinelope, and Pavcnik, Nina. (2008). "Distributional Effects of Globalization in Developing Countries." Journal of Economic Literature 45 (1): 39–82.

Heal, G. 2006. "Are Oil Producers Rich?" Initiative for Policy Dialogue Working Paper Series. https://policydialogue.org/files/publications/papers/Ch06.pdf.

Hidalgo, C.A., Klinger, B., Barabasi, A.L., and Hausmann, R. (2007). "The Product Space Conditions the Development of Nations." Science 317 (5837): 482.

Hinloopen, Jeroen, and van Marrewijk, Charles. (2001). "On the Empirical Distribution of the Balassa Index." Review of World Economics/Weltwirtschaftliches Archiv 137: 1–35.

Hirschman, O. Albert. (1958). "The Strategy of Economic Development." New Haven, CT: Yale University Press.

Humphreys, M., Sachs, J., and Stiglitz, J. (2007). "Escaping the Resource Curse." NY: Initiative for Policy Dialogue, Columbia University Press.

Innis, A. Harrold. (1950). "Empire and Communications." Clarendon, Oxford.

Kemp, Murray C., and Van Long, Ngo. "How to Eat a Cake of Unknown Size: The Case of a Growing Cake." Economics Letters 17.1–2 (1985): 67–69.

Kemp, Murray C., and Van Long, Ngo. "On Two Folk Theorems Concerning the Extraction of Exhaustible Resources." Econometrica: Journal of the Econometric Society (1980): 663–673.

Kemp, Murray C., and Van Long, Ngo. "The Role of Natural Resources in Trade Models." Handbook of International Economics 1 (1984): 367–417.

Lam, Ricky, and Wantchekon, Leonard. (2002). "Political Dutch Disease." Northwestern University.

Leamer, Edward E. 1984. "Sources of International Comparative Advantage: Theory and Evidence." Cambridge, MA: MIT Press.

Loayza, Norman, Mier y Teran, Alfredo, and Rigolini, Jamele. (2013). "Poverty, Inequality, and the Local Natural Resource Curse." Policy Research Working Paper; No. 6366. Washington, DC: World Bank. © World Bank. https://openknowledge.worldbank.org/handle/10986/13169. License: CC BY 3.0 IGO.

Mavrotas, G., and Kelly, R. (2001). "Old Wine in New Bottles: Testing Causality Between Savings and Growth." The Manchester School 69: 97–105.

Mironov, V., and Petronevich, A. (2015). "Discovering the Signs of Dutch Disease in Russia." Resources Policy 46: 100–110.

Mustapha, Ishaq Muhammad, and Masih, Mansur. (2016). "Dutch Disease or Nigerian Disease: A Prima Facie? New Evidence from ARDL Bound Test Analysis." MPRA Paper 69767. Germany: University Library of Munich.

Myint, Hila. (1958). "The Classical Theory of International Trade and the Under-Developed Nations." Economic Journal 68: 317–337.

Myint, Hila. (1965). "Economic Theory and the Underdeveloped Countries." Journal of Political Economy 73 (10): 477–491.

Nurkse, R. (1958). "Contribution to 'the Discussion of Professor Viner's Paper:' Stability and Progress in the World Economy." In D. Hague (Ed.), The First Congress of the International Economic Association (pp. 69–77). London: Macmillan.

Ohlin, Bertil. (1933). "Interregional and International Trade" (p. xvii). Cambridge: Harvard University Press.

Oomes, N., and Kalcheva, K. (2007). "Diagnosing Dutch Disease: Does Russia Have the Symptoms?" IMF Working Paper, 16–22.

Osmundsen, P. (2010). "Time Consistency in Petroleum Taxation: Lessons from Norway." In P. Daniel, M. Keen, and C. McPherson (Eds.), The Taxation of Petroleum and Minerals (pp. 425–444). Oxford, UK: Routledge.

Pesaran, M.H., Shin, Y., and Smith, R.J. (2001). "Bounds Testing Approaches to the Analysis of Level Relationships." Journal of Applied Econometrics 16 (3): 289–326.

Prebisch, Raul. (1950). "The Economic Development of Latin America and Its Principal Problems." New York, USA: United Nation.

Rodrik, D. (2015). "Premature Deindustrialization." NBER Working Paper Series.

Rowthorn, E. Robert, and Wells, R. John. (1987). "De-industrialisation and Foreign Trade." Cambridge: Cambridge University Press.

Rowthorn, Robert, and Ramaswamy, Ramana. (1999). "Growth, Trade, and Deindustrialization." IMF Staff Papers 46 (1): 18–41.

Sachs, Jeffery, and Warner, Andrew. (1995). "Natural Resource Abundance and Economic Growth." NBER Working Paper Series, No. 5398. Cambridge, MA.

Sachs, D. Jeffery, and Warner, M. Andrew. (1997). "Sources of Slow Growth in African Economies." Journal of African Economies 6 (3): 335–376.

Saeger, S. Steven. (1997). "Globalization and Deindustrialization: Myth and Reality in the OECD." Weltwirtschaftliches Archiv 133 (4): 579–608.

Seers, Dudley. (1963). "The Limitations of the Special Case." Bulletin of the Institute of Economics and Statistics, May, 77–98.

Singer, H. (1950). "The Distribution of Gains Between Investing and Borrowing Countries." American Economic Review, Papers and Proceedings 40: 473–485.

Smith, Adam. (1776). "An Inquiry into the Nature and Causes of the Wealth of Nations." London: Methuen & Co Ltd.

Stevens, P. (2015). "Energy, Environment and Resources: The Resource Curse Revisited Appendix: A Literature Review."

Toda, H.Y., and Yamamoto, T. (1995). "Statistical Inference in Vector Autoregressions with Possibly Integrated Processes." Journal of Econometrics 66: 225–250.

Torvik, R. (2002). "Natural Resources, Rent Seeking and Welfare." Journal of Development Economics 67 (2): 455–470.

United Nations Conference on Trade and Development (UNCTAD). (2012). "Trade Income Distribution and Poverty in Developing Countries: A Survey." United Nations, Discussion Paper, No. 207.

Van der Ploeg, Frederick, and Poelhekke, Steven. (2009). "Volatility and the Natural Resource Curse." Oxford Economic Papers 61: 727–760. https://doi.org/10.1093/oep/gpp027.

Watkins, H. Melville. (1963). "A Staple Theory of Economic Growth." Canadian Journal of Economics and Political Science 29: 141–158.

Wright, Gavin, and Czelusta, Jesse. (2004). "The Myth of the Resource Curse." Challenge 47 (2): 6–38.

Wolde-Rufael, Y. (2009). "Energy Consumption and Economic Growth: The Experience of African Countries Revisited." Energy Economics 31: 217–234.

CHAPTER 6

The Petrochemical Sector of T&T: With Reference to the Methanol Industry in T&T

6.1 Introduction

This chapter discusses the petrochemical sector of the T&T economy and builds on Chapter 3. Methanol is selected for special reference as the refinery in T&T was closed in 2018 and methanol blending with imported gas offers a real opportunity to help lower T&T's gas import bill whilst simultaneously help the country meet some of its Paris Accord targets.

6.2 The State as an Entrepreneur in Trinidad

The role of the state in fostering entrepreneurship in the market economy is considered by many, as one of the reasons that countries such as Singapore, Japan and Korea have experienced sustained economic growth and development, particularly between 1960 and 1990 (Gereffi 1995; Sarel 1996). Page (1994) argued that these countries were able to avoid market failure, not because of getting the basics right, but because of the role government played in the development process. The Governments in these countries altered the industrial structure where necessary and also provided technological learning. Page went on to point out that Taiwan and Japan which at the time were considered to be the two most productivity-driven economies in the world, also identified most

R. Hosein, *Oil and Gas in Trinidad and Tobago*,
https://doi.org/10.1007/978-3-030-77669-5_6

with "activist policies to promote technological learning" within their economies (Lall 1996; Loasby 1991).

In the Theory of Economic Development, Schumpeter described the development as a process of structural change, which he outlined as having several parts, one of which was the opening of a new market, which was not previously represented. In many regards by opening its resource-based petrochemical sector, the state in T&T followed this aspect of Schumpeter's innovation drive (this will be elaborated below). In Schumpeter's view innovation was at the centre of economic change as it helped to create gales of "creative destruction."

In the Caribbean region, Sir Arthur Lewis (1950) in his recommendations for Caribbean economies noted that industrializing by a process of inviting established foreign firms to come into the Caribbean and set up shop was one of the best strategies for the islands to implement in order to deal with their issues of "surplus labour," given the presence of foreign exchange, managerial, technological and market access bottlenecks. Lewis argued that the main constraint for Caribbean economies resided in the ability to find and penetrate foreign markets and by engaging in Industrialization by Invitation, Caribbean countries could benefit from the wholesale importation of technologies, capital and managerial skills. Given this, Lewis (1950) then noted that the process of industrialization must begin with the market, because an industry will not survive if it cannot dispose of its outputs. Even though a market can either be local or foreign, Lewis (1950), argued in favour of foreign markets, as the small size of local markets will not allow a country to benefit from economies of scale. (Lewis further argued that even the intra-regional market would be too small and should be used only as an extra-regional launching pad.)

Lewis (1950) was aware of the fact markets are difficult to find and penetrate so he went on to advocate that the Caribbean countries should invite foreign firms, who already have established markets, to do business in their countries. He noted that when industrialization is done for an export market, it is better pursued by firms that are already established in the foreign market and indicated that: "*It is hardly possible for the islands to break into the market in competition with existing suppliers. Breaking into a market involves great expenditure on sales promotion to establish new trade channels, and this will hardly be worthwhile for the limited amount of trade that the islands would do. The moral of this is that what should rather be done is to try to persuade existing suppliers, with established distribution channels...... to open factories in the islands to supply their trade*" (Lewis 1950, p. 31).

The capital needed to fuel the industrialization process is typically large, as the process of industrialization, Lewis emphasized, is very expensive and so he argued that this capital should also come from foreigners.[1] But Lewis was also careful to note that the contribution of the host country in the capital formation process should come in the form of having their government undertake the responsibility for constructing factories, which they could make available to the foreign firm at subsidized rates.[2]

In 1957, the T&T government, on the prompting of Lewis, established an Industrial Development Corporation (IDC). Lewis felt that an IDC was indispensable for the industrial development of a country. The task of the IDC was to assist the government in setting up its production platform and to assist investors (including foreign firms) with their investment problems. Lewis also argued that it was necessary to have a battery of incentives to encourage exporting firms. As a consequence the legislation to facilitate the industrialization process in T&T was enacted between 1946 and 1967 and took the form of: (a) Hotel Development Ordinance 1946, (b) Aid to Pioneer Industry Ordinance 1950, (c) the Income tax Aid to industry 1950, (d) Cement Industry Ordinance 1956, (e) Income tax in Aid of Industry 1955, (f) Nitrogenous Fertilizers (Industry Development Ordinance 1958), (g) Lube Oil and Greases Ordinance (1961), (h) Petrochemicals Development Act (1967), and (i) the Manufacturing Industry Development Act (1967).

These different pieces of legislation set the tone for industrial activity in T&T in the years ahead.

6.3 Black Power Movement and the First Energy Boom

At the dawn of the 1970s, the T&T economy prospered from an oil boom (aspects of this was partly highlighted by Table 2.4 in Chapter 2). For example, between 1965 and 1975 the government collected TT$3216.5 mn in oil revenues but with the surge in oil price

[1] Lewis highlighted that this was true of the industrialization experience of not only the British in the fifteenth century but of every industrial country thereafter, except the USSR.

[2] Lewis also noted that the foreign capitalist would supply initiative.

and production, the state collected TT$14.3bn in the period 1979–1982 alone (Table 6.1).

This boom emerged in an environment that was sympathetic to change as in 1962 this country gained its political independence. In 1970, there were massive street protests concerning unemployment and growing discontent with regards to the presence of "foreign control over the commanding heights of the economy." One of the basic arguments of the protestors was that "*Black capitalism disguises white control just as Black government disguises colonialism. It is insulting to Black people to tell us that we should be contented with a little co-operative here and a shop or store there on the fringes of the economy, when we know that this country is ours. Black business will have to operate within the rules of the system which means all our basic problems remain*" (National Joint Action Committee 1970). NJAC went on to note that "*We need to destroy…the system from its very foundations…to get out of our economic mess*" (Black entrepreneurs in Post-Independence T&T).

Table 6.1 Impact of oil and gas on rents, revenues, and expenditures

	Oil price US$	*Oil production (mns) of barrels*	*Oil revenues TT$mn*
1965	1.8	48.86	85.3
1966	1.8	55.6	85.2
1967	1.8	64.99	88.2
1968	1.8	66.9	109.8
1969	1.8	57.42	108.2
1970	1.8	51.05	112
1971	2.24	47.15	138.4
1972	2.48	51.21	148.2
1973	3.29	60.67	197.3
1974	11.58	68.14	889.1
1975	11.53	78.62	1254.8
1976	12.8	77.67	1447.8
1977	13.92	83.62	1770.5
1978	14.02	83.78	1733.5
1979	31.61	78.25	2371.1
1980	36.83	77.61	4136.5
1981	35.93	69.11	4253.1
1982	32.97	64.62	3274.2

Source Synthesized data sources

The Black Power uprisings of the 1970s motivated a strong political push for the government to become the prime mover in the economy.[3] Initially the government of T&T, although ambitious in its intent, was constrained by a lack of resources but the occurrence of the first oil price boom, changed the government revenue position, for the better. In 1972 and 1975, two white papers on Public Participation in Industrial and Commercial activities were published, highlighting the following three objectives of the government:

- a localization objective: the acceleration of the process of the transferring of control into local hands,
- a development objective: to encourage and support local industry, particularly new ones,
- and an employment objective: to stabilize employment by reducing job loss.[4]

Like many economies in that era, the T&T economy in the period 1958–1973 engaged three five-year development plans to help drive the economy forward. The third five-year development plan for the period 1969–1973 paid attention to the need for greater investment in the commanding heights of the economy. Almost at the same time entrepreneurs from the South Trinidad Chamber of Industry and Commerce congregated and formulated the idea of building a Deep-water port at Point Lisas to serve an export industrial cluster. In parallel, the IDC began to focus considerable attention on the gas discoveries of Amoco and the best use to make of these discoveries.

The rapid increase in price and production of crude oil led to a sharp change in the economic fortunes of the state and it partially took the role of a Schumpeterian entrepreneur by entering the petrochemical arena in which it did not participate previously. This was in part as the state "suspected the political loyalty of the domestic private sector whose leaders were drawn largely from expatriates or European settlers, though long established in Trinidad and Tobago. Furthermore, both the politician and

[3] The Black Power demonstrations took place in T&T between 26 February and 21 April 1970. On the 21st April a state of emergency was declared. The demonstrations were carried out mainly by young black urban unemployed youths protesting domination of the business sector by a ruling white minority.

[4] See Sargeant and Forde (1992).

the elite public service derided the competence of the domestic private sector beyond trading, doubting its capacity to engage in the massive industrial undertaking that was being contemplated. The state therefore took on the prime role as entrepreneur" (Mottley 2008, p. 15).

Initially, the government required that foreign partnerships provide technology, managerial expertise and market contacts, much along the lines of Lewis' industrialization by invitation proposition. In 1975, the government concluded agreements with W.R. Grace to build a large ammonia plant and with three steel firms to build a large steel unit. In 1976, it agreed to a joint Amoco fertilizer plant. The government eventually withdrew from the joint steel venture and in 1977 began a steel venture of its own—the Iron and Steel Company of Trinidad and Tobago (ISCOTT). No doubt these decisions were partly politically motivated for as one researcher noted:

> *in a democratic setting there are certain constraints to economicmanagement and optimal resource allocation. Playing to the public gallery to get elected is part of that process.* (Ramsaran 1993, p. 239)

By 1988, the government had set up four ammonia plants, with 51% shareholdings in three, and complete ownership of the fourth. In addition, they had complete ownership of the steel plant and a methanol-producing firm. In 1984 the government would also commission a granular urea plant.

Apart from investments in these petrochemical plants downstream, the state also spent a considerable amount of its first oil windfall on infrastructural, human and physical capital as is indicated by the revenue outlays in Table 6.2. These infrastructural outlays helped to facilitate a change in the infrastructural base of the economy.

The momentum from the economy's independence movement was still very much alive in the time period just proceeding it, and on January 17, 1976, Dr. Eric Williams, the then Prime Minister of T&T stated, "*There have been attempts to persuade us that the simplest and easiest thing to do would be to sit back, exportour oil, export our gas, do nothing else and just receive the revenues derived from such exports as it would lead a life of luxury at least for some limited period. This, the Government has completely rejected, for it amounts to putting the entire nation on the dole. Instead, we have taken what may be the more difficult road and that is accepting the challenge of entering the world of steel, aluminum, methanol, fertilizer,*

Table 6.2 Funds allocated to long-term development projects in T&T ($USmn), 1976–1983

	Education	*Health*	*Electricity*	*Housing*	*Roads*	*National transport*	*Water*	*Telecommunications*
1976	27.39		7.8	0.47	6.11	9.11	7.24	1.93
1977	19.62	0.5	9.11	6.67	19.36	9.28	26.46	13.7
1978	22.2	1.22	8.07	37.09	22.88	13.74	64.58	18.66
1979	27.58	6.82	9.27	49.45	55.85	9.12	78.19	25.76
1980	17.23	4.89	15.92	86.05	98.91	22.23	44.76	29.17
1981	27.37	10.07	17.34	111.18	16.09	13.22	45.24	29.57
1982	47.39	13.13	3.61	195.1	189.48	8.64	34.98	41.81
1983	55.7	24.35	17.2	191.8	116.3	87.67	42.1	38.73

Source Ministry of Finance (1983)

petrochemicals. We have accepted the challenge of using our hydrocarbon resources, in a very definite industrialization process."

Mottley (2008) noted that from these resource-based industrialization outlays, the T&T government expected to get a "double bottom line." In the first case, the economy should benefit from a long-term viable investment. In the second case, a huge social return was expected. This social return took the form of a new category of middle-class professionals at the frontier of knowledge in these technical areas of productive activity. In an assessment of whether the state met its second objective Mottley (2008, p. 3) noted that "*the government's energy investments unquestionably transformed the lives of those nationals caught up in the operations of the enterprise created. Skills were upgraded; a 'first world' working culture was created within the walls of the enterprises; nationals mastered elements of high technology and improved their skills in marketing and finance. Compensation, though less than prevailing US rates, nevertheless won beneficiaries a ticket to the middle class or better.*"

6.4 Real Value Added in the Petrochemical Sector

Some of these plants are now ageing (the Yara plant which produces ammonia was closed in 2019, some 53 years after it start up-see Table 6.3) and policy makers would have to keep this in mind in their various decision-making.

Table 6.3 Capacity and age of plant data on some of the petrochemical plants in T&T since 1966

Start up date	*Plant*	*Current ownership*	*Former ownership*	*Product*	*Capacity—MT ('000)*	*Age of plant*
1966	Yara	Norsk Hydro/Yara	WR Grace	Ammonia	285	53
1977	Tringen 1	Yara	WR Grace/GORTT	Ammonia	500	42
1981	O1	Nutrien (PCS Nitrogen)	GORTT/Amoco; Arcadian	Ammonia	445	38
1982	O2	Nutrien (PCS Nitrogen)	GORTT/Amoco; Arcadian	Ammonia	445	37
1983	Urea	Nutrien (PCS Nitrogen)	GORTT/Arcadian	Urea	710	36
1984	M1	Consolidated Energy		Methanol	480	35
1988	Tringen 2	NEL/GORTT/Yara	GORTT/Yara	Ammonia	495	31
1993	M2	Consolidated Energy		Methanol	550	26
1996	M3	Consolidated Energy		Methanol	580	23
1996	O3	Nutrien (PCS Nitrogen)	Arcadian	Ammonia	250	23
1998	M4	Consolidated Energy		Methanol	580	21
1998	PLNL	Kock/CF Industries	Farmland Misschem	Ammonia	650	21
1999	O4	Nutrien (PCS Nitrogen)	Arcadian	Ammonia	650	20
2000	Titan	Methanex	Methanex/BP/Beacon	Methanol	860	19
2002	CNC	Consolidated/EOG/Kock/Process Energy (Trinidad)		Ammonia	650	17
2004	M5	Consolidated Energy		Methanol	1890	15

Start up date	*Plant*	*Current ownership*	*Former ownership*	*Product*	*Capacity—MT ('000)*	*Age of plant*
2004	Nitrogen 2000	Consolidated/EOG/Kock/Process Energy (Trinidad)		Ammonia	650	15
2004	Atlas	Methanex/BP		Methanol	1650	15
2009	AUM Ammonia	Consolidated Energy		Ammonia	650	10
2010	Melamine 1	Consolidated Energy		Melamine	30	9
2010	Melamine 2	Consolidated Energy		Melamine	30	9
2010	UAN	Consolidated Energy		UAN	1400	9
2019	CGC	Mitsubishi/Massy		Methanol		0

Table 6.4 Real value added in petroleum and chemical products (2012 = 100) and real GDP, 2012–2018

Industry	*Manufacture of petrochemicals (TT$mn)*	*GDP TT$mn (2012 = 100)*
2012	11,867.2	164,744.9
2013	11,772.9	166,360.8
2014r	11,700.9	165,794.3
2015r	11,874.7	170,853.5
2016r	11,119.2	160,095.8
2017r	11,516.4	155,394.2
2018r	11,378	156,010.7
2019e	12,470.8	154,101.1

Source ROTE, various years

In terms of real value added, using data from the recently revised national income account, the real value added declined from TT$11,867.2 in 2012 to TT$11,378.1 mn in 2018 (see Table 6.4).

This is not surprising as the petrochemical sector of the T&T economy, however, has been recently plagued with several challenges including some of the following considered below.

(a) Increased cost of natural gas feedstock prices.

The price paid for natural gas was recently increased to the industries on the estate. As a consequence, some of the firms on Point Lisas Industrial Estate have found it difficult to subsist as their cost of production on the one hand increased, whilst the price of the associated end product (based on direct government intervention that led to an increase in the price of feedstock gas), decreased. Specifically, and as Table 6.5 shows, methanol prices in 2020 (average January–July) was US$289.1 per tonne as compared to US$517.3 per tonne in 2013. With such price decreases, only the nimblest of methanol firms can survive.

Even more the fall in per unit profits meant that firms would find it difficult to reinvest into their business and this would affect their medium-term cost efficiency as well. In some cases, the older plants with outdated or out dating technology may find it difficult to continue (see the last column of Table 6.3 that shows the ages of the various plants).

(b) Competition from American plants.

The petrochemical industry in TT and other parts of the world are facing stiff competition from like firms in the USA. This is mainly on account of the surge in shale gas production in that country motivated by hydraulic fracturing. Indeed, as Fig. 6.1 illustrates the extraction of natural gas from the USA surged from 2.34 bcf per day in 2005 to 4.07 bcf per day in 2019.

Table 6.5 Methanol prices 2010–2020

	(US$/Tonne)
2010	338.3
2011	430
2012	429.7
2013	517.3
2014	513.5
2015	381.9
2016	272.1
2017	399.1
2018	474.2
2019	363
2020p	289.1

Source CBTT online data

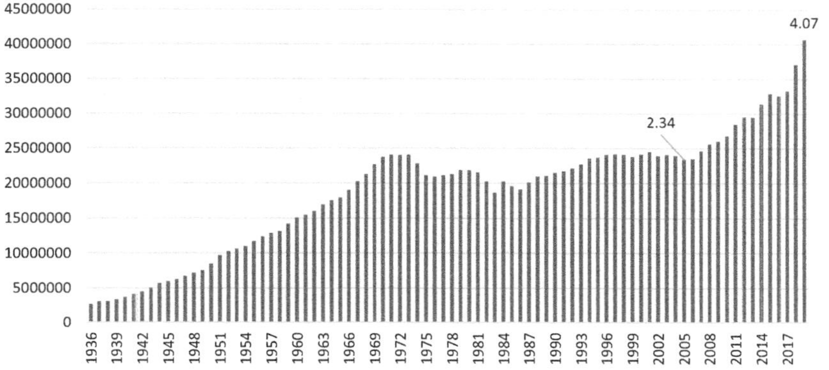

Fig. 6.1 U.S. natural gas gross withdrawals million cubic feet, 1936–2019

(c) Lower gas supply.

In T&T there are 4 main sectors that utilize over 200 mmcf/d of natural gas, these are power generation, ammonia, methanol and LNG. In 2015 they utilized 295 mmcf/d (see Table 6.6), 555 mmcf/d, 539 mmcf/d and 1967 mmcf/d, respectively. By 2020 (January–July average) this changed to 228 mmcf/d, 541 mmcf/d and 1873 mmcf/d, respectively. Note of these large utilizers of natural gas, methanol experienced the sharpest decline.
The Natural Gas Master Plan points in the direction that the ammonia and methanol plants in T&T can make more money for Trinidad and Tobago per gas molecule than LNG and so policymakers should ensure

Table 6.6 Changes in the utilization of gas, 2005–2020p

	2005	*2010*	*2015*	*2019*	*2020p*	*% change in gas utilized between 2010 and average for 2020*	*% change in gas utilized between 2015 and average for 2022*	*% change in gas utilized by sector between 2019 and June 2020*
Power generation	252	293	295	254	228	−22.30	−22.82	−10.4
Ammonia manufacture	526	612	555	551	541	−11.60	−2.52	−1.7
Methanol manufacture	564	561	539	547	487	−13.19	−9.65	−10.9
Iron and steel manufacture	74	104	79	47	33	−68.27	−58.23	−29.4
Cement manufacture	13	12	13	12	9	−29.17	−34.62	−27.2
Ammonia derivatives	12	18	20	26	21	14.81	3.33	−20.2
Gas processing	35	39	27	23	23	−40.17	−13.58	−0.2
Small consumers	12	10	9	8	8	−21.67	−12.96	−3.4
LNG	2010	2321	1967	1972	1873	−19.28	−4.76	−5.0
Total	3536	4010	3578	3439	3222	−19.64	−9.94	−6.3

Source CBTT online database and own derivations

that the share of the utilized natural gas in T&T that goes towards these industries, increases (Farrell 2019). Farrell argued that this position has already been articulated by two natural gas master plans: the first by Gaffney Cline and Associates in 2002 and the second by Poten and Partners in 2015. Thus far the sector has seen the closure of MHTL M1 and it is likely that as gas production falls into 2021, that the other plants will have to be mothballed or closed altogether.

Alongside all of this is the change in the reserves to production ratio which declined from over 35 years in 2002 to less than 10.53 years by 2019. Basically, then T&T migrated from a high reserve low cost scenario, to a high cost (based on the government raising the feedstock cost of gas to the estate in 2017) low reserve scenario. This will not do the petrochemical industry any good and policy makers would have to push hard to bring more gas on stream so that they could likely negotiate a lower feedstock price.

6.5 Methanol Blending?

As the previous Table 6.6 illustrated, between 2019 and June 2020 of the four largest (over 200 mmcf/d) of natural gas users in T&T the methanol sector realized the greatest degree of contraction. In this regard and given the deadline in the production of natural gas in T&T. Mixing methanol with gasoline and exporting to other CARICOM economies. Methanol blending has several distinct benefits for the Trinidad and Tobago economy. These maybe classified into three distinct categories: economic cost savings, environmental benefits, and job creation.

In terms of cost savings, it displaces a more expensive gasoline with a less expensive fuel option, methanol. By substituting some gasoline for methanol, the Trinidad and Tobago government can save on foreign exchange utilization (Fig. 6.2 shows T&T's fuel imports and its net official reserves). The figure shows the fuel imports from T&T and the stock of foreign exchange at the Central Bank. The information in Fig. 6.2 does provide some basic suggestion that the stock of reserves may have been adversely affected by the requirements of fuel imports.

At the T&T Methanol blending Forum (2019) last year it was shown that under a range of assumptions that a 5% blend of methanol with gasoline would reduce imports by 30 mn gallons per annum and save T&T almost TT$300 mn. Policymakers must reflect on this and consider even higher blends and the cost savings for T&T.

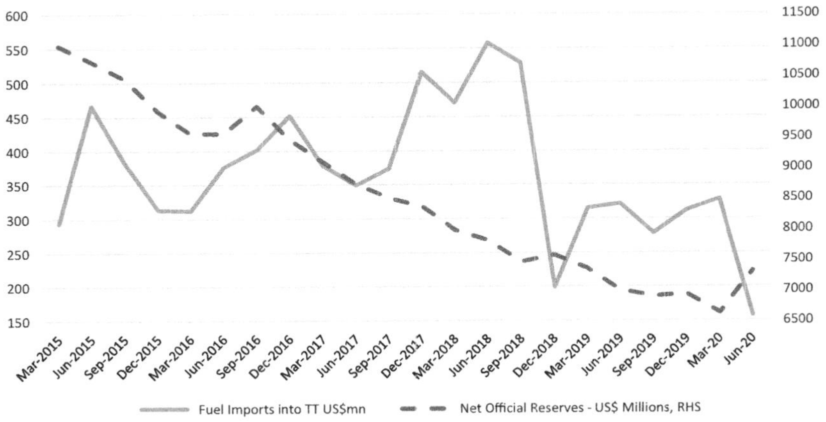

Fig. 6.2 Trends in fuel imports and net official reserves for T&T, March 2015 to June 2020

The introduction of methanol blending would also help to reduce the amount of volatile organic compounds and particulate matter emitted by the T&T economy and this is good for the environment. Indeed, according to World Bank data in 1960, the T&T economy had a CO_2 emission level of 2581.6kt in 1960 and this escalated to 47,931.3kt in 2010 although by 2019 it decreased slightly to 42,123kt. Whilst a 5% methanol blend will not dramatically alter these numbers, it would provide a further step in the right direction. Indeed, the Sustainable Development Goal #13 as outlined by the United Nations states that nations should "Take Urgent Action to Combat Climate Change and its impact." In this regard, by blending gasoline with methanol, T&T can reduce its particulate emissions. If T&T can get CARICOM states to use this blend, then the region can benefit environmentally and T&T can fetch more foreign exchange, which would be a welcome development. (19.7% of all St. Lucia's imports for example for 2016 was on fuel with the corresponding number for Belize, Barbados and Jamaica being 9.9, 15.5 and 19.8%, respectively.)

Methanol blending will also create jobs in blending operations and associated logistics. These jobs would be especially welcome now as the closure of the Petrotrin refinery and the idling of some petrochemical plants have combined to reduce energy sector employment in recent times. Indeed, for the oil and gas sector, CSO data indicates that in September 2015 employment stood at 22,500 workers and by September 2018 this collapsed to 15,100. This is a sizable decline and wherever jobs can be sustainably created it should be pursued, welcome and promoted.

Indeed, given the high level of production of methanol there are other possibilities available including the use of methanol as an efficient replacement for cooking fuels such as LPG. Above all the government should consider a task force to undertake an economic feasibility study of the blending possibilities. This should be done urgently as already in June 2020, the amount of methanol produced was 31% lower than the monthly average for 2019. This is troubling and where we can add more value for the benefit of T&T, it should be pursued.

6.6 Conclusion

The competitiveness of T&T petrochemical sector both from an external and internal perspective, has changed. On the external front T&T no longer has an abundance of natural gas nor does it have a high reserve to production ratio and so the cost of gas as a feedstock has increased.

In terms of the internal market, there is a decline in the production of gas and a greater proportion of the gas is now going towards LNG in 2020 as compared to 2014 and this raises the question of whether this is the best economic outcome for T&T or alternatively said "is the country making the best use of its natural gas?"

In terms of the way forward for T&T, this chapter suggests it must entail a dual approach. The government has to modify its fiscal rules so as to promote the exploration and production of more natural gas whilst at the same time, ensure that it is obtaining the most value added, per unit of natural gas.

The NGC may also have to raise the price of gas that it supplies to the power generation sector with a benchmark price being 90% of the price floor for other petrochemicals firms at the Point Lisas Industrial Estate. The Trinidad and Tobago Electricity Commission (T&TEC) is NGC's biggest customer and the country simply cannot afford to subsidize energy electricity prices, moving forward.

Also, because power generation obtains gas at a subsidized cost then the methanol sector is implicitly charged a higher price for feedstock gas to help compensate for the subsidy given to the power generation sector. This of course will hurt the competitiveness of the methanol sector and policy makers would have to consider whether this makes sense, in an economy where the stock of foreign exchange is already on the decline.

Finally, given the closure of the refinery, policy makers are urged to consider the option of methanol blending.

References

Farrell, Terrance. (2019). "At a Point of Inflexion: The Downstream Petrochemicals Industry in Trinidad & Tobago 2019." UTT Seminar. https://utt.edu.tt/files/cms/point_inflexion_presentation.pdf.

Gereffi, G. (1995). "State Policies and Industrial Upgrading in East Asia." Revue d'économie industrielle: 79–90.

Government of Trinidad and Tobago, Ministry of Finance. (1983). "Accounting for the petrodollar, 1973–1983 by Trinidad and Tobago." Government Printery.

Lall, S. (1996). "Learning from the Asian Tigers: Studies in Technology and Industrial Policy." New York: Palgrave.

Lewis, Arthur W. (1950). "Industrial Development in the Caribbean." Port of Spain.

Loasby, B.J. (1991). "Equilibrium and Evolution." Manchester: Manchester University Press.

Mottley, W. (2008). "Trinidad and Tobago Industrial Policy 1959–2008—A Historical and Contemporary Analysis." Jamaica: Ian Randle Publishers.

Page, J. (1994). "The East Asian Miracle: Four Lessons for Development Policy." National Bureau of Economic Research 9: 219–282.

Ramsaran, F. Ramesh. (1993). "Growth and Adjustment in a Petroleum Based Economy: Some Aspect of the Trinidad and Tobago Experience Since the 1970s." Social and Economic Studies 42 (4): 217–240.

Sarel, M. (1996). "Growth in East Asia: What We Can and Cannot Infer. Economic Issues 1." International Monetary Fund.

Sargeant, Kelvin, and Forde, Penelope. (1992). "The State Sector and Divestment in Trinidad and Tobago: Some Preliminary Findings." Social and Economic Studies 41 (4): 173–204.

CHAPTER 7

Dutch Disease, Baumol Disease and Labour Productivity in a Small Petroleum-Based Economy

7.1 Introduction

Economic growth in developing countries is tied to its production structures which work to bring about change by expanding value added and employment opportunities in higher productivity areas, at the expense of lower productivity areas. Thus, if factors are channelled from low productivity to high productivity areas the economy will grow even in a setting where there is no productivity growth, within individual sectors. In this regard, structural change can lead to economic growth even if there is no productivity growth. This chapter reviews the effect of structural changes in the economy and associated changes in labour productivity on account of the Dutch Disease. In this regard, this chapter sets out the Baumol Cost Disease Model and integrates a discussion of the Dutch Disease effect on the NBT and NT sectors into the model to establish that the long-term growth potential of the economy can be constrained as the very large NT sector realizes lagging growth in relation to the NBT sector. The chapter then uses shift share analysis to assess the breakdown of labour productivity into three parts: intra-industry productivity, static shift share and dynamic shift share effects. The chapter then outline various policy guidelines to boost employment in the lagging NBT sector and to enhance labour productivity in the NT sector.

R. Hosein, *Oil and Gas in Trinidad and Tobago*,
https://doi.org/10.1007/978-3-030-77669-5_7

7.2 Structural Change and Economic Growth

The interest in the relationship between structural change and economic growth is not a new one and indeed Joseph Schumpeter was an early proponent. Schumpeter proposed that innovation can act as a promoter for economic change. Schumpeter argued that economic development "*is a spontaneous and discontinuous change in the channel of the circular flow, disturbance of equilibrium, which forever alters and displaces the equilibrium state previously existing*" (Schumpeter 1934, p. 4). He noted that policy decisions should be based on historical, sociological, political and philosophical elements within the economy.

Young (1928) expanded on the division of labour as discussed by Adam Smith, by emphasizing how the division of labour and of market expansion were interdependent and cumulative (Young 1928). Kuznets (1971) in his Nobel laureate winning speech noted that modern economies are subject to high rates of structural transformation which include a migration of economic activity away from agriculture towards non-agricultural efforts, with a tendency towards industries and then services.

Myrdal argued that economic development is affected not only by economic factors, but also by historical, institutional, social and cultural factors. (Myrdal's work developed on the ideas of Knut Wicksell and Nicholas Kaldor.) He suggested that theories which disregard additional factors such as these are "*irrelevant and misleading*." He proposed a "circular cumulative causation approach" whereby economic change is thought to be the "endogenous phenomenon in the market system" rather than the exogenous factor, as stipulated in mainstream economics. Myrdal specifically noted "*circular causation will give rise to a cumulative movement only when a change in one of the conditions will ultimately be followed by a feed-back of secondary impulses big enough not only to sustain the primary change, but to push it further. Mere mutual causation is not enough to create this process*" (Myrdal 1968). Creating a cumulative causation is possible from virtual cycles of specialization and technical progress. (Paul Romer modelled this type of increasing returns argument implicitly made by Myrdal in his endogenous growth theories of economic development.)

Cumulative causation is embodied in the "new" economics geography literature which emerged in the 1990s and formalizes various cumulative causation mechanisms which account for uneven geographical distribution of economic activity. Regions tend to have a rich core and a poor periphery. In this setting, production of manufacturing goods locate where the population is high, and the population will grow where there are jobs.

Prebisch an Argentine economist argued that economic inequality and distorted development characterized the global system of exchange. In such a setting the outcome for developing countries trading with developed countries were disequilibrating. Prebisch was concerned that "*unlike the production structure of the periphery, which is specialized and heterogeneous, that of the centre is diversified and homogeneous.*" Prebisch argued in favour of a strategy of import substituting industrialization to change the structure of production in the developing world.

Structural change and its importance as a source of growth and productivity were also emphasized by Lewis (1954). Lewis stated that developing economies are characterized by large productivity differentials between the broad sectors of their economy, especially the traditional rural areas and the urban areas. Lewis emphasized that the economy was characterized by two main sectors—an overpopulated rural subsistence sector and an industrial sector into which labour from the subsistence sector gradually transferred. The Lewisian model emphasized the transfer of labour out of the subsistence sector and to promote the growth and employment of the modern sector. The whole process of labour transfer and modern sector employment is motivated by the expansion of output in the modern sector (Lewis 1954).

Hirschman (1958) argued in favour of production structures that promoted backward and forward linkages with the rest of the economy. He described the process of linkages by arguing that with the establishment of a business, there are distinct opportunities of a new expanding market for its inputs. He described a forward linkage associated with a particular mode of production as being one which is associated with downstream activities, whilst a backward linkage is one which encourages more upstream investment around a particular activity. Thus ammonia, methanol and urea are downstream or forward linkages of the gas value chain whilst exploration and production of natural gas are backward or upstream linkages of liquefied natural gas production. Hirschman argued in favour of investments to enhance the structure of production that fostered heavy backward and forward linkages. He was concerned that developing countries had to exist with industries offering only limited elements of backward and forward linkages. The deeper these backward and forward linkages the greater the scope for structural change.

Nurkse argued that international trade acted as an "*engine of growth transmission as well as a means of improved allocation of existing resources.*" Nurkse searched for ways in which less developed countries that were relatively abundant in their labour supply could focus on industrialization for export. After noticing the downfall of developing countries in the nineteenth century, Nurkse proposed the pursuit of export production and production mainly for markets within the developed economies as a means of boosting economic growth and motivating structural change (Nurkse 1953).

Chenery et al. (1986) illustrated that structural change is an important factor in explaining the growth performance of economies. They argued that growth in developing countries stems from an interdependent process best described as part of the overall transformation of the economic fabric of those economies. To them the process is twofold: income growth triggers a change in the makeup of domestic demand and production and consequently rising investment rates and the redistribution of labour increase aggregate growth. The transformation is not the same throughout the economy, because it is dependent on resource endowment and the initial economic infrastructure, compounded by the economic policy choice.

Against this backdrop of factors that influence the changing structure of an economy, the rest of this chapter proceeds as follows. The next section of this chapter discusses the relationship between the Dutch Disease and the "Baumol Cost" Disease and the implications of the induced change in the structure of the economy. The chapter then goes on to undertake an empirical assessment of the "cost" disease in T&T and the effects of a boom in the energy sector on the changing structure of production and productivity growth, in the economy. This is followed by a discussion of the variables entering the methodological base of the paper (shift share) followed by the actual shift share calculations and interpretations. The chapter then concludes with some relevant policy suggestions.

7.3 The Dutch Disease and the "Baumol Cost" Disease—Call the Doctor

Baumol (1967) noted that some sectors of an economy only have limited potential to benefit from labour productivity increases, on account of technical progress or capital deepening. The subsectors with these attributes are mainly in the service sector (hereafter NT sector). (Baumol identified some of these sectors as the performing arts, municipal government, education and restaurants.) Following Baumol, and to provide a clearer understanding of the concept of a "cost disease," a simple example can suffice. In the American car industry in 1913, Ford introduced assembly lines which facilitated the movement of vehicles from one workstation to another and limited the amount of time workers had to spend moving between workstations and the amount of tools they had to haul. In these types of sectors, output per worker increased considerably and firms were able to increase the wage rate of their workers. In other sectors of the economy, productivity gains are not as sharp, e.g. the number of calypsos Machel Montano can sing live in one night, has not really changed in the last twenty five years and if it did, has only done so marginally. Even so, wages in these entertainments and like sectors, according to the Dutch Disease model set out in Chapter 3, rise commensurately with the rest of the economy (especially with those in the BT sector). Firms in industries producing these types of "stagnant output" goods must increase their prices to meet rising costs per unit of production. The Baumol cost disease refers to the rise in salaries in jobs that have experienced little or no productivity increases but realize increases in wages on account of increases in productivity in more productive sectors.[1] Hereafter, this is called the Baumol Cost disease.

It is possible to relate the Dutch Disease outcomes in an economy to the Baumol Cost disease. In this regard note that output in each sector can be determined as stated in Eqs. (7.1) and (7.2)

$$Y_{NT} = aL_{NT} \tag{7.1}$$

and

$$Y_{NBT} = bL_{NBT}e^{rt} \tag{7.2}$$

[1] Several decades of data on productivity has confirmed Baumol's thesis, making it into a stylized fact of the economic growth literature.

L_{NT} and L_{NBT} are the employed labour force in the NT and NBT sectors respectively and a and b are two constants in the time period, *t*. Let the wage rate be conditioned by the productivity of the manufacturing sector, so that the wage rate may be expressed as:

$$W_t = We^{rt} \tag{7.3}$$

where W is a constant.

For a system of this type, the cost (of production) in the services and manufacturing sectors can be established as:

$$C_{NT} = W_t L_{NT}/Y_{NT} = We^{rt}L_{NT}/aL_{NT} = {}^{We^{rt}}/_{a} \tag{7.4}$$

$$C_{NBT} = W_t L_{NBT}/Y_{NBT} = We^{rt}L_{NBT}/bL_{NBTt}e^{rt} = w/b \tag{7.5}$$

This illustrates, following Baumol's logic that the per unit cost of output in the NT sector would increase continuously with time, but in the NBT sector would remain constant (Baumol referred to this as proposition 1). Against this backdrop one can form the ratio of (7.4) to (7.5) and via a process of simplification obtain:

$$C_{NT}/C_{NBT} = be^{rt}/a \tag{7.6}$$

which indicates that the relative cost of a unit of output in the NT sector to that of a unit of output in the NBT sector will behave as derived, regardless of if wages increase, as established in (7.3) above.

The Baumol perspective then investigated what would happen if regardless of the behaviour of the relative costs of the NT sector to the NBT sector, their relative outputs were maintained. In this setting we have:

$$Y_{NT}/Y_{NBT} = L_{NT}/L_{NBT}e^{rt} = K \tag{7.7}$$

For simplicity, the labour force may be stated as:

$$L = (L_{NT} + L_{NBT}) \tag{7.8}$$

This is not entirely unreasonable as the BT sector employs 3% of total employment

Drawing on Eq. (7.7) L_{NBT} can be re-expressed as follows:

$$L_{NBT} = L - L_{NT}$$

$$L_{NT}/L_{NBT}e^{rt} = K$$

And so

$$L_{NT} = KL_{NBT}e^{rt}$$

$$L_{NT} = K(L - L_{NT})e^{rt}$$

$$L_{NT} + KL_{NT}e^{rt} = KLe^{rt}$$

$$L_{NT} = KLe^{rt}/\left(1 + Ke^{rt}\right) \tag{7.9}$$

Substituting (7.10) into (7.9) and expanding and simplifying yields:

$$L_{NBT} = \left[L\left(1 + Ke^{rt}\right) - LKe^{rt}\right]/\left(1 + Ke^{rt}\right)$$

$$L_{NBT} = \left[L + LKe^{rt} - LKe^{rt}\right]/\left(1 + Ke^{rt}\right)$$

$$L_{NBT} = L/(1 + Ke^{rt}) \tag{7.10}$$

Thus, note that as $t \to \infty$, $L_{NBT} \to 0$.

Baumol made a third proposition linked to Eq. 7.10. He noted that if there is unbalanced productivity with the ratio of the sectors being held constant then more of the labour force would have to be transferred to the non-progressive sector and the amount of output in the other sectors will tend to zero.

To assess the impact on the overall growth rate of output in the economy in a situation in which the output ratios for the NT and NBT sectors are not allowed to change, we can proceed following Baumol 1967, and write:

$$I = \alpha_{NT}Y_{NT} + \beta_{NBT}Y_{NBT} \tag{7.11}$$

where α_{NT} and β_{NBT} are the weighted share of NT and NBT in the total output of the economy and I is an index of output.

Substituting Eqs. (7.1) and (7.2) into (7.11)

$$I = \alpha_{NT}\ aL_{NT} + \beta_{NBT}\ bL_{NBT}e^{rt} \tag{7.12}$$

By expansion (using 7.9 and 7.10)

$$I = \alpha_{NT}\ a(KLe^{rt}/(1 + Ke^{rt})) + \beta_{NBT}b(Le^{rt}/(1 + Ke^{rt})) \tag{7.13}$$

So that

$$I = (B_{NT}a\ LKe^{rt} + B_{NBT}bLe^{rt})/(1 + Ke^{rt})$$

Let.

$$R = L(\alpha_{NT}aK + \beta_{NBT}b)$$

So that:

$$I = Re^{rt}/(1 + Ke^{rt})$$

Using the quotient rule and by a process of simplification it may be shown that:

$$[dI/dt]/I = r/(1 + Ke^{rt}) \tag{7.14}$$

A careful observation of Eq. 7.14 indicates that as t increases dI/dt $\rightarrow$ 0. This is Baumol's classic cost disease problem. In terms of a Dutch Diseased small open petroleum exporting economy, given the enclave like structure of the petroleum sector, it transcribes that asymptomatically, if the NT sector has a lower level of productivity than the NBT sector and the NT sector's labour force keeps expanding, then this will compromise the long-term growth potential of the economy.

7.4 The Baumol Cost Disease in T&T

7.4.1 Data Overview

With the Dutch Disease (DD), the NBT loses labour to the BT sector (via the resource movement effect) and to the NT sector via the spending effect. The DD model also shows that the wage rate in all the sectors of the economy increases, so that the aggregate cost of production in all sectors of the economy, rises.

Table 7.1 Employment, employment shares and labour productivity in the booming tradable (BT), non-booming tradable (NBT) and non-tradable (NT) component of the T&T economy, 1999–2016

	BT	*NBT*	*NT*	*SUM*
1999	14,986	56,313	417,645	488,944
2008	18,800	56,700	511,600	587,100
2016	16,900	50,400	545,900	613,200
Employment shares in each sector				
1999	0.031	0.115	0.854	
2008	0.032	0.097	0.871	
2016	0.028	0.082	0.890	
Labour productivity in the booming tradable (BT), non-booming tradable (NBT) and non-tradable (NT) component of the T&T economy, 1999–2016				
1999	933,798.2	73,329.4	72,025.5	98,588.8
2008	1,946,824.5	141,377.4	93,440.4	157,418.7
2016	1,743,011.8	149,396.8	96,354.5	146,096.5

Source Author's calculations

The Table 7.1 shows the trend in the share of the BT, NBT and NT segments of the economy in total employment, in the T&T economy for the period 1999–2016. The clear indication from the data is that the long-term secular trend is one of a decreasing relative share of labour employed in the NBT sector, as compared to the NT sector. This is indeed a cause for concern, particularly as Table 7.1 illustrates that output per worker in the NT sector, increased at a slower pace than output per worker in the NBT sector and also output per worker in the NBT sector is considerably more than output per worker in the NT sector.

7.5 Shift Share Methodology

This section elaborates on the pattern of specialization in the T&T economy and examines how the attendant change in the structure of production outlined above can influence labour productivity in the economy. The methodological base used here is shift share analysis. Following Timmer and Szirmai (1997), let us define the share of workers in sector I, as s_i. Here L_i is the number of people working in sector i and L is the employed labour force. This allows labour productivity to be expressed as:

Equation (7.1)

$$LP_t = \frac{Q_t}{L_t} = \sum_i \cdot \frac{Q_{i,t}}{L_{i,t}} \cdot \frac{L_{i,t}}{L_t}$$

where LP is aggregate labour productivity.
L is number of employees.
Q is real value added.
i and t are individual manufacturing industries and time.
Subscripts without i are in aggregate.
$\frac{L_{i,t}}{L_t}$ is labour share in industry i in total labour.
$\frac{Q_{i,t}}{L_{i,t}}$ is labour productivity in the same industry.

Equation (7.2)

$$LP_t = \sum_i LP_i \cdot sl_i$$

where aggregate labour productivity is the weighted sum of individual industries.

Equation (7.3)

Changes in labour productivity are defined for a specific period of time [0,1] where 0 is the beginning year and 1 is the end year. The change in labour productivity can be written by subtracting the level of productivity at the end of the year [1] with productivity at the beginning of the year [0].

$$LP_1 - LP_0 = \sum_i LP_{i,1} \cdot sl_{i,1} - \sum_i LP_{i,0} \cdot sl_{i,0}$$

Equation (7.4)

Rearranging with algebraic manipulations and dividing by LP_0 to arrange in growth terms we now get.

$$\frac{LP_1 - LP_0}{LP_0} = \frac{1}{LP_0} \sum_i (LP_{i,1} - LP_{i,0}) \cdot sl_{i,0} + \frac{1}{LP_0} \sum_i (sl_{i,1} - sl_{i,0}) \cdot LP_{i,0}$$

$$\frac{1}{LP_0} \sum_i (sl_{i,1} - sl_{i,0}) \cdot (LP_{i,1} - LP_{i,0})$$

The first term in the formula is intra-industry productivity (IIP) which gives a value for productivity growth within individual industries weighted by the share of these industries in an initial period. This term reflects changes in aggregate labour productivity growth when labour shares are held constant. The second term shows the static shift effect (SSE) and sets out the contribution to productivity growth that arises on account of a change in the distribution of labour between industries, holding labour productivity at the initial level. As labour shifts away from low productivity industries, the value of the SSE increases, and this should be the desired effect for policy planners. The last term shows the dynamic shift effect (DSE) and outlines the interaction between labour productivity changes in individual industries and changes in labour market shares in industries. If both terms are high and positive, then LP would increase. Ideally the government would want the industries whose labour productivity is growing to also benefit.

When the two shift effects are taken together, they determine how a structural change in the economy impacts on the overall productivity of labour.

7.6 Empirical Outcomes

Table 7.2 shows this intra-industry productivity effect between 1999 and 2008 and then between 2008 and 2016. For the period 1999 to 2008 the intra-industry productivity effects were high and favourable for all the 3 sectors. Understandably, it was highest in the BT sector as the natural gas sector and petroleum sector increased as FDI flowed into these sectors and helped to spur higher output levels therein. The NBT sector also increased as per capita GDP increased, and the adverse impact of an appreciating real effective exchange rate did not fully set into the economy at that point. In the NT sector, the intra-industry productivity effect for 1999–2008 increased as the spending effect took root in the boom phase, of the boom bust cycle.

Table 7.2 Intra-industry productivity effect, various years, TT$mn (2000 = 100)

	BT	*NBT*	*NT*	*Contribution to overall LP % growth*
1999–2008	31,049.0	7837.3	18,292.1	58.00
2008–2016	−6526.4	774.5	2539.3	−2.04

Source Author's calculations

In the second period 2008–2016, however, the intra-industry productivity effect led to a negative contribution to overall labour productivity growth. This is because in this second period, the output of the BT sector fell and so the associated output per worker fell, holding labour shares constant at 2008 terms. In the NBT and NT sectors the intra-industry productivity effects remained positive but were outweighed by the size of the contraction in the BT sector so that the contribution of the intra-industry productivity effect from the three sectors was overall negative for the period 2008–2016.

As concerns the static shift share effect the BT sector experienced an increase in the share of labour for the period 1999–2008 on account of the resource movement effect but a fall in employment share from 2008–2016 as the bust phase of the boom bust cycle started to set into the economy. However, it is in this static shift share component of labour productivity that a crunching blow was landed to the contribution of the NBT sector to overall labour productivity growth, as the share of employment in this sector fell both in the period 1999–2008 and 2008–2016, precipitated by the combined resource movement and spending effects. For the NT sector, employment shares did increase, and hence the contribution of the NT sector to the SSE was positive for both time periods. Overall, the static effect was positive for the period 1999–2008 but negative for the period 2008–2016 (Table 7.3).

The third aspect of labour productivity growth is an interactive one and occurs when both the share of employment and sectoral labour productivity improves. For the BT sector in both time periods the DSE was positive. In the first period labour shares and labour productivity improved in this sector and in the second period, both labour productivity and labour share fell together, again yielding a positive DSE effect. The DSE for the NBT sector was negative for both time periods because of direct deindustrialization and indirect deindustrialization. In the NT sector the DSE was positive for both time periods but small (Table 7.4).

Table 7.3 Static shift effect, various years TT$mn (2000 = 100)

	BT	*NBT*	*NT*
1999–2008	1281.2	−1363.7	1240.6
2008–2016	−8685.7	−2033.7	1761.0
DSS			

Source Author's calculations

Table 7.4 Dynamic shift effect

	BT	*NBT*	*NT*	
1999–2008	1389.9	−1265.4	368.9	0.50
2008–2016	909.3	−115.4	54.9	0.54

Source Author's calculations

Table 7.5 Aggregate labour productivity growth rate (%)

	1999–2008	*2009–2016*
	59.67	−7.19
IIP	58.00	−2.04
SSE	1.17	−5.69
DSE	0.50	0.54

Source Author's calculations

Overall, for the time period 1999–2008 labour productivity increased by 59.7% in all T&T mainly on account of the IIP effect. For the time period 2009–2016, though there was a 7.19% contraction in labour productivity mainly on account of the SSE (Table 7.5).

7.7 Conclusion

This chapter outlined and assessed the Baumol cost disease and emphasized its relation to the Dutch Disease. The chapter also used shift share analysis to decompose the labour productivity changes in T&T into three subcomponents: within sector, static shift effects and dynamic shift effects. In the period 1999–2008, the main addition to overall labour productivity in T&T occurred on account of changes in sectoral labour productivity in the BT sector. In the period 2009–2016, the main reason for the fall in labour productivity was the decline in the share of the BT sector in total employment.

The government of T&T would have to work hard to change both the share of labour going to the NT sector as well as the level of productivity within that sector. This would require a solid effort by the government has already the economy's real effective exchange rate is 27%

appreciated as compared to 2010 (82% more than 2000). Later chapters would propose a variety of policy suggestions to help improve labour productivity in T&T.

References

Baumol J. William. (1967). "Macroeconomics of Unbalance Growth: The Anatomy of Urban Crisis." The American Economic Review 57 (3): 415–426.

Chenery, H. B., Robinson, S., and Syrquin, M. (1986). Structural Transformation. In Chenery, H. B., Robinson, S., and Syrquin, M. (eds.). Industrialization and Growth: A Comparative Study. Oxford: Oxford University Press: 11–12.

Hirschman, O. Albert. (1958). "The Strategy of Economic Development." New Haven, CT: Yale University Press.

Kuznets, Simon. (1971). "Economic Growth of Nations: Total Output and Production Structure." Cambridge: Cambridge University Press.

Lewis, W. Arthur. (1954). "Economic Development with Unlimited Supplies of Labor." Manchester School of Economic and Social Studies 22: 139–191.

Myrdal, G. (1968). "Asian Drama: An Inquiry into the Poverty of Nations." The Swedish Journal of Economics 70 (4): 242–245.

Nurkse, Ragnar. (1953). "Problems of Capital Formation in Underdeveloped Regions." Oxford: Oxford University Press.

Schumpeter, A. Joseph. (1934). "The Theory of Economic Development: An Inquiry into Profits, Capital, Credit, Interest, and the Business Cycle." Harvard Economic Studies 46.

Young, Allyn. (1928). "Increasing Returns and Economic Progress." The Economic Journal 38: 527–542.

Timmer, P. Marcel, and Adam, Szirmar. (1997). "Growth and Divergence in Manufacturing Performance in South and East Asia." Papers 37, Groningen State, Institute of Economic Research.

CHAPTER 8

An Assessment of the Macroeconomic Landscape: 1955–2020

8.1 Introduction

This chapter provides a long wave overview of the macroeconomic situation from 1955 to 2020 and details the extent of dependence on the petroleum sector. The discussion in this chapter previous chapters as well as provides a seamless steppingstone to the policy comments which unfold in the chapter. To structure the discussion in this chapter the analysis is divided into the period 1955–1972, 1973–1982, 1983–1993, 1994–2008 and 2009–2020. These periods coincide with pre first boom (1955–1972), first boom (1973–1982), first recession (1983–1993), second boom (1994–2008) and second recession (2009–2020).

8.1.1 Trends in Basic Macro Economic Variables

Economic rents in the petroleum sector of the T&T economy climbed from US$33.2 mn in 1955 to US$79.6 mn in 1972 at the dawn of the 2nd petroleum boom. The average for the period 1955–1972 was US$44.6 mn (see Table 8.1). The rapid increase in the price and production of crude oil in the time period 1974–1982, however, saw an escalation in the level of petroleum economic rents averaging US$968.16 mn per annum. Note though, there was a collapse in petroleum economic rents from US$2009.2 mn in 1980 to US$381.5 mn in 1998. In the period 1994–2008 petroleum rents averaged US$1611.7 mn per annum

R. Hosein, *Oil and Gas in Trinidad and Tobago*,
https://doi.org/10.1007/978-3-030-77669-5_8

Table 8.1 Basic macroeconomic trends in the T&T economy, various time periods

	Economic rent (US$mn)	*Real growth rate (%)*	*Inflation rate (%)*	*REER*	*Unemployment rate (%)*	*CAB (% GDP)*	*HHI*
Average 1955–1972	44.6	2.4	3.7	86.4	11.6	−12.9	0.61
1973–1982	968.2	5.5	14.4	102.2	12.7	2.0	0.80
1983–1993	792.1	−2.8	9.8	124.2	18.3	−1.9	0.52
1994–2008	1611.7	6.2	5.2	105.8	11.4	9.5	0.42
2009–2020	3049.9	−0.9	6.5	163.7	4.7	10.7	0.41

Source CBTT

and for the period 2009–2018 averaged US$3049.1 mn per annum. The high level of rents in the final period is partly on account of the elevated price of oil and gas during this time period.

The real growth rate of the T&T economy in the period before 1955–1972 averaged 2.1% but during the period of the first oil boom, real economic growth accelerated and indeed in the period 1973–1982 averaged 5.5%. In the 1980s, however, the real growth rate of the T&T economy collapsed, and the economy fluctuated between stagnating or recessing until 1993 and real economic growth averaged −2.8% in this time period. Thereafter, the real growth rate improved, and T&T entered its "Golden era" of growth, from 1994 to 2008. In this golden era of economic growth, real GDP growth averaged 6.23%. From 2009 to 2020, however, the economy entered a period of secular stagnation, although not as sharply as the first recession, with an annual average growth rate of −0.85% (see Table 8.1).

The challenge for T&T, however, resided in the realm of controlling expenditures in relation to non-energy revenues. Indeed, government expenditures escalated from US$51.7 mn in 1955 to US$3948.8 mn in 1982 before collapsing to US$1132.4 mn in 1993 and thereafter remaining moderately suppressed until 2000. After 2000, government expenditure escalated rapidly and peaked at US$8592.5 mn in 2014 although by 2020, it fell to US$7142 mn. Non-energy revenues in 2020 stood at US$4542.5 mn. As a consequence of these trends, the economy's non-energy fiscal balance is in significant deficit and will require a huge effort by government to reverse (Fig. 8.1).

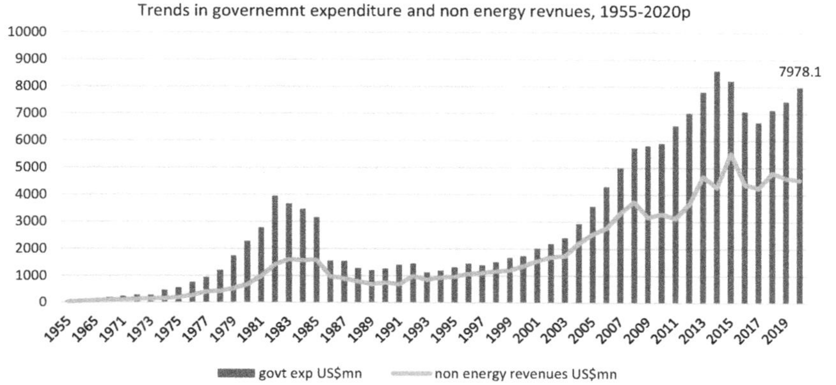

Fig. 8.1 Trends in government expenditure and non-energy revenues 1955–2020p

The comparative trends in government expenditure and non-energy revenues prompted a sharp deterioration in the non-energy fiscal balance of the economy which in 2014 was as deep as—US$4311.1 mn in and for the period 2009–2020 averaged—US$2963.2 mn per annum.[1] This reflects the extent of dependence on energy rents and also underscores a structural flaw in the T&T economy in that the energy revenues were increasingly used to offset the non-energy fiscal balance rather than being stashed away as savings, which could be in turn used to smooth long-run consumption (Fig. 8.2).

In the first oil boom the government set about sowing the petroleum rents and capital expenditure was comparatively more buoyant than transfers and subsidies. This was a golden era of investment and the economy developed competence in its petrochemical sector. However, after 1983 transfers and subsidies remained continuously above capital expenditures and disappointingly the gap widened with the progress of time as indicated by Fig. 8.3. This indicates a greater inclination of the state to distribute the rents as compared to saving the rents. Part of the reason for this may be that for the first time the party that held political power from 1956 to 1986 lost office and part of the public purse was thereafter used in a rentier way, to bring votes.

[1] 2020 was an anomaly because of Covid-19.

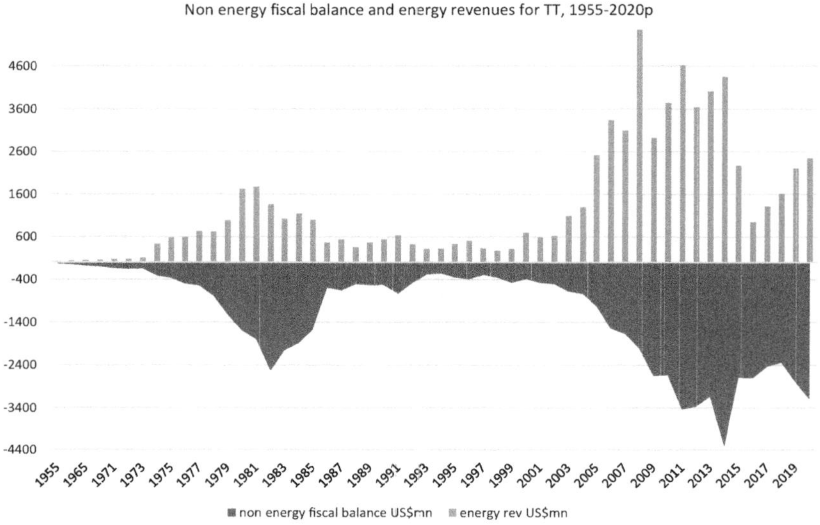

Fig. 8.2 Non-energy fiscal balance and energy revenues for T&T, 1955–2020p

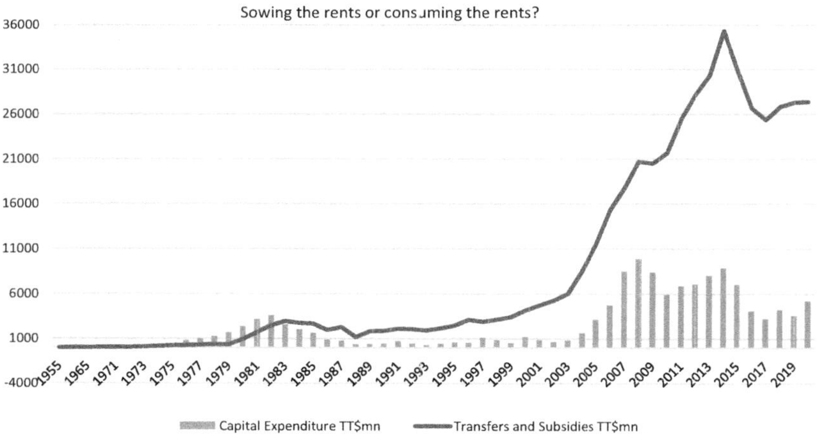

Fig. 8.3 Capital expenditure and transfers and subsidies 1955–2020p

The use of a Hodrick Prescott filter that the non-cyclical aspect of government transfers and subsidies continued to rise (Fig. 8.4) even after 2009, although the non-cyclical component of rents from the petroleum sector, was on the decline, providing clear evidence of fiscal imprudence.

Prior to the second oil boom, the inflation rate averaged 3.7% per annum. However, by the 1970s amidst the rapid increase in domestic demand, inflation reached an annual average of 14.4% as the economy overheated (in 1980, the inflation rate reached 17.5%). During the 1980s the inflation rate moderated only slightly as the fall off in demand was partially countered by contractions in supply, as real output decreased. For the period 1983–1993 the inflation rate averaged 9.8%. For the period 1994–2008 the average annual inflation rate declined to 5.2%. Note though that in the dormant period of economic activity from 2009 to 2020 the inflation rate averaged 5.1%, with 2020 having an inflation rate of 0.9%.

As the economic growth progressed the real effective exchange rate (REER) in the context of the trend in the domestic inflation rate in the economy climbed and by 1985 the REER had appreciated by 83% above

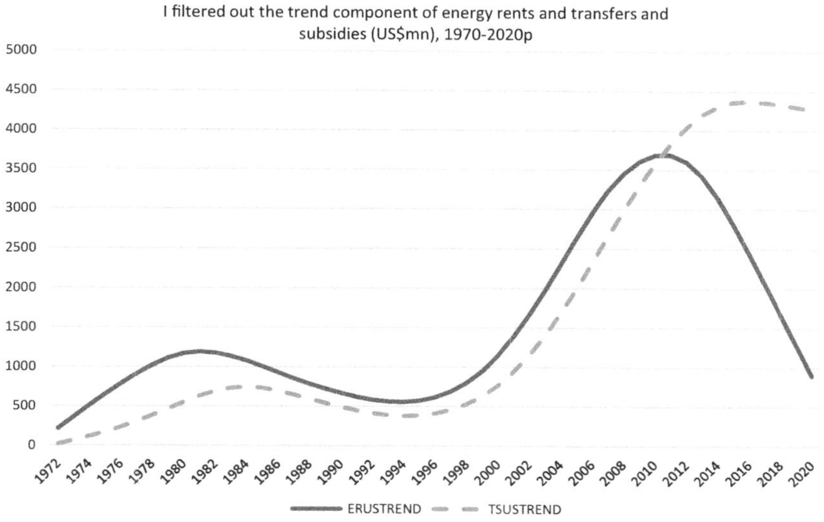

Fig. 8.4 Energy rents and transfers and subsidies 1970–2020p

that in 1955. Devaluations in 1985 and 1988 and the depreciation associated with the floating of the T&T dollar in 1993, however, resulted in a substantial amount of correction to the value of the REER. However, as the economy prospered in the second petroleum boom, the REER once again appreciated and in 2020, was 80.2% higher than in 1999 (when LNG production started).

The unemployment rate in the T&T economy stood at 15.4% in 1973 as compared to an annual average of 11.7% in the time period 1955–1972. However, the rapid growth of the T&T economy in the period 1973–1982, motivated a decline in the unemployment rate, which for the first time reached single digit values in 1980, of 9.9%. Part of the reason for this, however, was that the state became an increasingly large employer. (In particular, state sector employment increased from 27,909 in 1973 to 43,100 in 1982, an increase of almost 54.4%, no doubt this was partly on account of political rent sharing activities).

As economic growth fell in the 1980s, the unemployment rate increased and by 1987 it perched at 22.3% and until 1993, averaged 20.6% per annum. However, after 1993 with the recommencement of real economic growth in the economy, the unemployment rate fell (and with the assistance of a series of Make Work programs), stood at 3.8% in 2018. (The average unemployment rate in the period 2009–2018 was 4.6%.)

The economy's current account balance (CAB) as a percentage of GDP for the period 1955–1972 was persistently negative, averaging –12.06%. During the first boom (1973–1982) the CAB improved to an annual average of 1.9%, as petroleum export revenues, soared. In the recessionary period that followed (1983–1993), both oil prices and oil production fell, and in this setting, the current account balance reverted to deficit (annual average −1.9% for the period). In the period of the second boom as natural gas output from the economy improved, and the price of crude oil improved (this occurred after 1998) the CAB again improved and remained generally in surplus with an average annual value of annual average 9.5% for the period 1994–2008. Significantly, in the period 2009–2020, the CAB remained healthy (averaging per annum, 9.7%).

8.2 Towards a Greater Dependence on the Petroleum Sector

Failure to adequately sterilize the energy rents resulted in a greater dependence of the T&T economy on the energy sector. In the time period 1974 to 1982 the average annual value of the ratio of petroleum GDP to aggregate GDP stood at 40.3% whilst for the period 1983–1999 this ratio had an annual average value of 25.4%. Since 2000 though, the value of this ratio climbed reaching 42.1% in 2006 as the natural gas sector boomed. With the decline in natural gas production in T&T after 2010 and of crude oil after 2005, the share of petroleum value added in total GDP subsided to 36% in 2018 (see Table 8.2).

As a percent of total government revenues, energy revenue declined from 47.7% in 1955 to 35.5% in 1970, as the production of crude oil fell without any considerable upward migration of oil prices. Thereafter though, the share of energy revenues as a percentage of total government revenues increased to 73.2% in 1975, as both the price and the production of crude oil improved at the same time. The rapid increase in government energy revenues led to an increase in state led and state funded activities and set the economy on a very unsustainable consumption pathway. As both the price and production of crude oil waned during the 1980s, so too did the share of energy revenues in total revenues and by 1998, this ratio receded in value to 18.8%. The buoyancy of oil and gas prices for most of the period after 2009 helped to keep the ratio of energy revenues to total revenues afloat and for the period 2009–2014 this ratio averaged 39.4%.

Table 8.2 Aspects of the dependence of the T&T economy on the energy sector, various time periods

	Petro GDP/GDP	*Energy revenue/tot rev*	*Energy exports (sitc 3 and sitc 5)—% share*
Average 1955–1972	24.5	40.2	65.6
Average 1973–1982	37.6	62.6	88.9
Average 1983–1993	25.4	36.6	80.4
Average 1994–2008	32.4	34.9	78.3
Average 2009–2020	37.0	39.4	87.0

Source Computed from *Handbook of Key Economic and Financial Indicators*

Even more, the share of energy sector exports, treated as the exports of international trade classification Sect. 8.3 and 8.5, accounted for 55.3% of total export revenues in 1955. This ratio averaged 65.6% in the period 1955–1972. Thereafter, however, energy exports as a proportion of total exports escalated to 88.9% on average per annum in the time period 1973–1982, and remained buoyant at 80.4%, in the time period 1983–1993 as the economy sagged. In the period of rapid economic growth from 1994 to 2008 the share of energy exports as a proportion of total exports averaged 78.3% on average per annum. By 2009, however, energy exports as a percentage of total exports climbed to 89.5% of total exports and in the final period of the analysis, 2009–2018, energy export revenues as a proportion of total revenues stood at 87%, on average per annum.

8.3 Petroleum Is a Sunset Industry Globally

The Paris Agreement is an agreement with the UN's Framework Convention on Climate Change (UNFCC) signed in 2016 and signed by 195 UNFCC members of which 187 are a party to it (Paris Agreement, United Nations Treaty Collection). The long-term goal of the Paris Agreement is to keep the long-term increase in global temperatures below 2 °C above pre-industrial levels and to pursue effects of such a form so as to limit global temperature increases to 1.5 °C on the basis that this would significantly reduce the risks and impact of climate change.[2] Ideally, this requires a movement away from a reliance on fossil fuels.

Table 8.3 tells a story of the sunset nature of the energy industry in the world at large. The data indicates that the consumption of crude oil will peak around 2035. Coal consumption will start to fall after 2020 although natural gas consumption will continue to increase.

Significantly, the consumption of renewable energy, is expected to increase from 45 metric tonnes of equivalent energy in 1995 to 2740 metric ton of oil and gas equivalent in 2040. The Trinidad and Tobago economy needs to be aware of this in planning its way forward, as there will be a range of emergent opportunities in the sunrise renewable energy sector.

Consistent with these expected consumption trends, the world continues on a pathway of fossil fuel phase out which is the gradual

[2] https://unfccc.int/process-and-meetings/the-paris-agreement/the-paris-agreement.

Table 8.3 Consumption (Mtoe) unless otherwise noted

	World	*Oil*	*Gas*	*Coal*	*Nuclear*	*Hydro*	*Renewables*
1995	**8565**	3391	1816	2224	526	563	45
2000	**9356**	3691	2065	2356	584	601	59
2005	**10,894**	4030	2368	3106	627	660	103
2010	**12,119**	4145	2731	3606	626	777	234
2015	**13,060**	4396	2987	3765	583	881	449
2017	**13,511**	**4538**	**3156**	**3731**	**596**	**919**	**571**
2020	**14,304**	4675	3382	3779	673	993	802
2025	**15,264**	4790	3736	3710	696	1101	1231
2030	**16,095**	4829	4041	3647	739	1164	1674
2035	**16,980**	4876	4344	3628	739	1205	2189
2040	**17,866**	4860	4617	3625	770	1245	2748
1995–2017 (%)	**2.1**	1.3	2.5	2.4	0.6	2.3	12.3
2017–2040 (%)	**1.2**	**0.3**	**1.7**	**−0.1**	**1.1**	**1.3**	**7.1**

Source BP statistical yearbook
World, 2017 and 2017–2040 bolded to enable comparison

reduction of the use of fossil fuels to zero (0) in the context of climate change. Efforts to phase out fossil fuels involves replacing fossil fuels with alternative renewable energy sources. Already, there are significant efforts to reduce coal consumption, and as of 2018, 13 countries and many governments and businesses became members of the Powering Past Coal Alliance making a declaration to advance the transition away from coal power generation. However, some of the countries in the world which use the most coal, did not join; these include China and India.[3] Institutional support for the Powering Past Coal Alliance is strong and recently the United Nations, Secretary General, said that countries should stop building new coal powered plants, from 2020 (Blondeel et al. 2020).

Fourteen (14) countries and about twenty (20) cities from across the world have proposed banning the sale of passenger cars which are powered by gasoline, liquefied petroleum gas and diesel. China is currently researching a timetable for the ban; Japan has comprehensive plans for the formation of a hydrogen economy by 2040 and other countries such as the UK, Thailand, Denmark, Sweden, Norway, Germany,

[3] https://poweringpastcoal.org/about/members.

France, Netherlands, Portugal and Costa Rica have also proposed timelines. The intention here is to ban vehicles which are powered by fossil fuels to help reduce carbon dioxide emissions, many automotive companies are trying to work with these bans by trying to introduce electric vehicles. For example, in California in the USA, the emission requirements for automakers to make and sell any vehicle in the state is such that between 2018 and 2025, it is expected to force 15% of the new vehicle sales to be zero emissions. Globally, electric vehicle sales are on the rise and whilst in 2010, there were only 17,000 electric vehicles on the road, by 2020 this had soared to 7.2 mn with China hosting 47% of this stock but with nine other countries having in excess of 100,000 electric cars.

Some cities have signed the Fossil Free Streets Declaration and this a big step forward in trying to reduce carbon dioxide emission in the streets. The declaration was signed in 2017[4] as an initiative to transition the most economically important cities towards zero-emissions forms of transport by 2030.

8.4 Petroleum Is a Sunset Industry Locally

Even more than this in the T&T economy the reserves of oil and gas have been declining and whilst it is possible that more oil and gas may be found as it stands, the proven reserves are definitely moving southwards. In this setting policy makers must think ahead to have a concrete plan B (Table 8.4).

8.5 Conclusion

The T&T economy benefitted from a surge in petroleum-based economic rents in the period 1955–2018 totaling US$75.2bn. This surge in economic rents helped to breed a sense of dependence and successive governments failed to aptly diversify the production base away from the petroleum sector. The real economic growth of the economy ebbed and flowed with the petroleum rents and periods of boom were followed by periods of recession and or secular stagnation. The rents stimulated a sharp increase in transfers and subsidies, inflated domestic price levels and in so doing prompted an appreciation of the economy's REER, even

[4] https://cleantechnica.com/2017/10/27/c40-fossil-fuel-free-streets-declaration-signed-mayors-12-major-cities/.

Table 8.4 Proven oil and natural gas reserves in T&T

	Proven oil reserves (mns of barrels)
1964	510.0
1970	592.0
1980	620.0
1990	522.0
2000	716.0
2005	620.0
2018	243
Year	*Proven natural gasreserves (bcf)*
2000	19,674.0
2001	20,348.0
2002	20,758.0
2003	18,809.0
2004	18,775.0
2005	17,913.5
2006	17,052.0
2007	16,997.0
2008	15,374.0
2009	14,416.0
2010	13,460.0
2011	13,257.0
2012	13,106.0
2013	12,240.0
2014	11,503.0
2015	11,500.76
2016	10,593.76
2017	9,469.08
2018p	

Source Handbook of Key Economic and Financial Indicators

though the nominal exchange rate, was adjusted several times along the way. The rapid economic growth used up spare capacity in the economy during the 1970s and then again in the period 1999–2015 and in so doing the unemployment rate in the economy tumbled and to the extent that the period after 2003, it was persistently less than 10% and after 2012 always less than 5%. In 1988 the unemployment rate was 22.3%.

The Trinidad and Tobago economy are now at a critical juncture in which its reserves of oil and of gas are considerably lower than it was in the past and also in a world where the petroleum sector itself in the context of the Paris Accord is considered a sunset industry. The way forward must embrace three clear strategic interventions:

(a) Harvesting remaining oil and gas to maximize the total economic rents collected.
(b) Cutting back on rent subsidies and rent absorption.
(c) Opening new corridors of foreign exchange earnings, as the sun sets on crude oil as a source of fuel.

These three interventions are explained in greater detail in the next three chapters.

Reference

Blondeel, Mathieu, Thijs Van de Graaf, and Tim Haesebrouck. (2020). "Moving Beyond Coal: Exploring and Explaining the Powering Past Coal Alliance." Energy Research & Social Science 59: 101304.

CHAPTER 9

Rent Absorption in the T&T Economy

9.1 Introduction

This chapter focuses on channels to reduce rent absorption in the T&T economy. The amount of rents in circulation helps to shape the expectations of the elites in an economy and influences economic policies as well as it helps to drive the long-term political economy process. A high level of rents triggers competition and contests for its use. The elites may resist the need to modify the exchange rate if it is overvalued especially when they benefit from import distribution businesses. But this creates a problem in the bust phase of the boom bust cycle as the stock of foreign exchange shrinks in the context of an underdeveloped non-energy sector, which cannot carry the adjustment. This chapter has three parts. The first part commences by briefly outlining the relationship between consumption and investment in a small oil-based economy. Here four permutations are mentioned these are the Permanent Income Hypothesis (PIH), the Bird in Hand (BIH), the optimal strategy (D^{op}), and the Hand to Mouth (resource curse strategy). The chapter then outlines various steps that can be considered to improve the Heritage and Stabilization Fund (HSF) as linked to the BIH permutation in the T&T economy. The chapter then discusses how to minimize the adverse impact of rents subsidies with two such subsidies elaborated the "Make Work Program" and the "GATE" program. In each case policy measures are suggested on how to improve on rent dependence.

R. Hosein, *Oil and Gas in Trinidad and Tobago*,
https://doi.org/10.1007/978-3-030-77669-5_9

9.2 Reduce the Pace of Rent Absorption by Modifying the HSF

9.2.1 *Understanding Consumption and Investment Decisions in a Small Capital-Starved but Resource-Abundant Economy*

In a small, capital-starved but resource-rich developing country, the state will have to make important decisions regarding both consumption and investment.

The generalized volatility of oil revenues means that the state will have to make special efforts to smooth out these revenues, whilst the exhaustibility of these resources means that it must consider saving part of the resource rents for the future. Figure 9.1 relates to various consumption paths given the resource revenue pathway. These four different consumption pathways are discussed below.

(a) Permanent Income Hypothesis (PIH)

The PIH hypothesis introduced by Friedman in 1957 solves the problem of optimal consumption in the context of maximizing a social welfare

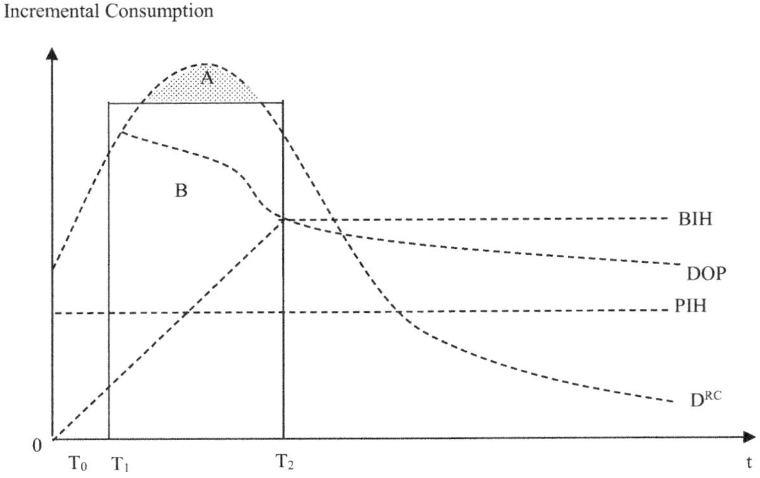

Fig. 9.1 Consumption of natural resource rents (*Source* Author additions from Collier et al. (2010). D^{OP}: optimal case for developing countries. D^{RC}: rent redistribution strategy for developing countries)

function in an environment characterized by uncertainty. The literature on the revenue management of non-renewable natural resources recommends that the state smooth expenditure overtime. However, the challenge with smoothing is that the state will need to determine the long-run value of the resources from the commodity, which in turn involves forecasting both long-run extraction costs and long-term pricing. This can be difficult, as oil prices are subject to a multiplicity of influences and tend to fluctuate.

The PIH line regarding consumption is flat, indicating that the change in consumption according to this theory is constant. The change in consumption at T_0 is equal to the interest income that the "stock of resource wealth" valued at T_0 using the world interest rate, would fetch. The challenge with the PIH is that it involves borrowing in the period T_0–T_1, when the economy receives no income from the resource wealth, and repaying in the period T_1–T_2, when the resource wealth forms a stock of savings. The size of the savings fund and level of consumption increment at all dates are such that interest payments on the fund (once resource revenue has come to an end) exactly finance the consumption increment.

The policy prescription from the PIH thus helps the economy with:

- stabilization and saving some of the wealth for future generations
- avoiding procyclical tendencies.

The obvious challenge with the PIH approach is the uncertainty over the size of the permanent income.

(b) Bird in Hand (BIH)

A more conservative strategy is the BIH approach. With this approach, no resources are borrowed, and consumption is only slowly built up between T_1 and T_2 so that the incremental asset base peaks at T_2 when the resource is exhausted. Under a BIH strategy, consumption benefits are pushed into the future. With the BIH approach, all the resources are placed in the SWF and consumption is then conditioned by the interest earned on the asset.[1] Once the revenues to be collected have been

[1] Once the oil revenues have dried up, there should be enough money in the cumulative stock of assets so that the non-oil deficit can be sustained, thereafter.

exhausted, the BIH follows the same pattern as the PIH. The major disadvantage of this approach is that consumption is displaced into the future. In a poor economy, this may not be politically practical. In common, the BIH and PIH convert the resources into a financial asset and then streamline consumption from the financial asset to the benefit of the future generation, although it is more pronounced with the BIH. As reserves decline, the amount of uncertainty is reduced, and a meaningful understanding of the stock of wealth ascertained (the amount of oil in the ground consequently becomes less of an issue). The BIH approach is the underlying strategy used by Norway to manage its oil revenues.

The BIH approach has several advantages over the PIH, including the following:

- It facilitates increasing expenditure overtime, and this may be politically appealing.
- It provides more effective stabilization to expenditures in the economy, as it is based on predictable levels of revenue flows.

If the country wants a lowered level of poverty and expects higher per capita income in the future, then it makes sense to spend today to alleviate poverty. The BIH may not be the best strategy for such a setting.

(c) Optimal Strategy (D^{OP})

As capital expenditures on infrastructure improve, there can be a crowding-in of private capital. In this regard, Collier et al. (2010) address the issues associated with efficiently managing natural resource revenues in developing countries with a low level of capital. They break rank with theories such as the PIH and argue that capital-stunted economies should place priority on domestic investment. These researchers refer to their expenditure strategy on upfront capital investments as the "optimal approach." Collier et al. conclude by highlighting that the message from the "optimal approach" is that consumption is important to the relatively poor generation but investment is also important to put consumption on a rising pathway over time and the best way to do this is by bringing forward the economy's growth trajectory through more investment in the current period to benefit all generations.

(d) Hand to Mouth (HtM)

Another permutation but which must be avoided by developing countries at all cost, is the HtM. It occurs when the resource curse sets in, and the relationship between non-productive government expenditure and energy revenues moves out of sync so that debt mounts and consumption overshadow investment. In this type of setting the state exhausts all its collected energy revenues on non-productive expenditures. In many regards as the Table 9.1 shows this overall type of strategy the T&T economy followed in the period 2005–2020. Specifically, the state collected TT$293 bn in energy revenues and spent TT$385.9 bn on transfers and subsidies alone and in the process built up a net public sector debt of TT$130.2 bn as capital.

Table 9.1 Trends in government spending, revenues, transfers and subsidies and debt 2005–2019

Fiscal year end date	*Central government energy revenue (TT$Mn)*	*Central government expenditure on transfers and subsidies (TT$Mn)*	*Central government capital expenditure (TT$Mn)*	*Net public sector debt outstanding (TT$M)*
2005	13,961.3	10,821.6	2798.6	34,581.8
2006	21,416	14,830.4	4615.3	35,374.3
2007	20,025.9	16,780.9	7781.9	35,648.2
2008	32,463.2	20,114.1	9684.5	36,463.8
2009	19,335.4	21,173.6	8414	41,587.4
2010	23,881.4	20,833.3	6399.2	46,203.5
2011	27,709.6	25,099.5	6952.6	49,166.4
2012	23,467.8	27,206.1	6987.7	64,924.4
2013	25,878.1	30,068.4	8439.8	66,096.1
2014	27,913	34,663.5	8434.8	71,081
2015	14,513.8	30,701.9	7620.8	77,341.1
2016	6361	27,856.1	4398.3	88,308
2017	3821	26,030.3	3448.5	93,647
2018	10,964.1	25,391.1	3492.1	95,543.8
2019	14,791.1	26,743.8	3747.2	103,214
2020	6532.1	27,638.2	4329.1	130,271.3
Sum	293,034.8	385,952.8	97,544.4	

Source Central Bank of Trinidad and Tobago

9.3 The HSF in T&T

The Heritage and Stabilisation Fund (HSF) fund in the T&T economy was established in March 2007, with the intent to save and invest the revenues government received in the energy sector above what it budgeted. The HSF replaced the Interim Revenue Stabilization (IRSF) fund by an Act of Parliament. The IRSF in turn was introduced in 2000 with the designed intent of promoting fiscal discipline in the economy and also to help cushion the impact on the economy and on the budget, should there be a sharp unexpected fall in oil prices. The thrust for the HSF came out of the economy's experience in the 1970s when the economy made substantial amounts of economic rents and did not save the surplus, but rather engaged in expansionary fiscal policies. The HSF in T&T follows the basic principles, established for foreign wealth funds as set out in the Santiago Principles.[2] The HSF can initiate both savings and withdrawals.

Savings is triggered when actual energy revenues (AER) exceed forecasted energy revenues (FER), by 10%.

i.e. AER-FER $\geq$ 10%, savings occurs.

The savings rule states that if actual energy revenues are more than 10% of forecasted energy revenue, then 60% of this excess revenue (ER) at a minimum, goes into the HSF. Alternatively said, $HSF_{t+1} = HSF_t + \lambda ER$.

where $0.6 \leq \lambda \leq 1$.

For the TT economy, although these rules provide a framework for stabilization, in practice the various energy price assumptions especially after 2005/06 limited deposits into the HSF by narrowing the differential between the last actual price and the new forecast.

Thus, in the Table 9.2 note the BP_t is the current forecasted price of oil and AP_{t-1} is the actual price in the last time period. Observe that after 2005/2006 there was a "chase after the goose that laid the golden egg" and the budgeted price of oil increased from US$25 in 2005/2006 to US$80 in 2012/2013 and remained at a budgeted price above US$75.

[2] The Santiago Principles are a set of guidelines to run Sovereign Wealth Funds (SWF). These principles were developed by the IMF in collaboration with the International Working Group of Sovereign Wealth Funds (IWG-SWF). The backbone of these principles is to offer transparency and global financial risk management. According to Truman (2010), T&T's HSF does well in terms of public disclosure, even when compared to other funds such as the Norway Government Pension Fund, and the Alaska Permanent Fund.

Table 9.2 Relationship between real price of oil and budgeted price of oil

	WTI oil prices	*Budgeted oil prices*	*Ratio (BPt / Apt–1)*
1991/92	21.54	22	
1992/93	20.58	23	1.118
1993/94	18.43	21	1.139
1994/95	17.2	19	1.105
1995/96	18.43	16.5	0.895
1996/97	22.12	17.5	0.791
1997/98	20.61	20	0.970
1998/99	14.42	19	1.318
1999/00	19.34	14.1	0.729
2000/01	30.38	16	0.527
2001/02	25.98	22	0.847
2002/03	26.18	22	0.840
2003/04	31.08	22	0.708
2004/05	41.51	25	0.602
2005/06	56.64	25	0.441
2006/07	66.05	32	0.497
2007/08	72.34	50	0.691
2008/09	99.67	70	0.702
2009/10	61.95	55	0.888
2010/11	79.48	65	0.818
2011/12	94.88	75	0.790
2012/13	94.05	80	0.851
2013/14	97.98	80	0.816
2014/15	93.1	80	0.859
2015/16	48.7	80	1.643
2016/17	43.2	45	1.042
2017/18	50.9	48	0.943
2018/19	64.8	52	0.802
2019/20	57.1	65	1.138
2020/21		**45**	

Source Author's computations

Against this backdrop, it is critical that the government redesign its Heritage and Stabilization Fund (HSF) as part of a medium-term fiscal strategy. As reserves are declining (international reserves fell from US$11.5 bn in 2014 to US$6.9 bn in 2019) the government will need to be clear about the balances amongst saving, consuming and investing its energy resources. Note though that the formula carries the indication that money can go into the HSF in a period t, when the economy has a fiscal balance which is zero or even negative! This raises the question as to where these revenues will come from, and the indication is that it will have to be borrowed. Indeed the economy has been borrowing and building up debt alongside an increasing HSF balance and so it may make more fiscal sense to link deposits to the fiscal balance, especially if the economy is borrowing at rates of interest in excess of what the economy is receiving on the HSF! This chapter argues that deposits should only be placed into reserves, provided that the economy has a fiscal surplus.

Further, the HSF has worked more as a heritage fund in the past, than as a stabilization fund (the government of T&T did draw down resources from the HSF during the lock down of the economy from March to June 2020). Thus in 2008/09 when withdrawals from the fund became necessary, none were made (see Table 9.3). The government would want to review the mechanics of the fund so that it does not unnecessarily resort to borrowing.

Table 9.3 HSF withdrawals and contributions US$mn

	Gas rents	*Oil rents*	*Oil rents and gas rents*	*Energy revenues*	*HSF contribution/withdrawal*	*Non-energy fiscal balance*
2000	291.6	907.5	1199.2	699		−379.442
2001	336.6	608.3	944.9	592.7		−466.746
2002	349.5	700.7	1050.2	629.2		−498.005
2003	476.9	912.1	1389	1096.8		−672.184
2004	589.9	1117.5	1707.4	1295.4		−728.276
2005	864.7	1968.4	2833.1	2516.3		−1013.7
2006	1341.4	2290.1	3631.4	3344.6		−1536.82
2007	1509.1	2000.7	3509.7	3098.5	2.088	−1661.65
2008	1722.3	2575.5	4297.8	5451	1.054	−2002.75
2009	1915.4	1185.3	3100.8	2926	0	−2642.92
2010	1633.3	1568.3	3201.6	3745.7	0.477	−2626.52
2011	2439	2262.1	4701.1	4623.3	0.451	−3428.36
2012	2794.1	1950.8	4745	3647	0.207	−3361.48
2013	2967.5	1830.5	4798	4016.7	0.042	−3129.66
2014	2131.6	1640.3	3771.9	4355.3	0	−4311.2
2015	1310.7	622.6	1933.3	2275.8	0	−2685.92
2016	677.2	417.2	1094.4	953.5	−0.375	−2694.25
2017	1006.4	697.1	1703.5	1318.6	−0.252	−2428.21
2018	904.7	951.8	1856.5	1616.8	0	−2329.32
2019	1039.9	1323	2362.9	2207.6		−2787.01
2020p	926.3	1200.6	2126.9	2146.7		−3187.46

Source Online CBTT database

9.4 What the HSF Balance Could Have Been

As mentioned before, between 1908 and 2020 Trinidad and Tobago produced 10,331.4 million barrels of oil and gas equivalent of which 3707 million barrels were oil and 6623.5 million barrels were of gas, in barrels of oil equivalent. Since 1956 (adult suffrage of Trinidad and Tobago) 6470.9 of gas in millions of barrels of gas oil equivalent was produced or 97.7% of the total to date, with the corresponding number for crude oil being 3186.9 million barrels or 85.9%. To be clear a significant aspect associated with economic rents generated from the energy sector accrued in the time period when we had control over our economy and so we cannot blame profit repatriation by foreign oil firms for a low degree of accumulated energy rents as savings.

In 1998, the price of crude oil plummeted to US$12.7 per barrel but thereafter escalated to US$99.6 per barrel in 2008 and although oil prices dipped in 2009 to US$61.7 per barrel for the period 2010–2014 it averaged US$91.4 per barrel. Gas prices in 1998 stood at US$2.8 per mmbtu but escalated to US$8.9 per mmbtu in 2008.

In 2000, when the IRSF was started oil prices stood at US$30.3 and the production of crude oil stood at 119.1 million. For natural gas, prices in 2000 stood at US$4.3 per mmbtu and gas production stood at 1498.1 mmcf/d. By 2008, the HSF benefitted from a deposit of US$3.142 bn (see Table 9.3) although in that same time period (2000–2008) energy revenues tallied to US$18.7 bn.

It is here argued that instead of spending out all the energy revenues on transfers and subsidies policy makers should have instead adopted a strategy in which they saved 25% at an average annual compounded rate of interest of 5.6%.[3] If such a strategic approach were adopted, today the T&T economy would have had a stock of money in the HSF of US$22,460.5 mn. The approach of policy makers in T&T left the fund with a mere US$5.9 bn as of September 2018 of which US$2.6 bn was investment income. The ills of this type of policy failure would remain with the T&T economy for many years to come.

In moving forward, to improve the HSF and also to help insulate the T&T economy from frittering out its energy revenues, it is here proposed that policy makers consider saving all of the remaining energy revenues. This is a BIH approach and will strengthen the economy's Savings fund

[3] This is the average return on the fund, to date.

from a rainy-day fund to a transformational fund. A BIH strategy will require tremendous discipline by the government and will not likely be possible until BHP brings the projected 16,000 barrels of additional oil on stream in Q1 2022 (Energy Chamber 2019) but it is a real consideration in safeguarding the future. To complement this type of thinking it is recommended that T&T consider implementing Fiscal Responsibility Legislation and this is discussed in a later chapter.

9.5 Inefficient Application of the Hartwick Rule: Tertiary Level Education Funding

This section addresses the deployment of the Hartwick rule in the T&T economy as relates to tertiary level education financing. As the petroleum rents started to flow in a more abundant way in the T&T economy, the government proceeded to variously increase its funding support for tertiary level education. These educational interventions did not properly respect the Hartwick Rule and as applied, paid little attention to the vertical and horizontal aspects of the associated efficiency outcomes.

In the context of the Hartwick rule, education takes on a particularly important depth. The Hartwick rule defines the amount of investment in produced capital such as buildings, roads and knowledge stocks that are needed to exactly offset declining stocks of non-renewable resources. The rule is often abbreviated as "invest resource rents" and requires that a nation invest all rents earned from exhaustible resources currently extracted, where "rent" is defined along paths that maximize returns to owners of the resource stock. However, because of scarcity issues the application of the Hartwick rule should be done efficiently and the "investment" outlay should not be used for consumption purposes (Akitoby and Coorey 2012).

It is widely known that a sound primary education is critical for an economy to benefit from an improved level of literacy and numeracy skills but Hezemans and Ritzen (2004) have noted that it is critical for the economy to have an improved amount of tertiary education skills as the economy matures. One source states, "…higher education plays a key role in training qualified individuals who will be capable of implementing new technologies and using innovative methods to establish more efficient enterprises and institutions and thus allocate resources more effectively. Through research and increased knowledge, higher education can also help to address the challenges arising from population growth, limited arable land, endemic diseases, urbanization, energy costs and climate change" (Mpofu et al. 2013, p. 327). In fact, this "trained labour" not only formulates technology, but determines its use in production.

This chapter discusses the history of funding TLE in T&T and elaborates that the funding formula which prevailed in the boom phase of the petroleum rents cycle as well as the strategy that is currently being deployed is not the best funding strategy in the context of the economic reality of the country and recommends an Income Contingent loan (ICL) approach, to fund tertiary level education, in T&T.

9.5.1 *Brief History of Tertiary Level Education Funding in T&T*

In the aftermath of the recession in the 1980s the T&T government introduced the Student CESS Act in 1989. The CESS amounted to a 10% charge on the economic cost of going to university. Commercial banks made loans available after various criteria were satisfied, for students who met matriculation standards, but who could not afford the tuition fees. However, as energy sector rents cumulated, the government made several adjustments to the funding of tertiary level education. The Dollar for Dollar (DfD) program was one such initiative, which was introduced in 2001. Basically, the DfD program provided a lump sum subsidy paid by the government of T&T to local students enlisted in selected tertiary level institutions in the country. According to the Ministry of Science, Technology and Tertiary level Education (MSTTE 2003); DfD was available to students applying for enrolment at any of the following institutions:

(1) The three campuses of the University of the West Indies (UWI)
(2) The UWI/Institute of Business and the Institute of International Relations
(3) The National Energy Skills Centre
(4) Trinidad and Tobago Institute of Technology[4]
(5) Cipriani College of Labour and Cooperative Studies
(6) All of the campuses of the College of Science, Technology and Applied Arts of Trinidad and Tobago (COSTAAT)
(7) Trinidad and Tobago Hospitality and Tourism Institute.

[4] Later this became the University of Trinidad and Tobago.

DfD paid 50% of the student's tuition fees with the prime objective of reducing the costs of tertiary level education to the average household and to increase tertiary level education enrolment by 20%. In 2004, the government introduced the Government Assistance for Tuition Expenses (GATE) program, which in addition to 50% of tuition fees, relied on a means test as a basis to offer additional funding to the student, up to a maximum of full payment of tuition fees to suitable applicants. In 2006, GATE was modified, no doubt as a partial result of the massive natural gas windfall (hereafter $\text{GATE}_{\text{petroleum rents}}$) which financed the full cost of tertiary level education for all students. Qualification for the $\text{GATE}_{\text{petroleum rents}}$ required registration in an approved program at an accredited institution, upon meeting the stipulated requirements in that program. The intention of $\text{GATE}_{\text{petroleum rents}}$ was to extend the tertiary participation rate to 60%, over a ten-year period. The GATE program required that the graduated student worked in T&T for 3 years, irrespective of the level of tertiary level funding received. In 2017/18 amidst a sharp decline in economic activity in T&T, a new permutation of the GATE program was started (hereafter $\text{GATE}_{\text{recession}}$). The $\text{GATE}_{\text{petroleum rents}}$ and $\text{GATE}_{\text{recession}}$ programs are discussed below, in the context of the Hartwick rule.

9.5.2 *GATE Petroleum Rents and the Hartwick Rule*

The $\text{GATE}_{\text{petroleum rents}}$ program involved the removal of the means testing and introduced 100% tuition funding for TLE for all households.[5]

In order to see this, consider the Fig. 9.2. The line labelled Y_0^d shows the initial distribution of income in T&T and the line labelled Y_1^d shows the new distribution of income when everyone is given a lump sum income outlay to help with their tertiary level education fees, once they meet matriculation criteria. The horizontal axis ranks households by financial need. The poorest household is Hp and the richest household is Hr.

[5] "Mr. Speaker, the GATE Programme replaced the Dollar for Dollar Education Plan in September 2004. In my 2005 Budget Statement I indicated that we intended to provide free tertiary education in public institutions by the first of January 2008. Since then, our revenue situation has improved considerably. I am therefore pleased to announce, Mr. Speaker, that with effect from January 1, 2006, all nationals of Trinidad and Tobago enrolled at public tertiary institutions, namely UWI, UTT, COSTAATT and other institutions where the Government sponsors students, will be eligible for free tuition, that is free public tertiary education. Budget 2006—accessed from http://ctrc.sice.oas.org/TRC/Articles/trinidad/Budget%20Statement%202006.pdf, on Saturday 11 January 2016".

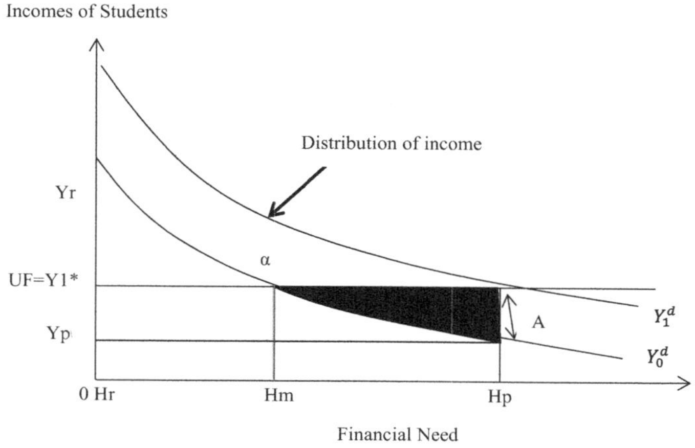

Fig. 9.2 Illustration of wastage under GATE petroleum rents

When universal funding is applied, it shifts the income distribution line outwards away from the origin (Y_0^d to Y_1^d) so that the distribution of income remains the same. With the GATE$_{\text{petroleum rents}}$ windfall program, what was created in T&T was a situation in which the poorest household was able to go to University as they received $A in funding which allowed them to be able to meet their university fees. The lump sum subsidy of $A facilitated horizontal efficiency. However, because every other (richer) household in terms of financial needs such as Hm, received the same lump sum of $A and every household with an income level above $A then the entire α area represented wasted resources, as only the shaded area is needed to ensure all "poor students" meet their fee obligations.

Evidence of vertical inefficiency is seen in the income classifications of households accessing the GATE program. From the column "% Distribution of Households by Household Income Group (HIG)," in Table 9.4, observe that the 4.6% of households from the income group $9000–$10,999 accessed GATE funding, 2.9% from the income group $11,000–$12,999, 5.5% from $13,000–$14,999, 1.5% from $15,000–$16,999 and 12.9% from $17,000 and over.[6] Note though, households

[6] This data is from the T&T Household Budget Survey 2008/09. A Survey of Living Conditions was undertaken in 2014 but the government challenged its credibility.

Table 9.4 Comparison of household expenditure and access to GATE by income group of head and household income group

Income group (TT$)	*% Distribution of households by household income group (HIG)*	*% Accessing GATE funding by IGH*
All Income Groups	100	0.9
Less than 1000	2	0.5
1000–2999	10.4	0.2
3000–4999	17	0.3
5000–6999	17.2	1
7000–8999	14	1.8
9000–10,999	11.7	4.6
11,000–12,999	7.6	2.9
13,000–14,999	5.2	5.5
15,000–16,999	3.9	1.5
17,000 and over	11.2	12.9

Source Trinidad and Tobago household budget survey 2008/2009

earning less than $9,000 per month comprised 60.4% of the households surveyed but showed lower access to GATE funding. Using the available data in Table 9.4, observe that 2% of all households fell in the less than $1000 income category but only 0.5% of this group, accessed GATE funding. In the $1000–$2999 group, there were 10.4% of households of which a mere 0.2% accessed GATE funding. Indeed, a careful assessment of the data illustrates that students from the richer households (above $9000) accessed GATE in a much greater way than households in income groups, less than TT$9000.

Apart from favouring richer households, the GATE petroleum rents strategy had a variety of other shortfall, as it did not focus on skills production specifically tied in some way to export development. This is, however, where an efficient Hartwick Rule intervention has to be targeted given the limited stock of petroleum reserves in T&T and the maturing of the existing hydrocarbon fields.

9.6 GATE Recession and the Hartwick Rule

The government revised the GATE program, effective August 2017 ($GATE_{recession}$). The $GATE_{recession}$ funding formula is based on the scale outlined below. Thus students pursuing an undergraduate degree from households with a monthly income of less than TT$10,000 are eligible for 100% of GATE funding whilst households in the income group TT$10,000–TT$30,000 are eligible for 75% of funding and households with income in excess of TT$30,000 receive 50% funding.

This section argues that in designing a funding formula for tertiary level education in TT, some basic facts must be borne in mind, these include:

- That the population less than 19 years old stood at 512,000 in 1991 and by 2018 had fallen to 380,500. This is a sharp decline and must be factored into the decision-making process.
- That the economy contracted −17% between 2009 and 2020.

These facts together with those shown in the Table 9.5 collate to infer that the demand curve for the TLE in T&T would have shifted leftwards. (In particular observe the decline in the number of people less than 19 years of age and the decline in GDP per capita [US$].)

Table 9.5 Trends in energy revenues and other data that can adversely impact on demand for university education

	Energy revenues TT$mn	*University graduates (Labour Force)*	*Population less than 19 years*	*Real GDP growth %*	*GDP per capita US$)*
2002	3931	47,200			7104.3
2010	23,881.4	73,300	478.5	3.32	16,683.36
2011	29,709.6	83,067	371.8	−0.29	19,184.8
2012	23,467.8	95,550	373.8	1.27	19,374.8
2013	25,878.1	107,450	375.3	2.23	20,427
2014	27,913	117,275	376.6	−0.91	20,604.7
2015	14,513.8	141,975	377.9	1.82	18,639.1
2016	6361	139,125	379.0	−6.30	16,523.2
2017	8821	141,850	379.8	−2.31	16,629.1
2018	10,964.1	139,240	380.5	−0.25	17,553
2019	14,791.1	138,271	379.1	−0.8	17,541.2
2020p	6532.1	–	378.7	−7.1	16,371.1

Source World Development Indicators and the *Handbook of Key Economic Indicators*

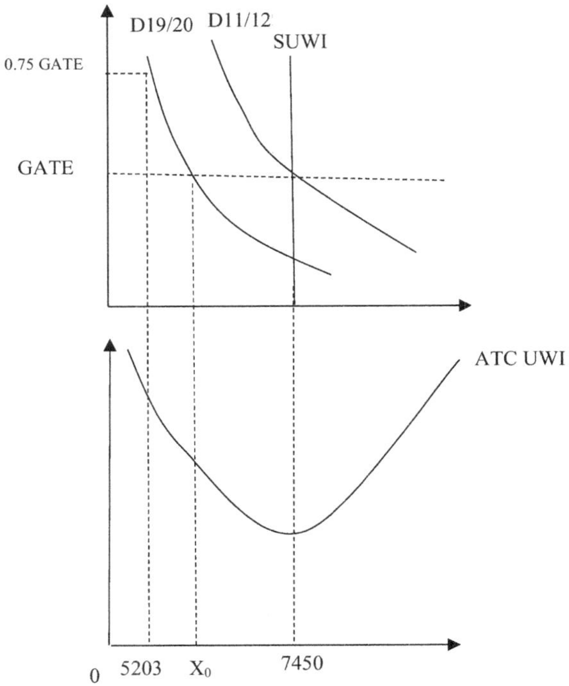

Fig. 9.3 GATE changes and its impact on enrolment at UWI St. Augustine

The Fig. 9.3 shows the impact of the $\text{GATE}_{\text{recession}}$ intervention. Using Fig. 9.3, observe that for the academic year, 2019/20[7] there were 10,625 applicants to UWI's undergraduate program of which 7432 were admitted but only 5203 were enrolled. In 2011 some 7450 students were enrolled out of an application pool of 13,515. These numbers translate into a selectivity rate (admitted as a % of applications) of 65% in 2011 and a yield rate (enrolled as a % of admitted) of 85%. In 2019/20 the corresponding selectivity rate was 73% and the yield rate was 75% (as compared to 84% in 2011).

Thus, UWI's selectivity rate is increasing but its yield rate is falling. This may be reflecting the declining per capita GDP of the economy and

[7] 2019/20 was used to avoid any exogenous shock influences from Covid-19.

hence a decline in demand because of "affordability" by some households. Note that there is also a leftward movement along the $D_{2019/20}$ curve on account of the rise in the price of tertiary level education.

It is here argued that the best use of the energy rents at this point is to fund tertiary education free for all students upfront so that the number of students undertaking undergraduate and post graduate education does not fall and in so doing possibly compromise the stock of human capital at the disposal of the economy, in the long run. However, because the energy rents are decreasing and given the significant fall in the size of real GDP the Hartwick rule as applied here, should be more in the form of a low cost human capital formation loan, which students repay later when their human capital has appreciated. This loan should follow the logic of an income contingent loan.

9.7 Income Contingent Loan

An ICL has several potential advantages due to its nature and the repayment method. These loans are undertaken by the student and not their parents and it is the graduated student who repays the loan based on their income levels in the future. The hinging of repayment on the income of the graduate allows for "consumption smoothing by reducing the burden on disposable income from student debt, particularly for those at the lower end of the earnings spectrum" (Chapman 2016). This tying of the loan repayment to the graduate's income also provides "insurance against default." Once a system of unique personal identifiers for each debtor and an efficient tax collection system is in place in the country, the repayment process can work well.

In cases where the student cannot repay the loan immediately or at all, "repayment holidays" or "cancellation of outstanding debts" are valid options. The latter may be achieved if a low-income earner reaches the maximum period of time for the repayment of the debt and the outstanding debt is forgiven. With this loan type, the loans are guaranteed by the state "with potential losses being assumed by the taxpayer." Furthermore, the interest rates are state subsidized in many cases and are therefore, lower than that of private banks.

ICLs are monitored by the state which also determines the rules concerning eligibility for the loan and the characteristics of the loan. In general, this allows the loans to be available to students "following all courses and at all institutions" so that they all "borrow on similar terms."

It is possible to design a system that offers working-class students priority access and better payment conditions, than other groups.

The nature of an ICL brings with it certain disadvantages due to the innate conditions which allow for moral hazard and adverse selection. These issues arise as the loan may be more readily taken by students who expect to earn a lower income in the future (adverse selection) in addition to graduates purposefully remaining below a predetermined income threshold so as to avoid repayment of the loan once employed (moral hazard). Table 9.6 provides a basic comparison of an ICL and the $\text{GATE}_{\text{recession}}$ program.

Furthermore, a loan which is backed by the government as opposed to a bank comes with the challenge of the lack of the obligation to "chase" loan repayment, thereby increasing the instance of defaulting on the loan.

Policy makers, should they consider adopting an ICL approach, would have to determine how they can reduce the adverse selection and moral hazard aspects.

Table 9.6 A basic comparison of an ICL and the $\text{GATE}_{\text{recession}}$ program

	Equity	*Efficiency*	*Comment*
$\text{GATE}_{\text{recession}}$	Poor students from households with income levels less than $9999 receive full funding	Reduces consumption of HHs in the economy in the income group TT$10,000–TT$29,900 and for the students in the income group TT$30,000 and above as well as students over 50 years old	The fall in the size of the relevant age cohort and in per capita GDP would shift the demand curve for TLE leftwards. In such a setting it is not prudent to "increase" price as it will cause a further contraction in the quantity demanded of TLE
ICL	All households receive free education at the point of Matriculation. Students repay in accordance with the ability to repay	This is efficient as it is sensitive to the student's ability to pay	Eventually, as people start to repay, the same block of resources would be recycled to other students

9.8 Conclusion

The basic Hartwick Rule requires that the natural capital extracted from an economy be replaced as reproducible capital. The DfD and various permutations of GATE deployed in T&T had aspects of the Hartwick Rule attached to it as it helped to promote a dramatic increase in the number of people with a university education from 46,000 in 2002 to 137,425 in 2018/2019. However, the $\text{GATE}_{\text{petroleum rents}}$ program whilst being horizontally efficient, was vertically inefficient, and prompted wastage as the rich were funded beyond what they needed.

As the "bust" phase of the petroleum cycle set into the economy after 2015 the state intervened and changed its funding adopting a $\text{GATE}_{\text{recession}}$ program requiring students in the income group $10,000–$29,999 to pay 25% of their fees and those from households with an income level above $30,000 to pay 50% of their fees. However, by the time this intervention was made in 2017/18 the market was:

- Partially saturated in general with TLE graduates, as reflected in the fact that the number of students with TLE that were unemployed, escalated from 1100 in 2001/02 to 6113 in 2018/19 and
- The economy contracted so that by the end of 2020, the economy was 15% smaller than in 2015.

Against this setting, this section argued that it is best to eschew the entire GATE program and implement an income contingent loan program so that all benefitting students with an income above a particular level, pay for their tertiary level education upon graduating and finding an appropriate job.

9.9 Make Work Programs

This section focuses on the government "Make Work" program (The Community-Based Environmental Protection and Enhancement Programme) CEPEP and outlines aspects of the economic wastage associated with the program. Rent dispersion programs of this nature compromise the economy's long-run growth potential through a number of channels including the build-up of debt and limiting capital formation. Indeed, by syphoning labour off to sectors with very low levels of economic growth it slows the overall growth of GDP and stunts the process of structural reform. Further, individuals benefitting from the rents tend to resist the economic reform as it lowers their scope for rent seeking. This section traces the history of Make Work Programs in T&T and investigates the impact of the rent dispersion strategy, the CEPEP, on the economic growth performance of the T&T economy. The analysis compares economic output at the Rybczynski point of production associated with the natural gas boom (which occurred from 1999 to 2015) with the output level associated with the implementation of Make Work projects. The section demonstrates that on account of Make Work programs, the T&T economy experiences an approximate reduction in nominal GDP of TT$1.365 bn (2016). The section also traces the extent of underemployment in the Make Work sector, in comparison to other segments of the T&T economy.

Trinidad and Tobago have a long history with Public Work programs but the available data is at best patchy and very poorly documented and reliance has to be placed on snippets of information from Budget Speeches and newspaper clippings. The first special works program in Trinidad and Tobago was the Prime Minister's special work program of the 1950s (see Table 9.7 which provides basic summary data). This was followed by the Development Environmental Works Program (DEWD) of the 1960s. In 1988 the state introduced the Labour-Intensive Development Program (LIDP), the objective of which was to provide short-term opportunities to vulnerable individuals in Trinidad and Tobago. Although LIDP was a replacement for the DEWD program, it maintained the same type of work pattern as the DEWD. The URP program replaced the LIDP program but was very much of the same genre. The newest round of the Public Work programs in Trinidad and Tobago is the Community Environmental Protection Enhancement Programme (CEPEP). This program was started in 2002 whilst the Unemployment Relief Programme (URP) was started in 1992.

Cumulative expenditures on CEPEP by 2019 totaled in excess of TT$6.5 bn. Note that the program was introduced at a time when the economy was experiencing strong economic growth and the unemployment rate on its own accord was on its downward pathway. Specifically, the unemployment rate at the start of the sod turning for Atlantic 1 was 16.3% in 1996. By 2002 when the Make Work program started the unemployment rate had already declined to 10.4%. On account of the coming on stream of 3 more LNG trains and the associated economic activity, the unemployment rate tumbled to 6.2% by 2006. On its own momentum

Table 9.7 Legacy of public work programmes in Trinidad and Tobago

Program	*When started*	*Attributes*
Prime Minister's special work program	1950s	Objective: to provide short-term employment opportunities to vulnerable people in Trinidad and Tobago and to curb the gang warfare in Port of Spain Activities: maintenance works (cleaning roads, cutting grass)
Developmental environmental works division (DEWD)	1960s	Objective: to provide work for persons with limited skills Activities: maintenance works (cleaning roads, cutting grass) The program received widespread public criticism based on wastage of resources, ghost gangs and the negative impact on worker productivity
Labour-intensive development programme (LIDP)	1988	Objective: to provide short-term employment opportunities to vulnerable people in Trinidad and Tobago LIDP replaced DEWD in terms of title but generally targeted the same cohort of persons as in DEWD and continued to face the same economic challenges as regards efficiency
Unemployment relief program (URP)	1992	Objective: to provide short-term employment opportunities to vulnerable people in Trinidad and Tobago. The program seeks to reduce poverty, crime, high unemployment levels Activities: The upgrade of physical and social infrastructure Target population: unemployed nationals of Trinidad and Tobago seeking short-term employment opportunities The LIDP was essentially rebranded and continues to be criticized as a tool of political convenience

(continued)

Table 9.7 (continued)

Program	*When started*	*Attributes*
CEPEP	2002	Objectives: to provide environmental protection, enhancement, and beautification of environmental work areas (EWAs) Activities: provide employment opportunities to nationals in the areas of: environmental maintenance; coastal maintenance; wetlands maintenance; disaster and emergency response (DERT); dead animal removal (DART); waste removal Target population: nationals of Trinidad and Tobago seeking short-term employment opportunities. The original conceptualization of the program was that the intervention was targeted especially to single mothers Program is run in an environment where URP already exists and has been criticized for being a tool of political convenience and even more so for negatively impacting on worker ethic and productivity

Source Own compilation from newspaper clippings

the market was addressing the unemployment concerns in the economy and so the Make Work program, except for the extremely vulnerable in society, was not needed! Alternatively said, CEPEP came exactly at a point in time when the free market was addressing the needs of the labour market.

9.9.1 Public Work Programs and Surplus Labour

Public work programs can compromise the overall real output level in those economies in which they exist, by reducing the stock of workers for other more productive activities, in other sectors. If this is the case and if the output per worker in the Public Work sector of the economy is less than in other sectors of the economy (e.g. manufacturing), then it is possible that the real output of the economy as a whole could be compromised. Further, if some entrepreneurs pursue rents rather than pursue Schumpeterian innovation, then this can also compromise output levels of the economy.

Karl (2007) has argued that patronage programs exist in many primary exporting economies, but it is likely worst in oil-based economies because of the political systems which distribute rents through a system of patronage. For example, in 2011, there were a series of protests in Oman. The people of Oman demanded a lowered cost of living, jobs and a reduction in corruption. In response to such protests the government created 50,000 jobs in the public sector and increased the wages of public servants (Darke and Walsh 2017). Saudi Arabia also experienced protests in 2011. Subsequently, the government announced a US$10.7 billion social welfare package including new jobs and other handouts (The Wharton School of the University of Pennsylvania 2011).

The type of entrepreneurs mentioned by Schumpeter[8] and the type of entrepreneurs that are interested in rent seeking activity may be simplistically summarized by Eq. 9.1.

$$E_t = RSE_t + PE_t \tag{9.1}$$

RSE: rent seeking entrepreneurs,

PE: Profit (Schumpeterian) entrepreneurs,

E: Total stock of entrepreneurs.

Clearly as RSE increases, the stock of PE in any time period falls. The challenges for an economy occur when the returns to RSE supersedes PE, as in this setting, entrepreneurs may rationally choose RSE above PE. In this paper, we suggest oil rents can trigger such a change in the context of relatively weak institutions and this is one of the devastating side attributes of entrepreneurial rent seeking, i.e. it can lead to the dissipation of the economy's rents. This occurs when the entrepreneur "hires" a lobbyist to pursue contracts associated with the rents and in so doing

[8] According to Schumpeter (1965), entrepreneurs are "individuals who exploit market opportunity through technical and/or organizational innovation". He noted that entrepreneurs enjoy "the gale of creative destruction" to replace in whole or in part inferior innovations across markets and industries and in so doing, creating new products and new business models.

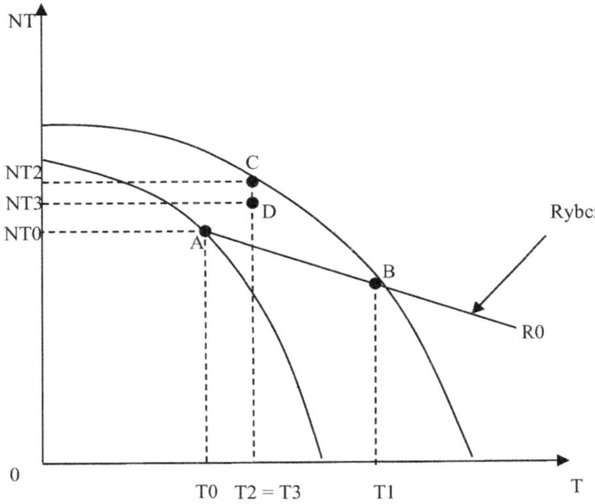

Fig. 9.4 Impact of public work program on economic growth

reduces monopoly profits.[9] Entrepreneurial rent seeking of any magnitude thus reduces the extent of competitive production and innovation in an economy.[10]

To elaborate on the influence of the CEPEP program in the Trinidad and Tobago economy consider Fig. 9.4. The rapid increase in the production of natural gas in the Trinidad and Tobago economy between 1999 and 2016 pushed its production possibilities curve outwards.[11] Specifically, assume that in 1999 the economy produced T_0 units of tradable goods (consisting of BT_0 units of the booming tradable good and NBT_0

[9] It is well known in the literature that monopoly profits in turn help to support the cost of innovation.

[10] One source notes that when "talented people become entrepreneurs, they improve the technology of the line of business they pursue, and as a result productivity and income grow. In contrast, when they become rent seekers, most of their private returns comes from redistribution of wealth from others and not from wealth creation" (p. 505) (Murphy et al. 1991).

[11] Natural gas output increased in Trinidad and Tobago from 72.1 mn barrels of oil equivalent in 1999 to 300.2 mn barrels of oil equivalent in 2010 although by 2020 it subsided to 228.7 mn barrels of oil equivalent.

units of the NBT good and NT_0 units of the NT good). With a natural gas resource boom, the associated economic forces working through a Rybczynski effect push the economy to the point B which is associated with a higher level of tradable output T_1. Note that the BT good is assumed to be natural gas intensive. Thus:

$$T_0 = NBT_0 + BT_0$$

$$T_1 = NBT_1 + BT_1$$

But $NBT_1 < NBT_0$, because of the resource movement effect associated with the boom and for the same reasons $BT_1 > BT_0$.

If the state at B intervenes and introduces Public Work programs in the economy of the nature of CEPEP, then the economy's composition of output changes and hence the value of output produced, can change. Let us consider such a point to be C. Note that at C the combination of goods produced is T_2, NT_2.

$$T_2 = NBT_2 + BT_2$$

But $NBT_2 < NBT_1$ ($< NBT_0$) on account of the spending effect associated with a boom.[12]

$BT_2 \cong BT_1$ ($> BT_0$) on the assumption that the spending effect only marginally impacts on the BT sector.

At C in a petroleum-based economy, workers can develop a compromised work ethic on the basis that some kind of work is entitled to them, from the state. In this regard and from a historical perspective, note that, Public Work programs as mentioned previously in Trinidad and Tobago started in the 1950s and because of their adverse impact on worker ethic and productivity (Ryan 2015, p. 32) noted "If it cannot be argued that Williams[13] was responsible for crippling black enterprise, it can nevertheless be said that he contributed greatly to its demise in the period after 1970 by pampering blacks with patronage and various make-work activities, thereby removing what was left of the incentive to work." Ryan

[12] This refers to the impact on the flow of labour when the government, which receives the majority of the resource rents in a developing economy and workers in the BT sector, spend the energy sector rents. The state is therefore the main conduit between the enclave energy sector and the rest of the economy.

[13] Dr. Eric Williams was the first Prime Minister of Trinidad and Tobago.

went on to note that "Helped along by the seasons of great wealth generated from energy resources, the all-pervasive state quickly morphed into a centre for distribution of the oil-generated national patrimony rather than an agency for development. The net effect of the make-work program was negative on the work ethic. If according to Williams 'Massa Day Done,' Williams was seen as the new political 'Massa' whose historic role was to 'run something' to the sons and daughters of the former slaves. They wanted him to distribute their 'grandfather's backpay.' His emphasis was therefore on consumption and distribution rather than on production' (Ryan 2015, p. 32).

To provide some basic corroboration of this point, Table 9.8 shows

Table 9.8 Most problematic factors for doing business in Trinidad and Tobago, 2006/2007, 2010 and 2013

Most problematic 2006–2007		*Most problematic 2010*		*Most problematic 2018*		*2020*
Crime and theft	21.7	Crime and theft	18.3	Poor work ethic in the national labour force	15.9	
Insufficient government bureaucracy	13.7	Poor work ethic in the national labour force	17.6	Insufficient government bureaucracy	3.3	
Corruption	13.02	Corruption	11.7	Corruption	12.2	
Poor work ethic in the national labour force	11.28	Insufficient government bureaucracy	10.9	Foreign currency regulations	11.4	
Inadequate supply of infrastructure	9.55	Access to financing	8.4	Crime and theft	7.1	
Inadequately educated workforce	6.34	Inadequate supply of infrastructure	7.4	Access to financing	5	
Access to financing	5.3	Inflation	6.8	Insufficient capacity to innovate	4.7	
Inflation	2.21	Inadequately educated workforce	4.9	Inadequately educated workforce	3.6	
Restrictive labour regulations	3.39	Tax rates	2.6	Inadequate supply of infrastructure	3.2	

Source Global competitiveness index (various years)

the most problematic areas of business in Trinidad and Tobago for 2006, 2010 and 2018, drawn from the Global Competitiveness Report. The clear indication is that with the passing of time, worker ethic in Trinidad and Tobago according to the results of this survey, became worst.

A compromised work ethic pushes the economy from C to D. Note at D, we have the combination of output being T3 (T3 = T2), NT3. At D, the economy produces more BT good than at A and relatively the same amount as at B and C (see Table 9.9). The NBT sector good, however, is produced in a smaller way at D, than at B or A. This reflects both the direct deindustrialization of the economy from A to B and the indirect deindustrialization of the economy from B to C. The NT sector with a Rybczynski effect would be smaller at B, as compared to A. At C, the NT sector is larger than at A or B, as the Rybczynski effect on the NT sector, is countered by the spending effect of the Dutch Disease. If import consumption has inertia and given that income falls from C to D, then the average propensity to import will rise. At C, imports increase as the economy produces less NBT sector goods, some proportion of which is presumably imported (at C, per capita GDP is higher

Table 9.9 The possible impact of public work programs on output, employment, the non-energy CAB and the fiscal balance

Output				
	A	*B*	*C*	*D*
Tradeable	T_0	T1	T2	T3
BT	BT_0	↑	≡	≡
NBT	NBT_0	↓	↓	≡
NT	NT_0	↓	↑	↓
Make work	0	0	↑	↓
Employment				
BT	BT_L^0	↑	≡	≡
NBT	NBT_L^0	↓	↓	≡
NT	NT_L^0	↓	↑	↓
MW	MW_L^0	0	↑	≡
Underemployment	0	0	0	↑
Non energy current account balance (CAB) and fiscal balance (FB) impact				
Non-energy CAB	0	↑	≡	↓
FB	0	↑	↓	↓

than at A). Note that an increase in the economy's per capita GDP with decreasing manufacturing and export agricultural sectors (these are both part of the NBT sector) as well as a rising domestic inflation rate (as the NT sector overheats) and hence appreciating real effective exchange rate, spurs a rise in import expenditure and the non-energy current account balance, consequently deteriorates. The fiscal account can also worsen as the government amongst other things, incurs a budgetary cost to implement these Public Work programs and also lose tax revenues on account of the fall in the output of non-tradable goods, that occurs between C and D.

9.9.2 A Closer Look at the Economy at C and D and the Effects of Public Work Programs

The economy at C.

Patronage programs can compromise the value of the economy's output if the average productivity of workers in the Public Work program, is less than in the tradable sector (in this case, specifically the NBT sector). These patronage programs keep the economy at full employment, but the change in the structure of output can compromise the value of GDP. To see the effect on GDP, it is possible to proceed as follows:

$$GDP_t = VA_t^m + VA_t^{ps} + VA_c^o$$

where VA: value added.

m: manufacturing (used as a proxy for the NBT sector).

ps: personal services (where Public Work programs such as CEPEP in Trinidad and Tobago are recorded in terms of value added).[14]

o: other value adding sectors

$$GDP_t = L_t^m l_t^m + L_t^{ps} l_t^{ps} + L_t^o l_t^o$$

L_{it}: employment in sector i in the time period t and

[14] National Income statistics in Trinidad and Tobago are produced in 2 substantive forms: Trinidad and Tobago Standard National Accounts (TTSNA) and Trinidad and Tobago Standard International Trade classification (TTSIC). Under the TTSNA format the CEPEP program is counted under the classification "personal and other services." In this study, TTSNA data was used, as labour force data in the Continuous Sampling Survey of the Population (CSSP) is also produced by the same industrial sector classifications.

λ_t^i: output per worker in sector i, in time period t.

In an economy with a Public Work Program, unfortunately, some of the workers from the manufacturing sector are lured away by higher effective wages and lower worker efforts required in the Public Work. In this regard, a Public Work program induced level of economic activity can be represented as:

$$GDP_t^* = L_t^{m*} l_t^m + L_t^{ps*} l_t^{ps} + L_t^o l_t^o \tag{9.2}$$

(For simplicity, the fall in the number of workers in the manufacturing sector is assumed to not affect output per worker, in that sector).
Let

$$L_t^{m*} = L_t^m - L_t^{pw} \tag{9.3}$$

and

$$L^{ps*} = L_t^{ps} + L_t^{pw} \tag{9.4}$$

L_t^{pw}: employment in the Public work sector.
where L_t^{m*} and L_t^{ps*} are the levels of employment in the manufacturing and personal services sector, at point C, respectively. Substituting (9.3) and (9.4) into (9.2) yields,

$$GDP_t^* = (L_t^m - L_t^{pw}) l_t^m + (L_t^{ps} + L_t^{pw}) l_t^{ps} + L_t^o l_t^o$$

$$GDP_t^* = L_t^m l_t^m - L_t^{pw} l_t^m + L_t^{ps} l_t^{ps} + L_t^{pw} l_t^{ps} + L_t^o l_t^o$$

$$GDP_t^* = GDP_t - L_t^{pw} (l_t^m - l_t^{ps})$$

$$DGDP_t = L_t^{pw} l_t^{ps} - L_t^{pw} l_t^m \tag{9.5}$$

< 0 providing $\lambda_t^{ps} < \lambda_t^m$.

The economy at D.

To investigate the underemployment effects of the movement from C to D let us assume we can divide a 40-h week into j groups. For example, in the Continuous Sampling Survey of the Population (CSSP) the data on employed workers are collected by the following hourly worker groupings; 0 hours, 1–8 hours, 9–16 hours, 7–12 hours, 25–32 hours and

33–40 hours and 41 and over hours. In this regard, the total number of underemployed hours (U) can be determined as follows:

If there are n sectors, in the economy and each sector has U_i underemployed hours then:

$$U_h^* = U_1 + U_2 \ldots U_n \tag{9.6}$$

where U_h^* is the total number of underemployed hours in the n sectors of the economy.

Note that,

$$U_1 = U_{11}h_1 + U_{12}h_2 + \ \ldots U_{1j}h_j \tag{9.7}$$

where Eq. 9.7 indicates the number of unemployed hours by hourly worker groupings. Thus, $U_{11}h_1$ would be the number of workers in sector 1 that were underemployed for h_1 hours, U_{12} would be the number of workers in sector 1 that were underemployed for h_2 hours, and so on.

The total number of hours overall unemployed in the economy is the sum of the underemployed hours in the economy plus the number of unemployed hours on account of the number of people unemployed. Cumulatively this can be represented by:

$$U_{hours} = U_h + U_h^* \tag{9.9}$$

where U_h is the number of people unemployed times a 40-hour work week and U_h^* (the number of hours of work lost by the underemployed per week).

Where for simplicity Uh is the number of people unemployed times a 40-hour work week and U*h (the number of hours of work lost by the underemployed per week).

To estimate the welfare loss of moving from B to C, we can proceed as follows. Table 9.10 shows that GDP in Trinidad and Tobago increased from TT$38.1 bn in 1998 but surged to TT$175.3 bn in 2008, as the petroleum industry rents permeated the economy in various ways. As oil prices, gas prices and oil production and then gas production fell, GDP declined to TT$145.9 bn in 2016. In terms of employment, total employment in Trinidad and Tobago rose from 479,313 in 1998 to 636,850 in 2014 but thereafter declined to 613,200 in 2016. For the manufacturing sector, employment in 2004 was 57,100 or 15.1% more than in 1998.

Table 9.10 Output per worker in various sectors of the Trinidad and Tobago economy, 1998–2016

	TT$mn GDP		*Employment*					
	GDP	*Manufacturing*	*Personal and other services (includes CEPEP)*	*Other GDP*	*Total employment*	*Manufacturing*	*Personal and other services (includes CEPEP)*	*Other employment*
1998	38,065.1	3479.1	765.4	33,820.6	479,313	49,595	73,918	355,800
1999	42,889.1	3437.2	789.1	38,662.8	489,351	51,196	78,325	359,830
2000	51,370.6	3625.4	810	46,935.2	503,334	53,800	76,400	373,134
2001	55,007.2	4074.4	869.1	50,063.7	514,126	51,600	74,400	388,126
2002	56,290	4494.1	901.9	50,894	525,081	53,900	72,700	398,481
2003	71,169	4945.5	1108	65,115.5	534,153	53,600	77,000	403,553
2004	83,652.5	6250.2	1122.2	76,280.1	562,378	57,100	85,500	419,778
2005	100,682	5523	1092.2	94,066.8	574,025	54,000	84,600	435,425
2006	115,951	6444	1283.3	108,223.7	586,205	54,205	82,000	450,000
2007	136,952	7216.8	1447.4	128,287.8	587,892	53,000	82,400	452,492
2008	175,287	7042.6	1480.6	166,763.8	597,700	50,500	83,100	464,100
2009	121,281	6973.9	1634.3	112,672.8	588,300	49,900	87,700	450,700
2010	141,268	8503.1	1599.5	131,165.4	582,200	47,200	87,500	447,500
2011	163,008	9219.3	1921.2	151,867.5	585,346	49,400	91,400	444,546
2012	165,203	8884.2	2035.6	154,283.2	614,050	49,200	94,200	470,650
2013	170,318	10,122.4	2431.6	157,764	626,287	48,100	94,600	483,587
2014	167,764	8979.7	2565.8	156,218.5	636,850	48,100	94,200	494,550
2015	150,247	8549	2636.2	139,061.8	623,300	48,800	93,500	478,600
2016p	145,911	8288.8	2709.9	134,912.3	613,200	48,900	94,200	475,100

Source CBTT online database and the CSO's continuous sampling survey of the population (various years)

Table 9.11 Actual GDP and adjusted GDP current prices, TT$mn

	Other GDP	*Manufacturing*	*Personal services/Other services*	*GDP (TT$mn)*
2016	134,912.3	8288.8	2709.9	145,911.4
GDP new with labour reshuffling (current prices)				
2016	134,912.3	9957.2	2426.7	147,276.3
Change				1365.9

By 2016, however, employment in the manufacturing sector tumbled to 48,900. Thus, the manufacturing sector lost 8200 workers between 2004 and 2016.

As mentioned previously, CEPEP was introduced in 2002 at which point in time the number of people employed in all of Trinidad and Tobago was 525,081 and in the personal services/other services sector, the number of people employed was 72,700. Partly on account of the coming on stream of CEPEP, employment in the personal services sector escalated by 30.6% to reach 94,200 in 2016. By contrast in the national economy, the number of persons employed increased to 618,200 an increase of 17.7%. Surplus labour in the personal services/other services sector is here measured as the difference between actual employment in the personal services/other services sector less the number of people that would have been employed in this same sector, if its employment had grown at the same pace, as national employment.

On this basis the Personal Services/other services sector was found to have over 9000 surplus workers (9072 to be exact but treated here as 9000).

For simplicity, if these 9000 workers were transferred into the manufacturing sector as unskilled workers then the level of employment in the manufacturing sector would have increased to 58,000 which is similar to the level of employment in 2004, i.e. if the sector was not deindustrialized.[15] The top part of the Table 9.11 shows nominal GDP for 2016 from the CSO. The second part of the table shows GDP, assuming that the manufacturing sector employment increased by 9000 and the Personal Services/Other Services category decreased by 9000. The result of this

[15] According to the Trinidad and Tobago Manufacturing Association president, the main constraint now facing local manufacturers is a shortage of workers; he was quoted as saying "this is impacting negatively on our ability to expand our businesses"

adjusted GDP simulation is an increase in national GDP by TT$1.365 bn. The T&T economy cannot afford these welfare losses.

9.10 Underemployment Costs from C to D

Table 9.12 shows the number of employed hours by industrial group as data from the CSSP for underemployment was not available by industrial sector. Proceeding on this basis, Table 9.12 illustrates that the greater proportion of underemployment hours occurs in the community, social and personal services (CSP) sector where the Public Work program is counted. In 2016, the underemployment rate in CSP was 11.1% as compared to the national average of 8.6%. Note that the CSP sector accounted for approximately 43.92% of the underemployed hours for all Trinidad and Tobago in 2016 as compared 38.54% in 2002, when CEPEP started.

In 2016, the minimum wage in T&T was TT$15.00. The total lost value in terms of underemployed hours for the year in 2016 totalled to TT$1820.8 mn. Of this number TT$798 mn is attributable to underemployment in the CSP sector. The T&T economy experienced negative economic growth in the period 2016–2020 and can ill afford this type of wastage.

9.11 Conclusion

This chapter focused on rent dispersion and the importance of a stronger HSF formulation, the funding of TLE (with the suggestion of an Income Contingent loan as an option) and Make Work programs (to assess the size of the welfare losses). The chapter concludes that the HSF has to be strengthened so that even at very low oil and gas prices, this country saves part of its energy revenues, if not all. The Hand to Mouth strategy of consuming all of the energy revenues simply cannot work and indeed it has placed the country in a very uncomfortable position of having no economic growth since 2008 although the country produced 4 bn barrels of oil and gas equivalent and now has to straddle a huge debt of TT$135 bn.

An effort was made to invest some of the economic rents into tertiary level education, but the funding strategy was vertically inefficient and even the newer funding permutations are not fit for purpose given the contraction of GDP per capita in the T&T economy, in recent times. This

Table 9.12 Aspects of the underemployment situation in Trinidad and Tobago, 2001–2015

	% of work week lost because of underemployment by sector			*National Unemployment rate (%)*	*% share of underemployment by listed sector in total underemployment*	
	Trinidad and Tobago	*Manufacturing*	*Community social and personal services*		*Manufacturing*	*% share of underemployed hours of the community social and personal services sector*
2002	11.1	9.18	14.59	10.4	8.56	35.54
2016	8.6	5.3	11.10	3.8	5.8	43.92

Source CSSP (various years)

chapter recommended an income contingent loan as a strategy to reduce the extent of vertical inefficiency in the funding strategy and to eventually make students more responsible for their tertiary level education, given that it has properties of a private good.

The final section of the chapter examined the welfare loss to the country of the Make Work program, CEPEP. These losses are large and the maturation of the country's oil sector and the associated decline in its energy revenues makes it increasingly difficult to carry these types of welfare losses. The state should take heed and disband this program except for the most poor and vulnerable.

References

Akitoby, B., and Coorey, S. (2012). "Oil Wealth in Central Africa: Policies for Inclusive Growth." Washington, DC: IMF.

Chapman, B. (2016). "Income Contingent Loans in Higher Education Financing." Canberra, Australia: Crawford School of Public Policy.

Collier, P., van der Ploeg, R., Spence, M., and Venables, T. (2010). "Managing Resource Revenues in Developing Economies," IMF Staff Papers, 57, 84–118.

Darke, D., and Walsh, T. (2017). "Oman. Bradt Travel Guides."

Hezemans, Marijke, and Ritzen, Magda. (2004). "Communities of Practice in Higher Education. International Federation for Information Processing Digital Library; Information and Communication Technologies and Real-Life Learning."

Karl, T.L. (2007). "Oil-Led Development: Social, Political, and Economic Consequences." CDDRL Working Papers, 80, ss36 p.

Ministry of Science, Technology and Tertiary level Education. (2003). "Dollar for Dollar. Government of Trinidad and Tobago."

Mpofu, John, Chimhenga, Sylod, and Mafa, Onias. (2013). "Funding Higher Education in Zimbabwe: Experience, Challenges and Opportunities of the Cadetship Scheme." London: Palgrave Macmillan. https://doi.org/10.1057/9781137345783_13.

Murphy, Kevin M., Andrei Shleifer, and Robert W. Vishny. (1991). "The Allocation of Talent: Implications for Growth," Quarterly Journal of Economics, Vol. 106, pp. 503–30.

Ryan, Selwyn. (2015). "Black Entrepreneurship in Post-Independence Trinidad and Tobago: The Eric Williams Legacy."

Schumpeter, A. Joseph. (1965). Economic Theory and Entrepreneurial History. In: Aitken HG (ed) Explorations in enterprise. Harvard University Press, Cambridge, MA.

The Energy Chamber of Trinidad and Tobago. (2019). Retrieved from https://energynow.tt/blog/a-future-for-oil-in-tampt.

CHAPTER 10

Policy Interventions to Boost Competitiveness of the NBT Sector

10.1 Introduction

As indicated previously the production of crude oil has been on the decline in Trinidad and Tobago since 1978, except for a brief spike in 2005. Natural gas production has been falling since 2010 and whilst it did increase in 2016 and 2017 it has gradually commenced decreasing once again. As will be emphasized in this chapter and Chapter 11, the world is also moving increasingly away from non-renewable energy towards renewable energy. These facts combined, provide a powerful case for the T&T economy to invigorate its NBT sector which has not been doing very well. Specifically, exports excluding minerals decreased from TT$38.6bn in 2015 to TT$28.6bn in 2019.

This chapter outlines various policy measures to boost the NBT component of the Trinidad and Tobago economy. This is critical for the long-term economic stability of the T&T economy as regards economic growth, foreign exchange earnings and in the context of oil being a sunset commodity. In this regard the rest of this chapter outlines various policy suggestions which can help to improve the competitiveness of the local business environment. Some of the policy suggestions considered are:

1. Devaluing the currency to improve external competitiveness,
2. Improving the Ease of Doing Business setting,
3. Building on the "Rybczynski" gains from Venezuelan migrants,

R. Hosein, *Oil and Gas in Trinidad and Tobago*,
https://doi.org/10.1007/978-3-030-77669-5_10

4. Deepening trading ties with more natural trading partners,
5. Integrating the eTecK parks within a PPP dynamic,
6. Other enabling environmental changes.

10.2 Devaluing the Currency?

In 2020 the real effective exchange rate (REER) of the T&T economy was 81.2% higher than in 1999, when LNG production started. An appreciation of an economy's REER compromises the external competitiveness of its non-energy exports and policy makers would have to make deliberate attempts to improve the same.

To glean a basic idea of the extent of a nominal devaluation required to correct the T&T exchange rate, a reference can be made to the relative purchasing power parity information in the Table 10.1.

If we normalize and let 2000 be the base year, then by 2020 the RPI in T&T in relation to the USA's RPI was 1.9 times as high. To maintain relative purchasing power parity, it would mean that in 2020 the TT dollar would have to devalue to TT$11.8 per US$. The TT government has in recent times approached the overvalued exchange rate in T&T by focusing on an internal devaluation of cutting government expenditures and keeping the inflation rate low but without adequately stimulating the non-energy export component of the economy, to the extent that the real GDP contracted 17% between 2015 and 2020. The IMF 2018 used the EBA-Lite REER regression and found a REER gap of 42.1%. The IMF also used the Information Notice System (INS) and found a 21% appreciation of the REER between 2010 and the end of March 2018.

Policy makers have to be careful here though as Wilson and Mc Clean (2014), did not find support for the Marshall Lerner condition, in T&T. Even so it is here noted that the results on the ML condition should be carefully interpreted as services exports are not properly captured. Although T&T is not as dependent on services as other countries in the region our services exports have great potential for growth. With a devaluation the wage rate in T&T, other things constant, would drop and so would the price of these export services. Devaluation would help in some respect to boost the sale of our export services particularly to the rest of the region. It would also encourage more investment in areas such as hotels, export education and health services and professional services. T&T has a high level of human capital which gives it a distinct advantage in this region. It has a manufacturing sector which has allowed it

Table 10.1 Assessing the extent of overvaluation of the TT currency

	TT inflation (%)	*US inflation (%)*	*TT RPI (2000 = 100)*	*US RPI (2000 = 100)*	*Official exchange rate (LCU per US$, period average)*	*Relative PPP 2000 base year*
2000	3.6	3.4	100.0	100.0	6.3	
2001	5.5	2.8	105.5	102.8	6.3	6.5
2002	4.2	1.6	109.9	104.5	6.2	6.6
2003	3.8	2.3	114.1	106.8	6.2	6.7
2004	3.7	2.7	118.4	109.7	6.3	6.8
2005	6.9	3.4	126.5	113.4	6.3	7.0
2006	8.3	3.2	137.0	117.1	6.3	7.4
2007	7.9	2.9	147.8	120.4	6.3	7.7
2008	12.0	3.8	165.6	125.0	6.3	8.3
2009	7.0	−0.4	177.2	124.6	6.3	9.0
2010	10.5	1.6	195.9	126.6	6.30	9.7
2011	5.1	3.2	205.9	130.6	6.40	9.9
2012	9.3	2.1	224.9	133.3	6.40	10.6
2013	5.2	1.5	236.6	135.3	6.40	11.0
2014	5.7	1.6	250.1	137.5	6.40	11.5
2015	4.7	0.1	261.8	137.6	6.40	12.0
2016	3.1	1.3	269.8	139.4	6.70	12.2
2017	1.9	2.1	274.9	142.3	6.72	12.2
2018	1.0	2.4	277.6	145.8	6.73	12.0
2019	0.7	2.1	279.6	148.9	6.73	11.8
2020p	1.2	2.2	282.9	152.2	6.73	11.7

Source WDI online database and own additions

to acquire a wide range of technical skills not available in the rest of the region. Lower wages through devaluation should further stimulate that demand.

10.3 Improving the EODB Environment

The Doing Business annual report outlines the regulations that enhance business activity and those that constrain it in 190 countries. Sub-categories of the EODB index include starting a business, dealing with construction permits, getting electricity, registering property, getting credit, protecting minority investors, paying taxes, trading across borders, enforcing contracts, resolving insolvency and labour market regulation.

Doing Business has been used in thousands of articles published in peer-reviewed journals and informed debates about regulatory and institutional frameworks for economic development. Furthermore, Doing Business indicators indicate the ideal business climate to drive inclusive, sustainable economic growth (Klapper and Love [2010]; Djankov et al. [2002] and Ani [2015]).

T&T's EODB ranking has been worsening over the last few years, declining from a rank of 63rd in 2012 to a rank of 105th in 2020 (See Fig. 10.1 below).

In terms of the performance of the T&T economy on each of the associated pillars of the doing business index. Consider the Table 10.2 which shows that the economy's ranking on 8 of the 10 pillars worsened between 2014 and 2020. Specifically, T&T's (rank) performance deteriorated in terms of starting a business, dealing with construction permits, getting electricity, getting credit, protecting minority investors, paying taxes and trading across borders. These trends indicate that the business environment has become less facilitative of commerce and has effectively represented a deterrent to local businesspersons.

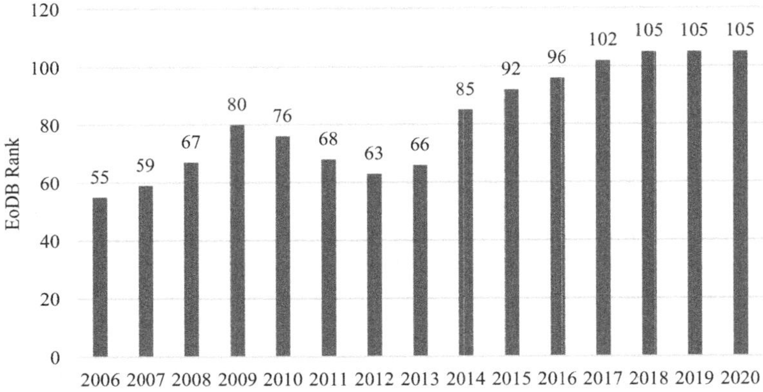

Fig. 10.1 T&T's EoDB Rank 2006–2020

Table 10.2 Pillars of the doing business index, 2014, 2020

	2014	*2020*	*Change in Rank*
Starting a business	67	79	−12
Dealing with construction permits	77	126	−49
Getting electricity	10	43	−33
Registering property	178	158	−20
Getting credit	28	67	−39
Protecting minority investors	22	57	−35
Paying taxes	97	160	−63
Trading across borders	73	134	−61
Enforcing contracts	174	174	-
Resolving insolvency	114	83	+ 31

Source Doing Business Report

10.4 Lessons Learned from Other Developing Economies

In the Fig. 10.2 below, the scatterplot shows that there is a negative relationship between the manufacturing sector as a proportion of GDP and the doing business rank. This implies that the higher the rank of an economy on the doing business index, the smaller is the relative size of the manufacturing sector. This observation implies that the lower the performance of an economy in terms of its doing business environment, the smaller would be its productive sectors.

Coincident with the increase in the EODB ranking in 9 of these countries was an increase in the size of the share of the manufacturing sector's value added in total GDP (the exception was Kenya). In 9 of the 10 listed economies, the relative size of the manufacturing sector to GDP expanded over the short period 2014–2019[1] (the exception was Kenya, in which the share declined marginally). In terms of the share of manufacturing and exports as a percentage of total exports, this increased in five of the top ten ranked developing countries except (those which declined were Mauritius, Thailand, Kazakstan, Maldova and Kenya) (Table 10.3).

[1] Note that data on GDP-related indicators, available for the selected economies is available up to 2019 only.

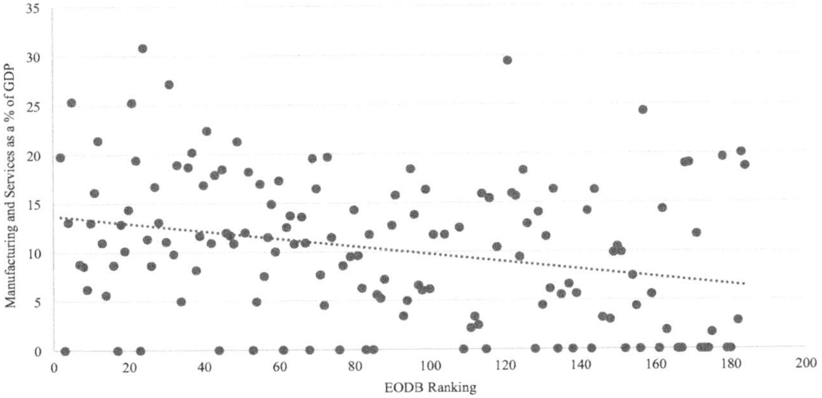

Fig. 10.2 Manufacturing as a % of GDP (2020)

10.4.1 Interventions for Consideration by T&T Policy Makers

From the discussions above, a list of possible interventions is proposed below for consideration by local policy makers to improve the doing business index (Table 10.4).

Improving these pillars of doing business can improve the overall ranking of the T&T economy over the short to medium-term period. What is needed however is a clear strategy, with SMART[3] objectives by which these improvements are to be measured and monitored to ensure that timelines and targets are being met.

[3] The acronym SMART—Specific, Measurable, Attainable, Relevant and Timely.

Table 10.3 Measures taken by selected developing economies to improve overall doing business rank, 2014–2020

Mauritius	• Simplified the process of plan approvals from utilities • Reduced the time to apply for wastewater connection • Made property registration faster • Made enforcing contracts easier by publishing performance measurement reports for the commercial division of the Supreme Court • Made resolving insolvency easier by improving the continuation of the debtor's business during insolvency proceedings
Macedonia	• Made dealing with construction permits easier by reducing the time required to register a new building and by authorizing the municipality to register the building on behalf of the owner • Made getting electricity easier by reducing the time required to obtain a new connection and by setting fixed connection fees per kilowatt (kW) for connections requiring a capacity below 400 kW • Made property registration faster and less costly by digitizing their real estate cadastre and eliminating the requirement for an encumbrance certificate • Strengthened its secured transactions system by providing more flexibility on the description of assets in a collateral agreement and on the types of debts and obligations that can be secured • Made paying taxes easier for companies by encouraging the use of electronic filing and payment systems for corporate income and value
Thailand	• Abolished a requirement to obtain a company's seal and eliminated the need for the approval of company work regulations from the Labour Department • Introduced an automatic risk-based system for selecting companies for a tax audit; reduced the property transfer tax rate • Adopted legislation to broaden the scope of assets that can be used as collateral • Use geographic information systems for access to electricity • Additional simplification of system for paying taxes

(continued)

Table 10.3 (continued)

Kazakhstan	• Implemented legislation to foster the development of the private sector • Implemented bolder reforms to support trade • Reduced time to start a business from 9 to 5 days • Trading across borders was made easier by introducing an electronic customs declaration system, as well as reducing customs administrative fees • Enforcing contracts was made easier by making judgments rendered at all levels in commercial cases publicly available and publishing performance measurement reports on local commercial courts
Azerbaijan	• Authorities leveraged digital technology and modern processes to reform how business is done • Streamlined electronic customs procedures implementations for faster cross-border trade • The Government implemented measures to support SME sector and to increase their participation in global value chains • The country has transformed into an important international transportation hub with its 6 functioning international airports and the biggest air cargo terminal in the region
Rwanda	• Exempting newly formed SMEs from paying the trading licence tax for their first two years of operations • Reduced the time to obtain water and sewage connections • Improved building quality control by requiring all construction professionals to obtain liability insurance on buildings which are in use • Improved reliability of power supply by upgrading power grid infrastructure and claims procedure • Reduced registering property to 7 days, 3 procedures and just 0.1% of property value
Serbia	• Implemented reforms to applications for construction permits • Improvements in business regulations • Reform of systems for trading across borders and paying taxes • Improvements to property registration systems

Armenia	• Strengthened construction quality control by imposing stricter qualification requirements for architects and engineers • Strengthened minority investor protections by requiring an independent review and immediate disclosure to the public of related party transactions, increasing shareholders' rights and role in major corporate decisions and clarifying ownership and control structures • Made paying taxes easier by extending value added tax cash refunds to cases of capital investment • Made exporting faster by allowing the online submission of customs declarations
Moldova	• Rationalized application for construction permits, where 18 out of 28 procedures were excluded • Implementation of a performance-based system which made authorities more accountable for implementing reforms
Kenya	• Introduced a Companies Act in 2015. This Act eliminated the requirement to have registration documents notarized before the Commissioner of Oaths, which reduced the procedural complexity and time for starting a business • In 2016 the stamp duty on the memorandum and articles of association and the statement of nominal capital was abolished • The Ministry of Land, Housing and Urban Development in Kenya made its service charter available online in 2016, which led to increasing transparency in registering property by giving clients access to critical information about the transactions they undertook at the Lands Offices • The establishment of an electronic construction permit platform to expedite the process of obtaining a construction permit • Introduced a Huduma Kenya Program, which has opened one-stop shops in 10 of the 11 counties in the country. The Huduma Centres offer a myriad of services, some of which facilitate local company registration and property transfers • Reduced the number of interactions with government for starting a business from 11 to just 3 simplified steps. This was supported by legal amendments, collapsing of some procedures into simplified ones as well as cost reductions

Table 10.4 Considerations for improving doing business pillars for T&T[2]

Pillar	*Recommendations for T&T*	*Expected outcome in T&T*
Starting a business	1. Establish a working committee in the Ministry of Labour Small and Medium-Sized Enterprises to address challenges faced by the business sector. Set performance standards and benchmarks regarding progress and performance 2. Organize regular meetings with members of the private sector (business associations) 3. Develop a country partnership framework in consultation with counterparts and civil society to guide investments and any quality technical assistance to the Government 4. Rationalize processes for starting a business—review steps required and eliminate unnecessary administrative requirements	1. Enhanced collaboration between public and private sector on specific industry relevant recommendations 2. Improves information flow between the private sector and Government Ministries

[2] Some of the interventions proposed in the National Budget 2021 related to an Electronic Funds Transfer Window to allow all payments to Government agencies such as taxes and custom duties to be done remotely. Plans were also announced to improve the efficiency of the Customs and Excise Division by modernizing, upgrading and automating procedures to reduce the time and cost associated with the import and export of goods. It was also suggested that National Trade Facilitation Committee be established. The budget also highlighted that plans were being proposed to reduce the time for obtaining approvals from state agencies to undertake construction.

Pillar	*Recommendations for T&T*	*Expected outcome in T&T*
Dealing with construction permits	1. Enable applications to be done via virtual system confirmed via e-mail 2. Rationalize the flow of information between arms of government, e.g. town and country planning and EMA to reduce processing time	1. Reduction in the time to obtain construction permits 2. Crowding in of private sector investment for construction projects
Getting electricity	1. Introduce an energy sector strategy plan (to include renewable energy opportunities) 2. To adopt environmental and social legislation 3. Establish a single hub to address client applications and provide timely feedback to applicants	1. Reduced time to access electricity for commercial purposes
Registering Property	1. Reduce the registration fee 2. Improve the quality of land administration system by publishing official service standards and court statistics on land disputes 3. Update all relevant land and property-related legislation 4. Improve efficiency in transferring property between agents	1. Reduced time for property registration 2. Quick turn over in terms of transferring property titles

(continued)

Table 10.4 (continued)

Pillar	*Recommendations for T&T*	*Expected outcome in T&T*
Getting Credit	1. Encourage state-owned financial institutions to develop products for non-energy sector 2. Encourage private sector f 3. Financial institutions to develop products for the non-energy sector 4. Offer guarantees to the Exim Bank to encourage non-energy investments and exports	1. Increased access to financial assets by the non-energy sector to expand production and exports
Protecting Minority Investors	1. Establish and enforce regulations to protect minority shareholders 2. Require an independent review and immediate disclosure to the public of related party transactions 3. Educate minority shareholders about their voting rights and obligations	1. Increase private sector appetite for commercial investments 2. Increased participation of private sector in PPPs
Paying Taxes	1. Fast track the Revenue Authority 2. Rationalize paying taxes (and obtaining tax returns) 3. Improve the VAT Returns system for businesses 4. Introduce incentives for capital accumulation for the purposes of increasing non-energy exports	1. Improved efficiency of tax system

Pillar	*Recommendations for T&T*	*Expected outcome in T&T*
Trading across Borders	1. Improve logistics at the various ports of entry 2. Improve capacity of customs divisions/departments: Rationalize customs systems: create a single hub to access trade related services 3. Undertake capacity building for small and medium sized firms on "how to export" 4. Encourage financial institutions to offer facilities to assist in trade logistics costs	1. Reduced time and costs associated with trading across borders 2. Increased amount of trade
Enforcing Contracts	1. To establish a specialized commercial division in its supreme court Reduce legal fees, filing and service times	1. Improved legal systems resulting in increased efficiency in enforcing contracts
Resolving Insolvency	1. Strengthen insolvency laws 2. Rationalize insolvency processes	1. Improved outcomes as regards insolvency sub ranking

Source Compiled from country cases

10.5 Building on the "Rybczynski" Gains from Venezuelan Migrants

To correct the overvalued exchange rate the T&T government has partially gone the route of an internal devaluation. In 2015, total government expenditure was TT$62.4bn but this was managed downwards to TT$52bn in fiscal year 2019/20 to TT$54.3bn. In tandem, the inflation rate in the economy fell to 0.9% in 2019, the lowest since 1973. But internal devaluations tend to work very slowly. Mackenzie (2012) indicated that internal devaluations tend to only be successful against the backdrop of higher inflation elsewhere and a substantial shift in relative prices via wage or price compression is doubtful. Pettinger (2019) stated internal devaluation relies on deflationary policies to reduce prices by reducing aggregate demand as opposed to a devaluation which can restore competitiveness without reducing aggregate demand. In this regard, it is here recommended that the government of T&T seize upon the opportunities presented from the inflow of Venezuelans that have landed onto its shores in recent times.

Table 10.5 shows a comparative sketch of the relationship between a devaluation of the TT dollar on a few key variables on the same and the impact of 20,000 Venezuelan unskilled workers added to the workforce. The simplistic assumption here is that these immigrants are all working. It is noted that 16,523 immigrants have been registered with the Ministry of Foreign Affairs and it is assumed that the difference in the Ministry's number and that of the UNHCR (40,000), refers to those that have not registered i.e. are in T&T, illegally.

A currency devaluation means that the price of the domestic good in the foreign market in US dollar term decreases and in so doing increases export sales whilst the price of the imported good in the T&T market rises, thereby decreasing imports expenditure. Additionally, wages can rise over time. The Current Account Balance (CAB) improves if over time there is a sharp enough adjustment in tastes, external competitiveness improves, and firm profitability and domestic investment is expected to increase, especially in the non-energy export sector.

As unskilled labourers entering the T&T market, output of goods produced by Venezuelans increase and wages in the sector employing these workers can fall. Furthermore, there is an improvement in the CAB, increased output volumes and decrease import volumes if sectoral work permits are issued in favour of exportables. These changes can improve

Table 10.5 Comparative assessment of a devaluation versus the contribution of 45,000 Venezuelans

	Devaluation	*Effects of 45,000 Venezuelans as "unskilled labourers"*
Output	Output of the exported good increases, imports of the imported good decreases	Output of the goods intensively produced by Venezuelans increase
Prices	The price of the domestic good in the foreign market in US dollar terms, falls. The price of the imported good in the T&T market, in TT dollar terms rises	Prices of the goods intensively produced by the Venezuelans decrease and the prices of the goods consumed by the Venezuelans increase
Wages	Can follow prices and rise over time. Hinges in part on the strength of the unions	Wages in the sector with abundance of Venezuelan workers can fall and trigger a downward levelling of wages. If this occurs, it is like a depreciation
Current Account Balance	The current account balance improves if the Marshall Lerner conditions hold	The current account balance depends on state-led policy. If sectoral work permits increase the output from the export sector and decrease imports, then the economy's current account balance can possibly improve
External Competitiveness	Improves as the price of domestic goods to foreign consumers, improves	Improves if the economy's cost of production falls. This seems to be occurring. In the past a labourer in T&T asked for around TT$300 per day in the construction sector. A Venezuelan worker now works for TT$200 and some cases TT$150 per day
Export Volume	Increases	Depends on the sectoral labour market strategy. If the workers are not part of the export sector, then export revenues will not increase

(continued)

Table 10.5 (continued)

	Devaluation	*Effects of 45,000 Venezuelans as "unskilled labourers"*
Import Volume	Decreases	Increases as at the same exchange rate most of the additional goods consumed by the Venezuelans would be imported
Firm Profitability	Those in the export sector are likely to benefit more than firms in the import sector	Firms that employ the Venezuelans at a lower wage to T&T nationals, will benefit
Domestic Investment	Can increase particularly in the non-energy export sector	Will increase in those areas that absorb the Venezuelans workers

the economy's external competitiveness due to a decline in the cost of production, increase firm profitability and domestic investment levels in areas where immigrant labour is employed.

If the inflow of Venezuelans is complemented by an appropriate domestic labour market policy, there can be an increase in investments and so output of the T&T economy as a whole can improve. If this output increase is in non-energy export-oriented areas of production, then the economy will overall benefit, as the current account balance can also improve.

The comments in the Table 10.5 are apart from the productivity benefits that can emerge because of an improved worker ethic associated with workers that are "hungry". There will also be distinct benefits to the labour force participation rate (LFPR) which is currently on a downward pathway. Indeed, the state should be thinking ahead as to how to motivate the LFPR from 58.7% in 2018 to 72% (the pre-COVID 19 level of The Bahamas economy), within the next 5 years and should be actively designing a guest worker program for the economy.

10.5.1 *More Widespread Use of Spanish to Help Promote Trade with Spanish Speaking Neighbours*

From a trade perspective, effective communication requires that the exporting and importing firm have a certain amount of proficiency in the same language. It is possible to estimate the probability that two randomly selected individuals from the HC and the PC can communicate in a language, L, as the product of the proficiency rate in the HC and the FC.

Column A of the Table 10.6 shows the probability that someone from the listed country can communicate in English. Thus, 6.5% of the people in Argentina can speak English. Crystal (2003) indicated that 87.7% of the population in T&T can speak English (Fidrmuc et al. in another setting explain that immigrants and or minorities do not possess adequate linguistic skills in the host country language). In this regard column B shows the probability that a randomly chosen person from T&T and from the listed bilateral trade partners can communicate in English. Thus, for T&T and Argentina, the probability that two randomly chosen people, one from either country, can communicate in English, is 0.0572. Grau-Perejoan and Gea-Monera (2018) indicate that 5% of the population in T&T can speak Spanish. In this regard, column D shows the probability that two randomly chosen people from T&T and the listed country can communicate in Spanish. For example, with Argentina, this value is 0.049.

Table 10.6 Probabilities associated with someone from T&T and the listed countries can communicate in English or in Spanish

Period 2000–2015	*Partner Countries Proficiency Rate for English (Author compiled various sources) (A)*	*Probability that T&T and the PC communicates in English (B)*	*Partner Countries Proficiency Rate for Spanish (Author compiled various sources) (C)*	*Probability that T&T and the PC communicates in Spanish (D)*
Argentina	0.065	0.057	0.981	0.049
Chile	0.095	0.084	0.959	0.048
Colombia	0.042	0.037	0.989	0.049
Costa Rica	0.082	0.072	0.992	0.050
Dominican Republic	0.015	0.013	0.976	0.049

In the past, the T&T government in preparation for an era of greater trade with Spanish speaking countries, adopted Spanish as an official second language. Indeed in 2005, the then Trade and Industry Minister, Ken Valley outlined five initiatives to facilitate the integration of T&T with those of Latin America when he addressed the "Remapping the Americas" (FTAA) Conference at UWI, St. Augustine. One of the five initiatives was the push for Spanish to become T&T's first foreign language. The strategy of the government at that time, was for T&T to become an effective intermediary between the Spanish speaking countries of the South and Central America and the English-speaking countries of the North.

To facilitate a greater degree of Spanish being spoken by T&T nationals the government of T&T formed the Secretariat for the Implementation of Spanish (SIS) on September 9, 2004 and it was formally launched on March 22, 2005. This Unit was specially created to drive Spanish as the First Foreign language (SAFFL) initiative in T&T.

In November 2016 as a continuation of the efforts of the government of T&T to improve the country's Spanish speaking proficiency, the government accepted an offer from the Republic of Colombia to provide Spanish as a foreign language course for public servants from T&T. The course was for a five-month period and started on the 7 November 2016.

The push to increase the proportion of the T&T population that communicates in Spanish must be accelerated in T&T.

10.5.2 Change in GDP

From another angle the Table 10.7 shows the real non-energy GDP of T&T that was realized for 2019 and then the level of real non-energy GDP assuming the gainful employment of a conservative 20,000 immigrant Venezuelan workers. The first column of the Table 10.7 shows the

Table 10.7 Various non-energy GDP sector (TT$bn) permutations based on different allocations of Venezuelan labour

	Non-energy GDP with Labour Market Strategy deploying Venes	*Non-energy non-man sector with "ad hoc" labour market strategy*
2019	120.7	116.6

GDP when the 20,000 immigrants are allocated in accordance with a guest worker program: 10,000 to manufacturing, 5000 to agriculture and 5000 to services.

The 2nd column shows the level of GDP if the 20,000 Venezuelan migrants are allowed to work "wherever" they find work in the non-energy and non-manufacturing sectors of the economy. When the guest worker program is compared with the ad hoc allocation, there is a difference in GDP of about TT$4bn, this is golden, given the current state of the T&T economy.

So, in many regards the discussion boils down to whether we can design an appropriate guest worker program. Can we?

10.5.3 *Impact on LFPR, Ageing Population and Increasing Dependency*

According to the Table 10.8, the number of young people in Trinidad and Tobago less than 19 years was 527,400 in 1987 but by 2019 this had declined to 381,900. The number of people 60 years and over in 1987 was 97,400 but by 2019 this had accelerated to 182,500. The ratio of over 60 to under 19 population was therefore 18.5% in 1987. By 2019 this ratio climbed to 47.8%. In the context of the rapidly ageing population, the labour force participation rate tumbled and by 2019 stood at 58.1%, or more than five percentage points less than in 2019.

The addition of 20,000 able bodied Venezuelan workers to the labour force in Trinidad and Tobago would help to improve on the ratio of over

Table 10.8 Various aspects of the labour force in T&T, various years

	Both sexes 19 years and younger 000s	*60 years and over (000s)—RHS*	*Ratio over 60 to under 19 population*	*Labour force participation rate %*
1987	527.4	97.4	18.5	59.8
1990	485.4	99.1	20.4	55.9
1995	487.1	109.6	22.5	60.2
2000	458.4	126.5	27.6	61.2
2005	470.1	129.7	27.6	63.7
2010	478.5	132.0	27.6	62.1
2015	377.9	175.6	46.5	60.6
2019p	381.9	182.5	47.8	58.1

60 to under 19 population by extension it would also help to improve the labour force participation rate. This would help to push the production capabilities of the T&T economy, outward.

10.6 Making Use of Our Trade Agreements

10.6.1 Establishing and Trading with the Economy's Natural Trading Partner

In the Fig. 10.3 below the oval shows the year in which the bilateral agreement was signed and the percentage share of T&T imports and exports which the indicated bilateral partner accounted for in 2017. Thus, for Costa Rica the regional trade agreement between CARICOM and Costa Rica was signed in 2005 and in 2017, Trinidad and Tobago imported 0.7% of its total imports from Costa Rica. Furthermore, exports from T&T to Costa Rica was a mere 0.1% of Trinidad and the Tobago's total exports in 2017.

T&T also has partial scope trade agreements with Panama (October 2013) and Guatemala (February 2015) and the Dominican Republic. This chapter proposes that instead of engaging in trade agreements and underutilizing them that Trinidad and Tobago adopt a two-pronged approach in the future when forming trading agreements. The first part

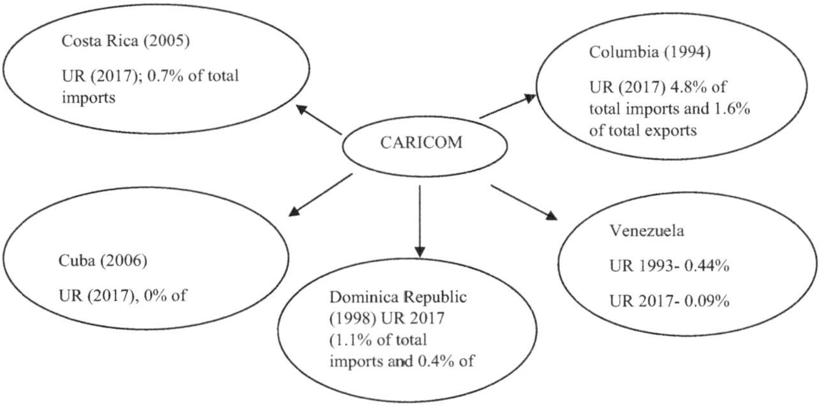

Fig. 10.3 The Utilization Rate (UR) of T&T with some of the signed CARICOM Bilateral Trade Agreements

of this two-pronged approach involves using TradeCan analysis to identify rising stars and missed opportunities associated with T&T's exports to these various markets and T&T's imports from these various markets. TradeCan is an analytical tool developed by UNECLAC to evaluate the competitiveness profile of a country's merchandise exports. Specifically, the tool maps the changing demand levels in an economy in a partner country with exports of the home country. Based on changes between a base year and a final year, export sectors are deemed to be either rising stars, missed opportunities, declining stars or retreats.

- A rising star reflects export areas that are dynamic products, and which are gaining market share.
- A missed opportunity is reflective of areas that have lost market share in dynamic products.
- Declining stars are reflective of areas that are gaining market share in stagnant export areas.
- Retreat areas reflect decreasing market share for stagnant export areas.

The second part involves researchers at the Ministry of Trade, researching the associated rising stars and missed opportunities to determine in which aspect of the 6-digit classification of possibilities, the T&T economy holds comparative advantage. By way of elaboration, the Table 10.9 shows the "Missed opportunity areas" of the T&T economy with CARICOM in which the T&T economy has either weak, medium or strong comparative advantage.

This type of approach should be formalized by an appropriate entity e.g. the Ministry of Trade (or the Chamber of Industry and Commerce) and circulated on a bi-annual basis to the Trinidad and Tobago Manufacturers Association (TTMA) and like entities in the T&T economy, so that local entrepreneurs can consider and assess which options best fit their entrepreneurial interest.

T&T would also want to consider deeper ties with countries such as China and India. In 1960, China accounted for a mere 1.13% of World GDP (at constant prices) whilst India accounted for 1.31%. By 2018, China accounted for 13% of World GDP and India 3.44%. These two economies are expected to continue to grow rapidly over the next two

Table 10.9 "Missed opportunity" areas which current have a RCA for T&T's export market to CARICOM countries

RCA Category	*RCA Score*	*SITC Rv-3 5 Digit Code*	*Description*
Weak RCA	1.153656	84,562	Spray-guns and similar appliances
	1.242548	5459	Other vegetables, fresh or chilled
	1.574334	65,215	Other pile and chenille fabrics, woven, of cotton (other than terry toweling or similar terry fabrics of headings 652.12 and 652.13 and subgroup 656.1)
	1.627557	84,521	Dishwashing machines (other than household-type)
	1.888818	65,839	Blankets and travelling-rugs (other than electric) of other materials
Medium RCA	2.030507	59,227	Glues based on starches, or on dextrins or other modified starches
	2.66208	1612	Bellies (streaky) and cuts thereof of Bacon, ham and other salted, dried or smoked meat of swine
	2.802007	84,692	Other gloves, mittens and mitts
	3.116062	66,339	Ceramic articles, n.e.s
	3.936405	64,293	Trays, dishes, plates, cups and the like, of paper or paperboard
Strong RCA	4.949655	67,912	Line pipe of a kind used for oil or gas pipelines, of iron (other than cast iron) or steel
	5.211319	89,721	Imitation Jewellery of base metal, whether or not plated with precious metal
	5.63682	4815	Germ of cereals, whole, rolled, flaked or ground
	6.340041	4811	Prepared foods obtained by the swelling or roasting of cereals or cereal products and from unroasted cereal flakes or from mixtures of unroasted and roasted cereal flakes or swelled cereals
	6.963052	7111	Coffee, not roasted, not decaffeinated
	7.562703	4849	Other Bread, pastry, cakes, biscuits and other bakers' wares, whether or not containing cocoa in any proportion; communion wafers, empty cachets of a kind suitable for pharmaceutical use, sealing wafers, rice-paper and similar products

(continued)

Table 10.9 (continued)

RCA Category	*RCA Score*	*SITC Rv-3 5 Digit Code*	*Description*
	7.735744	3418	Other fish, fresh or chilled (excluding livers and roes) Fish, fresh (live or dead) or chilled (excluding fillets and minced fish
	7.783457	5456	Cucumbers and gherkins, fresh or chilled
	8.908701	4842	Sweet biscuits, waffles and wafers, gingerbread and the like
	9.008604	5677	Sweet corn prepared or preserved otherwise than by vinegar or acetic acid
	10.07111	9891	Pasta, cooked or stuffed; couscous, whether or not prepared
	10.33887	9844	Vinegar and substitutes for vinegar obtained from acetic acid
	10.84013	5995	Juice of any other single fruit or vegetable
	11.0319	11,211	Grape must in fermentation or with fermentation arrested otherwise than by the addition of alcohol
	11.78125	2213	Cream of a fat content, by weight, exceeding 6% Milk (including skimmed milk) and cream, not concentrated or sweetened
	17.27475	69,919	Other mountings, fittings and similar articles; base metal hat racks, hat-pegs, brackets and similar fixtures; automatic door closer
	18.04815	68,231	Copper bars, rods and profiles of copper alloys
	18.51841	89,729	Imitation Jewelry of other non-precious materials

decades (Of course the approach would need sound scientific research to assess the possibilities in these economies that align with these strengths).

10.7 ETECK Parks

In 1959 the Industrial Development Corporation (IDC) was formed to stimulate industrial growth. Following that, in 1984 the Economic Development Corporation (EDC) was formed to develop policies for the non-oil and gas sectors. In 1988 the Tourism Development Authority

(TDC) was established to promote and formulate industries and by extension, the development and maintenance of the tourism sector. In 1995, the IDC and TDC joined to form the Tourism Industrial Development Company. In 1997 the Property Industrial Development Company of Trinidad and Tobago (PIDCOTT) was formed as a subsidiary of TIDCO which eventually became an independent entity in 2003 and was renamed the Enterprise Development Company Limited (eTecK) in 2004.

EtecK is in alignment with the Ministry of Trade and Industry's attempt to aid the diversification process "to drive the non-energy sectors for the sustainable long-term growth and development of diversified and knowledge-based economy that contributes to the creation of high quality jobs."

The general activities of the eteck parks include light manufacturing, manufacturing of cotton products, ceramic, sanitary ware, pharmaceutical items, food processing, crockery, construction and maintenance of marine craft, production of industrial materials and gas, automobile radiators, vinyl, engineering works, maintenance of industrial equipment, agro-processing, assembly of automobile components, vehicle maintenance, garment, Science and Technology, ICT, Business Services, Clean technologies, aluminium, paints, furniture, steel fabrication, manufacturing of paper, manufacturing foam, industrial chemicals, metal fabrication, cosmetics, lumber treatment, etc.

It is the opinion of this research effort that the E-Teck Parks in Trinidad and Tobago require a different structure and approach in order to help the economic transformation process in the economy. In the first instance the ETeCK Parks must be guided by an understanding of TradeCAN analysis in the sense that the Ministry of Trade should be involved by assessing the partial scope agreements and various trade agreements with CARICOM. The E-Teck Parks should be aligned with these trading agreements in the sense that firms in T&T should be encouraged to target the production of goods to these partial scope agreements that have increasing demand and in which the T&T economy has a comparative advantage.

Indeed, the government of T&T should closely examine the example of Singapore and its BioPolis industrial complex. Biopolis in Singapore is a custom-built biomedical research and development hub which started in 2001 for biomedical research to promote collaboration between private companies and public scientific and educational bodies on a five-phase basis and was completed in 2015. It was also noted that Biopolis is situated in close proximity to the National University of Singapore, the Institute of Technical Education, Singapore Polytechnic, National University Hospital, Singapore Science Park, Ministry of Education and Fusionopolis. The Agency for Science Technology and Research (2019) indicated that Singapore's Biopolis was opened to undertake the development areas such as research and development (R&D), manufacturing and healthcare. Furthermore, within a decade the company established a reputation as a world-class biomedical research hub.

La Lima Free Zone and Business Park (2019) started operations in December 2014 in Cartago, Costa Rica. The industrial park is a 79 hectares multipurpose complex for companies in advanced manufacturing, life sciences, logistics, supply and services sectors. La Lima offers industrial lots to build facilities that can range from 5000 m2 up to 20,000 m2, multitenant building with modules from 1500 m2 to 1800 m2 and leasing space to services companies ranging from 750 m2 to 3000 m2 per floor. The Park offers renewable energy, provides potable water through the Municipality and high-quality telecommunications.

Trinidad and Tobago would need to carefully study the experience of these other industrial parks and note the learnings. Similarly Costa Rica has Medical Manufacturing Industrial Parks and it is here suggested that policy makers in T&T would need to work with the University of the West Indies and the Ministry of Trade via foresighting to assess the right type of theme- based ETeCK Parks that are required to attract FDI in T&T.

10.8 Other Enabling Environmental Changes

10.8.1 Fiscal Responsibility Legislation (FRL) and a Fiscal Council

The government of T&T has to consider implementing Fiscal Responsibility Legislation (FRL). FRL is a strong legal framework that outlines for an economy fiscal policy reporting guidelines and rules. The IMF supports FRL because it makes it difficult to reverse decision-making without legislative backing. Trinidad and Tobago can benefit considerably from FRL as it will boost accountability, stability, and sustainability.

In terms of accountability of the executive to the legislature, FRL would require that the state be transparent in terms of executing on their fiscal responsibility. Transparency and accountability in FRL would require that the state be explicit about its fiscal plans and include a medium-term fiscal policy strategy and an annual budget strategy in its fiscal balance.

In terms of stability, FRL would require the government to publicize key objectives of its fiscal balance and public debt program. It would also include a targeted timeline which is recommended to be short run in nature, although rigid targets are not mandatory, but a clear statement on the medium-term fiscal objectives will be required. Strengthening FRL also involves strengthening the policies that could improve fiscal outcomes and fiscal discipline. In this regard, it mandates the government to commit to targeted macroeconomic objectives and strategies. Improving stability will reflect on improving clarity and the reliability, as well as timeliness of public fiscal reporting.

The sustainability aspect involves strengthening the agreed policies towards fiscal outcomes and fiscal discipline. FRL already exists in Grenada, Jamaica, and the Bahamas. Some considerations as targets for Trinidad and Tobago is to:

- restrict debt levels to 80% of GDP (this helps to cater for some of the spillover economic problems from Covid-19).
- to establish a fiscal council which has independent members and
- the government be required to have two-thirds majority in Parliament to change the legislation once it is in place.

FRL, when appropriately designed, reduces the probability that countries would engage in unsustainable budget deficits. FRL can also be designed in a way that in times of national emergencies such as natural disasters and pandemics, the budgetary and fiscal situation can be eased.

Fiscal Responsibility Laws provide the necessary teeth for fiscal rules. Table 10.10 provides some possible fiscal rules for T&T.

As part of the process of introducing FRL, the government of T&T should consider introducing a Fiscal Council, similar to that in Grenada, Jamaica and The Bahamas. Fiscal Councils are a complement to fiscal rules. They provide a monitoring authority that could help to monitor complex rules. For example, if a target was not achieved, it is difficult to mandate a reaction from a political directorate and so there will be weak incentives to achieve targets. A Fiscal Council in this kind of situation can play a crucial role in assessing the extent of the deviation from the targets and whether these deviations were caused by economic shocks or

Table 10.10 Outline of possible fiscal rules for T&T

Expenditure Rule	*Debt Rule*	*Other aspects*
Increase in expenditure must not exceed the projected 2 years non-energy GDP growth. 2 years ensures that the advantages of planning and forecasting in the medium term is captured Interest from HSF to help fund investment in non—energy sector	Restrict debt levels to 80% of GDP and with the intention of reducing it to 60% of GDP within 5 years of passing the legislation	Establish a Fiscal Council Introduce Fiscal Responsibility Legislation Well specified Escape Clauses allow for the temporary suspension of fiscal rules in the event of rare events. Clear guidelines on the determination of these events are important. Recommended events to be approved by the respective parliaments are: Natural Disasters (found in Brazil, Jamaica and Panama) Economic Recession Significant growth slowdown and of course, health pandemics

by government fiscal policies. A Fiscal Council can also play the role of recommending corrective actions and setting reasonable deadlines.

A Fiscal Council also acts as an impartial agency which helps to scrutinize fiscal policy. The existence of a Fiscal Council can act as a signal to the population, that the government is serious about fiscal rules. A Fiscal Council can also be used to maximize or increase social welfare by assisting voters and by encouraging elected officials to select budget deficits which are closer to the social optimum and the Council also ensures that policy makers run fiscal deficits, which are at a minimum.

10.8.2 Economic Development Board (EDB)

Trinidad and Tobago need to strongly consider re-establishing an EDB. The Board should have no more than ten (10) members from different professions with the chairperson being a Development Planner. The Board should have an independent budget where possible and operate autonomously and independently of the state. An EDB can have a positive impact on growth and development of Trinidad and Tobago and help to provide a strong institutional base for ideas to reverse the adverse effects of the resource curse and the Dutch Disease. The mandate of the EDB must be to facilitate the building of a strong economy with an adequate buffer of foreign exchange and one that is economically resilient and respects the principles of sustainable development. A properly functioning Economic Development Board can provide consultative and advisory support guidelines to the government in terms of what the medium-term framework and the steps to help achieve defined targets.

10.9 Specialized Economic Zones (SEZ)

In T&T there are two types of specialized economic zones currently in operation, light industrial parks and free zones. The light industrial parks fall under the responsibility of the ETecK program. There are 18 firms currently involved in the operation of the free zone enterprises and 11 of these 18 firms are single user enterprises, whilst the remaining 7 are in a free zone park or multi-user facility. As it stands the T&T government is making efforts to move towards a Specialized Economic Zones Policy in T&T.

This policy is geared towards modernizing the economy's existing economic/free zone regime, in terms of mechanisms and procedures for management, which will have the benefit of improving the backward and forward linkages amongst firms which use the zone. This can increase the social and economic impact of such spaces. Further the modernization of these zones can attract more international attention and encourage global firms to become more participative in the local market. It is recommended that this SEZ policy be legislated and activated for outcomes.

10.10 Public Procurement

An important part of the economy and public spending involves public procurement. Public procurement can demonstrate the level of government efficiency. Efficiency and integrity in public procurement is an essential steppingstone and helps citizens maintain trust in government. Indeed, governments from around the world are recognizing the potential importance of procurement to improve public sector productivity. Through savings and through economies of scale an efficient public procurement process can help reduce the fiscal deficit in a country. Public procurement can also be used as a strategic policy, to help attain the socio-economic and environmental objectives of the state.

No doubt, savings in money, time and surveillance from an improved public procurement process can be diverted to strengthening the economy's non-energy export infrastructural base.

10.11 The CSO and Evidence-Based Policy Making in T&T

The idea of "evidence-based policy making" has gained ascendency in the global economy. Policy decisions in the increasingly complex global economy should be informed by careful analysis using data that is sound and transparent. Evidence-based policy making must be the way forward for all economies in making decisions to recognize issues of national importance and in so doing to formulate important solutions.

In this regard, a vibrant Central Statistical Office (CSO) producing timely and reliable data is central to the planning process in this economy. One of the flagship publications by the CSO in my judgement is the Labour Force Report which uses data from the Continuous Sample Survey of the Population (CSSP). The CSSP provides a bloc of valuable data on the Trinidad and Tobago economy. It is designed as a multipurpose household survey (it started in 1963) and has as its objective to provide up to date data on the labour force characteristics of Trinidad and Tobago on a continuous basis.

The CSSP's survey design experienced several revisions with the latest revision being in 1994. The data in the CSSP is based on a stratified cluster design and covers data on the labour force by:

- Age
- Administrative area
- Gender
- Employment status
- Educational attainment
- Occupational group
- Industrial group
- Industrial sector
- Type of worker.

Data from the CSSP is also available on persons with jobs and unemployed persons, new entrance into the labour force and according to people by income group. The last CSSP bloc of data was in 2016 (This makes it really difficult to line up an understanding of the structural changes that took place in the economy during the depression and it is something that the government of T&T will need to address moving forward).

Successive governments of T&T have acknowledged the need to restructure the CSO to enable it to recapture its position as the premier statistical office in the Caribbean. Several studies, stakeholder consultations, meetings, committees, and reports have culminated in the decision to replace the CSO with the National Statistical Institute of Trinidad and Tobago (NSITT). It is anticipated that the NSITT will address the legislative, organizational structure, staffing and IT deficiencies of the current organization. The expectation is that the new organization will be resilient and dynamic enough to meet the changing needs of data users. It is imperative that the NSITT Bill that has been languishing before the Joint Select Committee (JSC) for over a year be sent back to Parliament. Further, both the current government and the opposition need to put their individual agendas aside and put country first to ensure the passage of the NSITT Bill both in the Upper and Lower Houses. Data is the key to development. Evidence-based decision-making by the government and business people cannot be made without sound and accurate data. Investors cannot invest in our economy without data. Rating agencies cannot report on our economy without data. A well-functioning, funded, independent statistical office is the hallmark of a forward-thinking economy.

10.12 Conclusion

This chapter focused on various policy interventions to help strengthen the T&T's economy's non-energy export sector. This is critical particularly as the primary export revenue (energy) earning sector weakens and becomes more sunset. The considerations mentioned include devaluing the currency (it was mentioned that two studies have found that the Marshall Lerner condition does not hold in TT), improving the EODB setting, enhancing the business environment by lowering the crime rate, deepening the country's trading ties with its more "natural trading partners", making wiser use of immigrant labour flows and pursuing ETecK Parks for the realization of more non-energy exports.

Several other enabling environment changes were suggested including the need for Fiscal Responsibility Legislation and a Fiscal Council, the formation of an Economic Development Board and the need for Specialized Economic Zones, alongside the formation of the NSITT.

Without doubt, T&T economy has deep structural problems. The cracks are growing, and the policy interventions must be strong and properly engineered. Ever present in the design of each intervention should be the need to stimulate non-energy exports, given the sunset nature of the crude oil sector. It simply cannot remain, business as usual.

References

Ani, T.G. (2015). "Effect of Ease of Doing Business to Economic Growth Among Selected Countries in Asia." Asia Pacific Journal of Multidisciplinary Research 3 (5): 139–145.

Crystal, D. (2003). "English as a Global Language (1st ed.)." Cambridge, UK: Cambridge University Press.

Djankov, S., La Porta, R., Lope-de-Silanes, F., and Shleifer, A. (2002). "The Regulation of Entry." The Quarterly Journal of Economics 117 (1): 1–37.

Grau-Perejoan, M., and Gea-Monera, M. (2018). "El Español en Trinidad y Tobago".

Klapper, L., and Love, I. (2010). "The Impact of Business Environment Reforms on New Firm Registration." World Bank Policy Research Working Paper 5493.

Mackenzie, K. (2012). Finacial Times. Retrieved from We'll Settle This Internal Devaluation Question Quicker Than We Thought. https://www.ft.com/content/7c326fa4-9d07-3327-a0df-8c5e070479eb.

Pettinger, Tejvan. (2019). "Inflation and Exchange Rates." Economics Help. Accessed April 14, 2019. https://www.economicshelp.org/blog/1605/economics/higher-inflation-andexchange-rates/.

Wilson, S.-A., and Mclean, E. (2014), "Understanding the Impact of exchange rate adjustment on the trade balance of selected Caribbean countries", (Working Paper Series).

CHAPTER 11

Benefitting from Existing Comparative Advantage: Maximizing Economic Rents

11.1 Introduction

A basic tenet of international trade theory is that economies should specialize in those commodities in which they have an abundance of factors of production and import those commodities that call for factor proportions in the opposite direction. Previous chapters illustrated the economic significance of the petroleum sector in T&T and there is good wisdom in maximizing the returns from this sector to sow elsewhere, preferably into areas with productive activity built around the development of reproducible capital (this is the Hartwick rule mentioned in previous chapters). In this regard, a twofold strategy is emphasized here: (a) maximizing the current rents from the energy sector (BT) this is elaborated in this chapter, whilst simultaneously trying to strengthen the non-energy sector (NBT and NT) this is emphasized in the next chapter. In this regard, the rest of this chapter focuses on several avenues that may be pursued by stakeholders in the T&T economy to maximize economic rents within the petroleum sector. This chapter will expand on the opportunities available by arguing in favour of policy makers strengthening the following areas:

1. Promoting even more deepwater exploration
2. Secondary and tertiary oil recovery
3. Restarting the Petroleum refinery under private sector ownership

R. Hosein, *Oil and Gas in Trinidad and Tobago*,
https://doi.org/10.1007/978-3-030-77669-5_11

4. Exploring all cross-Border Gas fields
5. Local content opportunities
6. Farm out/lease out program should be widened
7. LNG transfer pricing
8. T&T's educational supply infrastructure for energy sector workers.

11.2 Promoting Even More Deepwater Exploration

In a recent statement the MEEA noted that "*in house estimates for deep water oilpotential range from a low 3.1 billion to a high 8.2 billion barrels of OIP.*" In this regard, note that BHP Billiton a multinational oil company, has completed a seismic survey over 20,199 square kilometres offshore T&T.

However, continuing these deepwater exploration exercises is critical for the long-term survival of the economy's hydrocarbon sector. In order to push the deep-water prospects, the Trinidad and Tobago government needs to:

a) engage in more regular bid rounds and offer acreage to firms engaged in exploration activity (Fig. 11.1 shows that in recent times, there has been a decline in the average awarded acreage and in drilling activity),

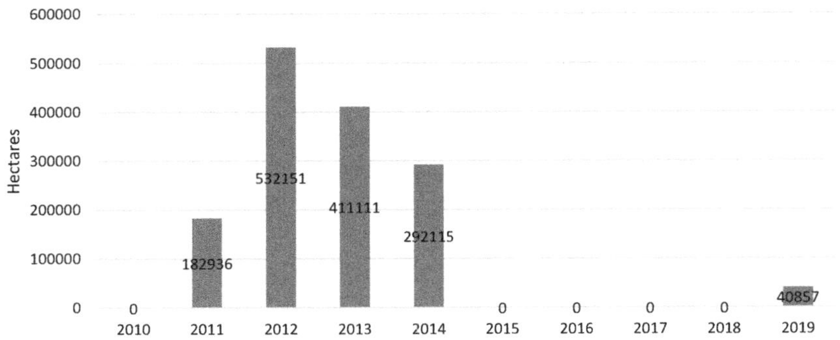

Fig. 11.1 Acreage awarded by Ministry of Energy 2010–2019

b) conduct seismic surveys in areas not already covered by the existing seismic surveys,
c) improve on the incentive regime by offering perhaps accelerated depreciation. Indeed, Trinidad and Tobago need to keep on benchmarking its fiscal package and contracted obligations to other oil producing countries, to ensure its hydrocarbon sector is competitive.
d) Make ALL the data at its disposal available to all interested parties so that those with superior technology and experience can use it to unlock hidden potential. The importance of data and technology cannot be over emphasized. (One of the recent discoveries of natural gas made by bpTT with the Ginger exploration well, uncovered the resource in what is considered a mature basin and illustrates in part how the right data and technology can help to unlock the resource potential of T&T).
e) The petroleum potential of the economy should be more aggressively marketed by professional and technical folks abroad and open proposals encouraged.

11.3 Modify the Supplemental Petroleum Tax (SPT) and Incentive Regimes in T&T to Encourage Production

The Supplemental Petroleum Act (SPA) was introduced in 1981 and has been amended on several occasions. The SPT is imposed on income generated from "income net of royalty". The SPT rates have varied over time and on 1/1/2013 the modifications shown in the Table 11.1 below were made, with the SPT kicking in only if oil prices crossed US$50 per barrel. In the FY2021 Budget, the SPT was raised to US$75 for small onshore oil producers.

It is recommended that the SPT has also be changed for large producers of oil as they can quickly bring more oil on stream.

Table 11.1 Sliding scale for SPT in T&T

Prices (US$/bbl.)	*Marine Licences*		*Land Licences /Deep Water*
	Marine	*New Field**	
P ≤ $50.00	0.0%	0.0%	0.0%
$50.00 < P ≤ $90.00**	33.0%	25.0%	18.0%
$90.00 < P ≤ $200.00	SPT Rate = Base SPT Rate + 0.2% (P – 90.00)		
P > $200.00	55.0%	47.0%	40.0%

*New Fields: Where recoverable reserves < 50mmbbls and production commences from 1/1/13,
**Base SPT
Source Ministry of Energy and Energy Industries (2019)

11.4 Providing Joint Ventures Between Huge and Small Producers

In 2017, EoG and bpTT reported the flow of 275 mmscf/d of gas from the Sercan field. Initially, this field was solely owned by bpTT, however, they were unable to profitably exploit the field because of its small size and the company's associated overhead costs. In this regard, the company successfully partnered with a smaller company and brought the gas on stream. This model where possible and relevant, should be replicated.

11.5 Secondary And Tertiary Oil Recovery Techniques

It is challenging to recover all the crude oil in an oil well. In this regard, crude oil production is categorized into three distinct categories: primary, secondary and tertiary. Primary oil recovery refers to the recovery of crude oil from a well using the natural pressure from that well. Although each oil well is unique in terms of its geology, primary recovery rates tend to be around 30% of the original oil in place. Secondary oil recovery refers to the use of methods to artificially lift the oil from a well. The most common means is water flooding. Water flooding involves the injection of water in wells to stimulate production. The water is used to support pressure of the reservoir (also known as voidage replacement) to increase oil production. Secondary oil recovery can allow for the recovery of an additional 15–25% of the crude oil (Cossé 1993). Tertiary oil recovery refers to the methods used to recover the crude oil from a well after primary and secondary methods have been exhausted. The main tertiary methods include thermal injection, gas injection, chemical injection and microbial recovery.

T&T's oil wells on land are mature with an estimated one billion barrels of oil already produced from onshore and over two billion produced from offshore acreage. This technique, however, has been largely limited to shallow heavy oil reservoirs. There is scope for the application of multiple secondary and tertiary recovery methods to improve T&T's oil production. To improve secondary and tertiary oil recovery efforts in T&T, policy makers should consider efficiency allowances to capex with respect to specialist equipment and chemicals. Oil is a sunset commodity and whilst it is commercially practical and profitable, we should extract whilst we can.

11.6 Reopening the Refinery at Petrotrin

The Petrotrin refinery was closed on October 2018 and the entire company was closed in November 2018. Using CSO's quarterly series on real GDP, one subcomponent of which is refining (including LNG). The average real value added for the first 2 quarters of 2018 (I am assuming that in the 3rd quarter of 2018 various downsizing activities to close the refinery would have started) was TT$2591 mn and in the first quarter of 2019, when the refinery was completely closed, value added on this sub component of GDP was TT$1723.4 mn. The difference between these 2 numbers gives an idea of "loss" GDP on account of the closure of Petrotrin's refinery and evaluates to TT$ 867.5 mn.

In terms of restarting the Petrotrin Refinery, the Minister of Finance in the 2020 Budget Speech stated that 70 bids were received for the mothballed Petrotrin refinery. The top three bidders were Patriotic Energies and Technologies Co Ltd, Beowulf Energy and Klesch. The Express Newspaper (September 20, 2019) indicated that the Government of Trinidad and Tobago awarded the Patriotic Energies and Technologies Company Ltd for US$700 million (TT$4.76 billion).

However, it has been several months since the award of the refinery to Patriotic, but no activity has been initiated. If this transaction is not yielding results the government of T&T should either return to the market or move on to the next bidder.

11.7 Cross Border Gas

In 2007, Trinidad and Tobago and Venezuela entered into a draft agreement on sharing gas deposits in the Loran-Manatee field. These fields straddle the territorial waters of both T&T and Venezuela. The total reserves in the field are estimated to be just over 10 TCF. The draft agreement gave Venezuela control of 73.75% (7.37 TCF) of the field whilst the remainder (2.625 TCF) goes to T&T.

To extract this cross-border gas, T&T and Venezuela have signed several cross-border treaties. The first Treaty was signed in 2007 and is called "The Framework Treaty." This Treaty is an overarching treaty that deals with any instance of cross-border deposits. In 2010, the governments of Trinidad and Tobago and Venezuela signed something called the Loran-Manatee Field Specific Treaty which declares how much of the natural gas is on Venezuela's side and how much is on TT's side (on Venezuela's side).

In 2013, another agreement was signed that created several committees: 1 committee would oversee the capital expenditure and 1 would oversee operations. Ultimately the companies involved would have had to come up with a "Field Development Plan." This is where the process stalled. The companies involved were Chevron on the Venezuela side and Shell on Trinidad's side. In the last 4 years very, little progress has been made because of the political situation in Venezuela and the sanctions that were placed by the US on persons doing business.

In 2020 the government of T&T and the government of Venezuela agreed to independent development of the part of the Loran-Manatee field that falls within their massive area.

It is here recommended that the same approach be adopted for development of the Cocuina-Manakin and Kapok-Dorado fields which collectively have an estimated 850 billion cubic feet of gas within the maritime area of T&T.

11.8 Local Content

Local content is the degree of local ownership, control and financing by citizens of a nation. According to Paul (2011) local content is the *"income received by locals, revenues accrued by owners of land and resources and income streams to local shareholders and creditors."*

A good example of local content captured from the oil and gas industry is the manufacture of offshore platforms in La Brea at the Labidco facility. The first platform developed as part of the local content and local participation initiative was the Cannonball platform (see Table 11.2). Whilst the project remained a tremendous success for bpTT's operations, it opened several doors that allowed for many other platforms to be built locally.

Table 11.2 Local content expenditure on platform fabrication in Trinidad and Tobago

Company	*Date*	*Capacity*	*Total expenditure*	*Local content*	*Expenditure (%)*
BHP Kairi 1 Platform	August 2004	700 ton	$340.1 mn		
Bp Cannonball Jacket & Deck	May 2005	1000-ton jacket/900 ton	$340.2 mn	$136.1 mn	40
EOG Oilbird Jacket & Deck	June 2006	1800-ton deck/2000 ton	$606.1 mn	$238.2 mn	39.3
BP Mango Jacket & Deck	March 2007	1000-ton jacket/900 ton	$504 mn	$126 mn	25
BP Cashima Jacket & Deck	March 2007	1000-ton jacket/900 ton	$655.2 mn	$163.8 mn	25
BG Poinsettia Deck	Dec 2009	1300-ton drill deck/2800 ton	$5040 mn	$1058.4 mn	21
EOG Toucan Deck	January 2009	1800-ton deck	$696 mn	$215.1 mn	30.9
BP Savonnete Jacket & Deck	February 2009	1000-ton deck/2000 ton	$472.5 mn	$94.5 mn	20
BP Serrette Jacket & Deck	2010	1000-ton deck/2000 ton			
BHP Angostura Ventboom & Bridge	On-going October 2009	500-ton bridge/120 ton	$648.9 mn	$356.9 mn	55

Adapted from Ministry of Energy & Energy Affairs (2013) http://www.energy.gov.tt/content/228.pdf

One of the strategies adopted by bpTT was the standardization or cloned approach which allowed for the delivery of the platforms with increased efficiency and significant content. Table 11.2 below provides some basic indication of local content expenditure on platform fabrication in T&T.

In 2017, however, bpTT announced it would build its Angelin project in Mexico instead of at the La Brea Site. When T&T lost the Angelin project it lost an investment of around US$80 mn, direct employment of 200 jobs, work for 10 contractors at TOFCO, business for about 100 suppliers to TOFCO and of course loss of corporation tax, indirect employment and the VAT on associated expenditures. The main reason this contract was lost is linked to the industrial relations climate in T&T. As a precursor to losing the Angelin Project, in mid-June the fabrication of the Juniper jacket was moved to Texas. At one point in time the President of the OWTU said to bpTT "Take your rig and go". To build local content, policy makers in Trinidad and Tobago have to shout louder (and support by action) "take your rig and come".

Since losing the Angelin platform, the Sercan platform and Ruby platform have also been lost. In this regard, the government of T&T should meet all the energy majors in T&T and negotiate conditions to restart platform construction activity in Trinidad and Tobago.

11.9 Farm Out/Lease Out Program

The T&T economy acquired over time the land-based assets of foreign multinational companies. These land-based assets fell under two state companies, Trintopec and Trintoc and these were later merged into Petrotrin. These two state enterprises inherited up to 3000 idle or marginalized wells. Indeed, the Draft Energy Policy of August 1992 noted *"There are several idle wells and blocks in shallow horizons in the country which can be viable cost producers given a lower cost regime. It is the view of the government that small independent operators especially those with small overheads and access to underutilized equipment acting alone or in consortia with local or foreign operators can be effective in this respect" (Draft Energy Policy1992, p. 10)*. In 1992, in an effort to stimulate economic activity in the petroleum sector the state noted that it will push alongside other strategic objectives, a farm out lease out program (FO/LO). In 2009/10 the state introduced another dimension the Incremental Production Service Contract (IPSC). This is a bit of a hybrid service contract, targeting specific fields. In practice the IPSC is

Table 11.3 Production of crude oil by Petrotrin (bpd)

Year	*FO/LO/IPSC*	*Petrotrin total*	*Petrotrin less FO/LO/IPSC*	*FO/LO/IPSC %*
2000	4692	60,677	55,985	7.7
2005	5144	58,020	52,876	8.9
2010	6080	42,397	36,317	14.3
2015	9897	44,630	34,733	22.2
2016	7029	40,841	33,812	17.2
2017	9766	42,243	32,477	23.1
2018	8350	37,588	29,237	22.2
2019	7868	33,331	25,463	23.6
2020*	7272	34,527	27,255	21.1

Source Ministry of Energy and Energy Affairs, various years
*As at June 2020

like a Lease Out but with some elements of a Farm Out and joint venture operations.

These contracted LO/FO/IPSC arrangements have been profitable for a variety of reasons, some of which have been cited by Lewis and Jaipaulsingh (2000) as:

a) The companies have ownership of the projects and this promotes a greater level of effort,
b) The area where the drilling occurs is smaller and this reduces operational costs,
c) In general, smaller companies experience lower overhead costs,
d) Response to issues such as an inactive well tends to be faster and more effective and this directly improves the productivity of the firm,
e) The companies' profits are tied to output as opposed to hours worked and this is a major difference that leads to these companies being more efficient.

Table 11.3 below shows that in 2000 the LO/FO/IPSC arrangements accounted for[1] 7.7% of the total output of Petrotrin. In 2020,

[1] Petrotrin was closed in November 2018. It was replaced by five (5) new SOE. One of them, The Heritage Petroleum Company Ltd now manages the exploration and production assets of the former Petrotrin Company Ltd.

it accounted for 22.2% of total output of Petrotrin. Given the performance of FO/LO/IPSC operators the state should consider delegating even more wells to these operators, especially the mature ones.

11.10 LNG Transfer Pricing

Poten and Partners in their analysis on the revenue impact of the LNG trains estimated that between 2011 and 2014 TT had a potential loss of US$6 bn per annum from the four LNG trains. Poten and Partners noted that for many transactions the offtake arrangements for the upstream companies involved sales to downstream marketing affiliates. The consultants went so far as to indicate that although transfer pricing exists with petrochemicals, its endemic in the case of LNG, in Trinidad and Tobago. The government of T&T needs to establish a committee to address the issue of LNG pricing and to seek redress. In June 2019, Shell agreed to pay the government TT$2.5 bn and in 2018 bpTT agreed to pay TT$1 bn. Nowhere, however, did either company agree to cheating the T&T government of revenues because of transfer pricing.

11.10.1 Regional Labour Market Possibilities

After several years of unsuccessful exploration, Exxon Mobil made a significant and successful discovery of oil 120 miles of Guyana's coast: this well was named Liza 1. After the Liza discovery, 17 other reservoirs were discovered of commercial value). Indeed, based upon the existing level of Guyana's reserves, it is ranked 12th globally (Guyana Chronicle, August 2019)[2]

The T&T economy has considerable expertise in training labour for the energy sector. Four institutions in T&T which train energy sector workers are:

i) The University of the West Indies (Petroleum Geosciences Unit)

The Petroleum Geoscience Unit St Augustine Campus of the UWI partners with the Government of Trinidad and Tobago and petroleum companies such as bpTT, EOG Resources, Shell, BHP Billiton, Petrotrin

[2] http://guyanachronicle.com/2019/08/14/guyana-12th-in-oil-reserves-league.

and NGC. The program at UWI are accredited by international bodies and include BSc Programme in Petroleum Geoscience, MSc Petroleum Engineering, Reservoir Engineering and MSc Petroleum Engineering.

ii) The University of Trinidad and Tobago

The University of Trinidad and Tobago offers a Bachelor of Applied Science (B.A.Sc.) in Petroleum Engineering there is also the option of pursuing a master's in petroleum engineering.

i) The National Energy Skills Centre (NESC)

NESC offers 2-year Diploma Programmes, 1-year Craftsman Program and several short courses in drilling trades, automotive services technician, heavy equipment technician, instrumentation, welding; building trades, millwright, pipefitting and fabrication and air conditioning and refrigeration amongst other skill areas. The NESC's Drilling Academy has a fully integrated, open-access technical training institute, designed to deliver robust curricula focussed on training for the energy sector.

ii) Metal Industries Company (MIC)

MIC offers program in TVET training, manufacturing, engineering and industrial maintenance services. This institution was established in 1974, has a tool and die making workshop that can support the manufacturing sector and the petroleum sector with the design and production of tools, dies and moulds. The MIC also operates as a commercial factory and is a leading provider of engineering solutions for the industrial sector both locally and regionally especially through its Design and Engineering Program, plastic services and industrial training.

11.11 Conclusion

This chapter reviewed various avenues through which the government of T&T could maximize the rents that the sector realizes from its comparative advantage-based productive activity. The chapter outlined and discussed the need to increase deepwater exploration and to further modify the Special Petroleum Tax (SPT). The chapter also emphasized the need to explore joint ventures between large and small producers to further explore secondary and tertiary oil recovery efforts and the importance of restarting the Refinery. Opportunities in cross-border gas is emphasized as well as the importance of enhancing local content opportunities. The critical importance of the LO/FO/IPSC program is highlighted and a call made to expand its width and depth. Finally, the "production" of skilled petroleum workers for "export" to Guyana and Suriname is raised as a niche opportunity given the established infrastructural base of educational systems in T&T.

The T&T economy in the years ahead that fossil fuel may still have some commercial value has to move quickly to maximize the economic rents it can collect. These rents will have to be wisely saved to create dynamic comparative advantage in vibrant emergent areas and not quickly and foolishly be frittered away.

References

Cosse, R. (1993). Basics of Reservoir Engineering: Oil and Gas Field Development Techniques.

Lewis, S.K., Jaipaulsingh, F., and Singh, D. (2000). "Entrepreneurial Success of Local Oil Operators." Journal of Petroleum Technology, December 2000.

CHAPTER 12

Conclusion: After 100 Years of Producing Oil and Gas

12.1 The T&T Economy is at a Crossroad

The T&T economy has been producing oil and gas for well over a hundred years. The crude oil part of the petroleum industry in particular is now in a sunset stage and the world economy is drifting more towards the use of renewable energy, although at a slow pace. A prudent question the ardent policy maker should ask is: what some of the missteps are the economy should avoid if it were to benefit from another boom. A simple summary is provided below:

- Sterilize the oil revenues from the economy, to prevent overheating. This in turn would limit the appreciation of the real effective exchange rate.
- Manage borrowing wisely and if possible don't borrow but use a proportion of the interest on the saved energy resources, each year.
- Encourage indigenous firms in the energy sector to increase local content and to increase the size of the associated multiplier.
- Promote downstream activity so as not to become trapped into the cycle of "drawers of water and hewers of wood."
- Reduce obstacles to the development of the energy sector by addressing ease of doing business constraints so that foreign firms won't find it difficult to set up shop. As the sector matures, modify

R. Hosein, *Oil and Gas in Trinidad and Tobago*,
https://doi.org/10.1007/978-3-030-77669-5_12

the above the ground fiscal rules so more exploration and production can take place.

- Manage the pace at which the services sector grows so that the Baumol cost disease does not emerge in the economy.
- Don't introduce Make Work programs as it reduces national welfare. Similarly, if free tertiary level education is offered, do it for a limited period so that moral hazard consumption does not result in a glut of tertiary level education graduates.
- Manage fiscal policy so as not to insert an excessive amount of transfers and subsidies into the economy as it can lead to a backward bending labour supply curve and a poor work ethic developing amongst some segments of the labour force.
- Manage rapid wage increases in the economy otherwise it can cause the manufacturing and other non-booming export sectors to become externally uncompetitive.
- If seasonal workforce from abroad can be deployed to keep the agricultural sector vibrant and thriving, then employ same as it can help to manage the level of food imports by maintaining a certain level of food production.
- Push for reforms to get the Ease of Doing business ranking within the top 25 in the world so vibrant non-energy industries can develop and thrive.
- Discourage rent dispersion as it can lead to infighting amongst various groups and a rise in the murder level.
- Promote policies to encourage exports based on economic analysis using Tradecan.
- Manage state sector employment sensibly so that the state does not crowd out the private sector.

The last 100 years of economic activity in the T&T economy, focussed heavily on fossil fuel energy.

In the remaining shelf life of Trinidad and Tobago's maturing petroleum fields it is recommended that they accommodate an even larger HSF pool whilst at the same time putting measures in place to strengthen its overall business environment and particularly the block of opportunities in the NBT sector.

With a spate of fiscal deficits since 2009, the economy is seriously in need of recalibration and the new normal working against one of its main comparative advantage products will make it even more challenging.

Policy makers would have to think outside the box and above all create an enabling environment for private sector capital to thrive. All of this will have to be undertaken in a post covid setting in which the demand for fossil-based fuels will decline in the context of greater utilization of renewable energy.

References

Adelman, I., and Taylor, J.E. (1998). "Is Structural Adjustment with a Human Face Possible? The Case of Mexico." Journal of Development Studies 26 (3): 387–407.

Akitoby, B., and Coorey, S. (2012). "Oil Wealth in Central Africa: Policies for Inclusive Growth." Washington, DC: IMF.

Alaska Resource Library& Information Services (ARLIS). (1990). "SPILL: The Wreck of the Exxon Valdez, Implications for Safe Transport of Oil." Alaska Oil Spill Commission Final Report.

Albu, Michael. (1997). "Technological Learning and Innovation in Industrial Clusters in the South." Electronic Working Papers Series, Paper No#7.

Alleyne, N.A., and Stoute, V. (2014). Options for Monetising Deep Water Gas in Trinidad and Tobago. SPE Energy Resources Conference. Society of Petroleum Engineers.

Amin, Sakib, and Murshed, Muntasir. (2017). "Remittance, Exchange Rate and Dutch Disease: The Case of Bangladesh (September 2017)." International Review of Business Research Papers 13 (2). Available at SSRN: https://ssrn.com/abstract=3070057.

Ani, T.G. (2015). "Effect of Ease of Doing Business to Economic Growth Among Selected Countries in Asia." Asia Pacific Journal of Multidisciplinary Research 3 (5): 139–145.

Arezki, R., Hadri, Kaddour, Loungani, Prakash, and Rao, Yao. (2013). "Testing the Prebisch-Singer Hypothesis Since 1650: Evidence from Panel Techniques That Allow for Multiple Breaks." IMF Working Paper 13/180, August.

R. Hosein, *Oil and Gas in Trinidad and Tobago*,
https://doi.org/10.1007/978-3-030-77669-5

Asmau, Y.J., Agility, M.S., and Amina, A.J. (2019). "Dutch Disease: Myth or Reality? An Analysis of the ARDL Model." International Journal of Business, Economics and Management 6 (3): 130–140.

Auty, M. Richard, and Kiiski, Sampsa. (2001). "Natural Resources, Capital Accumulation, Structural Change and Welfare." In R. Auty (Ed.), Resource Abundance and Economic Development: WIDER Studies in Development Economics, Chapter 2 (pp. 19–36). Oxford: Oxford University Press.

Auty, R.M. (1993). "Sustaining Development in Mineral Economies: The Resource Curse Thesis." London: Routledge.

Auty, Richard. (2001). "Why Resource Endowments Can Undermine Economic Development: Concepts and Case Studies." Proceedings of the BP-Amoco Seminar, Lincoln College Oxford University.

Badley, Olson. (2013). "Crude Export Ban No Match for Lightest U.S. Shale Oil." Bloomberg Business.

Balassa, Bela. (1965). "Trade Liberalization and Revealed Comparative Advantage." The Manchester School of Economic and Social Studies 33: 99–123.

Balassa, Bela. (1966). "Tarifi Reductions and Trade in Manufactures Among the Industrial Countries." American Economic Review 56: 466–472.

Baldwin, E. Robert. (1966). "Economic Development and Export Growth." Berkeley: University of California Press.

Bardi, Ugo. (2004). "Price Trends Over a Complete Hubbert Cycle: The Case of the American Whaling Industry in 19th century." Dipartimento di Chimica—Università di Firenze Via della Lastruccia 3, Sesto Fiorentino (Fi)—Italy and ASPO Association for the Study of Peak Oil (www.peakoil.net).

Barham, Bradford, and Coomes, Oliver. (2005). "Sunk Costs, Resource Extractive Industries, and Development Outcomes." In Paul S. Ciccantell, David A. Smith, and Gay Seidman (Eds.), Nature, Raw Materials, and Political Economy (Research in Rural Sociology and Development, Volume 10) (pp. 159–186). Emerald Group Publishing Limited.

Barsky, Robert, and Kilian, Lutz. (2004). "Oil and the Macroeconomy Since the 1970s." National Bureau of Economic Research (NBER) Working Paper 10855.

Bartholdson, Örjan, and Valentin, Mats. (2006). "The Dark Secret of Chocolate: A Report on the Working Conditions on the Cocoa Farms of West Africa." SwedWatch, Report No. 12.

Baumol J. William. (1967). "Macroeconomics of Unbalance Growth: The Anatomy of Urban Crisis." The American Economic Review 57 (3): 415–426.

Baumol, J. William. (1967). "Macroeconomics of Unbalance Growth: The Anatomy of Urban Crisis." The American Economic Review 57 (3): 415–426. Cambridge: Cambridge University Press.

Baumol, J. William, Batey Blackman, Sue-Ann, and Wolff, Edward. (1985). "Unbalanced Growth Revisited: Asymptotic Stagnancy and New Evidence." American Economic Review 75 (4): 806–817.

Beaubrun, Tony. (2008). "Memories of Pointe-a-Pierre". First Magazine Ltd.

Beckford, George L. (1972). "Persistent Poverty: Underdevelopment in Plantation Economies of the Third World." London: Oxford University Press.

Bekele, L. Francis. (2003). "The History of Cocoa Production in Trinidad and Tobago." In Re-vitalisation of the Trinidad & Tobago Cocoa Industry: Proceedings of the APASTT Seminar, Trinidad and Tobago: Association of Professional Agricultural Scientists of Trinidad and Tobago.

Belratti, Andrea. (2005). "The Complementarity Between Corporate Governance and Corporate Social Responsibility." The Geneva Papers on Risk and Insurance—Issues and Practice 30.

Ben, Lefebvre. (2014). "Shale-Oil Boom Spurs Refining Binge." Wall Street Journal. New York.

Besson, A. Gerard. (2008a). "Black Gold, Part 2: War and Peace." First Magazine Ltd.

Besson, A. Gerard. (2008b). "Black Gold, the Real El Dorado." First Magazine Ltd.

Besson, A. Gerard. (2008c). "Black Gold Part 3: The Road to Independence." First Magazine Ltd.

Besson, A. Gerard. (2008d). "History of Oil Part 2." The Caribbean History Archives. Paria Publishing Co LTD.

Best, Lloyd. (1968). "A Model of Pure Plantation Economy." Social and Economic Studies 17 (3): 283–326.

Best, Lloyd. (1971). "Independent Thought and Caribbean Freedom." In Norman Girvan and Owen Jefferson (Eds.), Readings in the Political Economy of the Caribbean. Mona: New World Group. Original in New World Quarterly, Vol. 3, No. 4 1967.

Best, Lloyd, and Levitt, Kari. (1968). "The Mechanism of Plantation-Type Economies: Outline of a Model of Pure Plantation Economy." Social and Economic Studies 17: 283–324.

Best, Lloyd, and Levitt, Kari et al. (1968). "Externally Propelled Industrialization and Growth in the Caribbea." Montreal, McGill Centre for Developing Area Studies, 4 Vols. (Unpublished MS).

Birdsall, Nancy, Pinckney, Thomas C., and Sabot, Richard H. (1995). "Inequality, Savings and Growth." Center for Development Economics 148, Department of Economics, Williams College.

Birdsall, Nancy, Pinckney, Thomas C., and Sabot, Robert H. (1999). "Equity, Savings and Growth." Working Paper No. 8. Brookings Institution, Centre of Social and Economic Dynamics, Washington, DC.

Blondeel, Mathieu, Van de Graaf, Thijs, and Haesebrouck, Tim. (2020). "Moving Beyond Coal: Exploring and Explaining the Powering Past Coal Alliance." Energy Research & Social Science 59.

Bogdan, Glavan. (2007). "Coordination Failures, Poverty Traps, 'Big Push' Policy and Entrepreneurship: A Critical View." MPRA Paper No. 5757.

Boodlal, Donnie, Furlonge, Hayden, and Williams, Rachel. (2008). "Trinidad and Tobago CO2 Inventory and Techno-economic Evaluation of Carbon Capture Options for Emissions Mitigation." University of Trinidad and Tobago.

Boopsingh, T., and McGuire, G. (2014). From Oil to Gas and Beyond: A Review of the Trinidad and Tobago Model and Analysis of Future Challenges. University Press of America.

Boyd, D.T. (2008). Stratigraphic Guide to Oil and Gas Reservoirs: Oklahoma Geological Survey SP2008–1.

Brennan, Lisa. (2010). "In Stunning End to Kazakh Bribe Case, Judge Lauds Giffen as a 'Patriot'." Just Anti-Corruption.

Brereton, Bridget. (1981). "A History of Modern Trinidad and Tobago 1783–1962." London: Heinemann International.

Brereton, Bridget. (1996). "An Introduction to the History of Trinidad and Tobago 1783–1962." Oxford: Heinemann.

Brewster, H.R. (1968). Exports, Employment and Wages in Trinidad and Tobago and Mr. Seers' Model of the Open Economy. CSO Research Paper (5).

Brigida, Matthew. (2014). "The Switching Relationship Between Natural Gas and Oil Prices." www.usaee.org.

British Petroleum. (2012). "BP in Azerbaijan Sustainability Report 2012." www.bp.com/caspian.

Broadman, G. Harry, Paas, Tiiu, and Welfen, J.J. Paul. (2006). "Economic Liberalization and Integration Policy: Options for Eastern Europe."

Bruce, C.J. (1972). The Open Petroleum Economy: A Comparison of Keynesian and Alternative Formulations. Social and Economic Studies 24 (2).

Busch, Joel H. (1968). "Asian Drama: An Inquiry into the Poverty of Nations." The Australian Quarterly 40 (4): 118–121.

Business Guardian. (2013). "IMF: T&T Borrowing to Save." http://www.guardian.co.tt/.

Cairnes, E. John. (1863). "The Slave Power: Its Character, Career, and Probable Designs: Being an Attempt to Explain the Real Issues Involved in the American Contest." Third edition, Follett F.

Carrington, Edwin. (1971). "Industrialization By Invitation In Trinidad Since 1950." In Norman Girvan and Owen Jefferson (Eds.), Readings in the Political Economy of the Caribbean Mona: New World Group (pp. 143–152).

Original in New World Quarterly, Vol. 4, No. 2, 1968. New York: Oster & Co., 1863.

Carroll B. Archie, and Buchholtz K. Ann. (2011). "Business and Society: Ethics and Stakeholder Management (8th ed.)." Australia: Thomson South-Western.

Cavalcanti, Tiago V. de V., Mohaddes, Kamiar, and Raissi, Mehdi. (2012). "Commodity Price Volatility and the Sources of Growth." IMF Working Papers 12/12, International Monetary Fund.

Caves, R.E. (1968). "Vent for Surplus' Models of Trade and Growth." In James D. Theberge (Ed.), Economics of Trade and Development (pp. 211–230). New York: John Wiley and Sons.

Chaitoo, Ramesh. (2013). "Public-Private Partnerships to Fit into Global Value Chains: Atlantic LNG in Trinidad & Tobago." ADB Training Seminar. Plugging Into Global Value Chains: A Strategy for Growth.

Chapman, B. (2016). Income Contingent Loans in Higher Education Financing. Crawford School of Public Policy, Australia.

Charles, Anthony. (2011). "Small-Scale Fisheries: On Rights, Trade and Subsidies." Halifax Canada: Saint Mary's University.

Chenery, B. Hollis, and Syrquin, Moises. (1975). "Patterns of Development 1950–1970." London: Oxford University Press.

Chenery, H. B., Robinson, S., and Syrquin, M. (1986). Structural Transformation. In Chenery, H. B., Robinson, S., and Syrquin, M. (eds.). Industrialization and Growth: A Comparative Study. Oxford: Oxford University Press: 11–12.

Churchill S. Winston. (1949). "The World Crisis." Published by Charles Scribner's Sons, New York.

Clark, Colin. (1940). "The Conditions of Economic Progress." London: Macmillan; New York: St. Martin's Press.

Collier, P., Van der Ploeg, R., Spence, M., and Venables, T. (2010). "Managing Resource Revenues in Developing Economies," IMF Staff Papers, 57, 84–118.

Copithorne, L. (1979). "Natural Resources and Regional Disparities: A Skeptical View." Canadian Public Policy/Analyse de Politiques 5 (2): 181–194.

Corby, Elowyn. (2011). "Ogoni People Struggle with Shell Oil, Nigeria, 1990–1995." Global Nonviolent Action Database.

Corden, W. Max, and Neary, J. Peter. (1982, December). "Booming Sector and De-Industrialisation in a Small Open Economy." The Economic Journal 92: 829–831.

Cosse, R. (1993). Basics of Reservoir Engineering: Oil and Gas Field Development Techniques.

Crystal, D. (2003). "English as a Global Language (1st ed.)." Cambridge, UK: Cambridge University Press.

Daily Express. (2012). "BPTT to Spend US$900m in 2012." www.trinidadexpress.com.
Darke, D., & Walsh, T. (2017). Oman. Bradt Travel Guides.
David, Renwick. (2008). "An Overview of Trinidad & Tobago's Petroleum Industry, Post-Independence." First Magazine Ltd.
Davis, A. Graham, and Tilton, E. John. (2008). "Why the Resource Curse Is a concern." Mining Engineering 60 (4): 29–32.
Demas G. William. (1976). "The Political Economy of the English Speaking Caribbean: A Summary View (Study Paper/Caribbean Ecumenical Consultation for Development." CEDAR Press; 4th edition (1976).
Demas, William. (1976). "The Political Economy of the English Speaking Caribbean: A Summary View, Caribbean Ecumenical Consultation for Development." Study Paper #4, Barbados.
de Roberts, L.C. (1980). "El Ecuador en la época cacaotera." Quito: Editorial Universitaria.
Djankov, S., La Porta, R., Lope-de-Silanes, F., and Shleifer, A. (2002). "The Regulation of Entry." The Quarterly Journal of Economics 117 (1): 1–37.
Dolin, E.J. (2007). "Leviathan: The History of Whaling in America." New York: W. W. Norton.
Down, A.L. (1960). History of Trinidad's Oil. Geological Society of Trinidad and Tobago.
Drysdale, Peter D. (1967). "Australian–Japanese Trade." PhD Thesis. Australian National University, Canberra, Australia.
Duesenberry, S. James. (1949). "Income, Savings, and the Theory of Consumer Behavior." Cambridge, MA: Harvard University Press, Harvard Economic Studies, LXXXVII.
Dvosky, George. (2012). "1846: The Year We Hit Peak Sperm Whale Oil." http://io9.com/5930414/1846-the-year-we-hit-peak-spearm-whale-oil.
Eaton, S.J.M. (1866). "Petroleum: A History of the Oil Region of Venago County, Pennsylvania." Philadelphia: J.P. Skelly & Co., 299 pp.
Eleco, de Groot. (2013). "Tackling the Resource Curse." http://www.thebrokeronline.eu.
Enill, Conrad. (2008). "Trinidad and Tobago: Overview of the Government's Energy Policy in the Second 100 Year Period Government of Trinidad and Tobago (Jan. 1981)". White Paper on Natural Gas. Keynote Address by the Honorable Conrad Enill, Ministry of Energy and Energy Industries, at the IBC Energy Caribbean 2008 Conference.
Erdős, Péter. (2012). "Have Oil and Gas Prices Got Separated?" Energy Policy, Elsevier 49 (C): 707–718.
Erunke, Candice Esidene, and Hafsat, Kingbu. (2012). "Historical Context of the Incorporation of Africa in International Politics." Afro Asian Journal of Social Sciences 3 (3.2),, Quarter II 2012.

Farell, Trevor. (2012). "The Underachieving Society: Development Strategy and Policy in Trinidad and Tobago: 1958–2008".

Gasmi, Farid, and Laourari, Imène. (2017). "Has Algeria Suffered from the Dutch Disease? Evidence from 1960–2016 Data." Revue d'économie politique, Dalloz 127 (6): 1029–1058.

Farrell, Terrance. (2019). At A Point of Inflexion: The Downstream Petrochemicals Industry in Trinidad & Tobago 2019. UTT Seminar. https://utt.edu.tt/files/cms/point_inflexion_presentation.pdf.

Fisher, B.G. Allen. (1939). "Production, Primary, Secondary and Tertiary." Economic Record 15.1 (1939): 24–38.

Forsyth, N. Peter, and Nicholas, Stephen J. (1983). "The Decline of Spanish Industry and the Price Revolution: A Neoclassical Analysis." Journal of European Economic History 12 (3): 601–610.

Friedman, Milton. (1970). "The Social Responsibility of Business Is to Increase Its Profits." The New York Times Company.

Frynas, Jedrzej George. (2000). "Oil in Nigeria: Conflict and Litigation Between Oil Companies and Village Communities." LIT Verlag Münster, 2000—Business & Economics.

Gbegi, D., and Adebisi, J.F. (2013). "Managing Local Content Policies in the Extractive Industries." Research Journal of Finance and Accounting. www.iiste.org. ISSN 2222–1697 (Paper) ISSN 2222–2847 (Online), 4 (7).

Gelb, Alan. "Economic Diversification in Resource Rich Countries." Center for Global Development (2010): 1–23.

Gereffi, G. (1995). "State Policies and Industrial Upgrading in East Asia." Revue d'économie industrielle, 79–90.

Ghosh, Palash. (2012). "Azerbaijan—A Repressive, Corrupt Country That the West Loves: There Must Be Oil." http://www.ibtimes.com.

Girvan, Norman, and Jefferson, Owen (eds.). (1968). "Readings in the Political Economy of the Caribbean" (pp. 143–152). Mona: New World Group. Original in New World Quarterly 4 (2).

Global LNG Info. (2014). "World's LNG Liquefaction Plants and Regasification Terminals." http://www.globallnginfo.com.

Global Witness. (2004). "Time for Transparency Report: Coming Clean on Oil, Mining and Gas Revenues." A Report by Global Witness, March 2004.

Goldberg, K. Pinelope, and Pavcnik, Nina. (2008). "Distributional Effects of Globalization in Developing Countries." Journal of Economic Literature 45 (1): 39–82.

Government of Norway. (2015). "Implementation of Seismic Surveys on the Norwegian Continental Shelf." Ministry of Fisheries and Coastal Affairs, Minister of Petroleum and Energy.

Government of Trinidad and Tobago. (1906). "Annual Administrative Report." Ministry of Energy and Energy Affairs Trinidad and Tobago.

Government of Trinidad and Tobago. (1908). "Annual Administrative Report." Ministry of Energy and Energy Affairs Trinidad and Tobago.
Government of Trinidad and Tobago. (1911). "Annual Administrative Report." Ministry of Energy and Energy Affairs Trinidad and Tobago.
Government of Trinidad and Tobago. (1913a). "Annual Administrative Report." Ministry of Energy and Energy Affairs Trinidad and Tobago.
Government of Trinidad and Tobago. (1913b). "Annual Administrative Report." Ministry of Energy and Energy Affairs Trinidad and Tobago.
Government of Trinidad and Tobago. (1914). "Annual Administrative Report." Ministry of Energy and Energy Affairs Trinidad and Tobago.
Government of Trinidad and Tobago. (1931). "Annual Administrative Report." Ministry of Energy and Energy Affairs Trinidad and Tobago.
Government of Trinidad and Tobago. (1932). "Annual Administrative Report." Ministry of Energy and Energy Affairs Trinidad and Tobago.
Government of Trinidad and Tobago. (1935). "Annual Administrative Report." Ministry of Energy and Energy Affairs Trinidad and Tobago.
Government of Trinidad and Tobago. (1940). "Annual Administrative Report." Ministry of Energy and Energy Affairs Trinidad and Tobago.
Government of Trinidad and Tobago. (1946). "Annual Administrative Report." Ministry of Energy and Energy Affairs Trinidad and Tobago.
Government of Trinidad and Tobago. (1947). "Annual Administrative Report." Ministry of Energy and Energy Affairs Trinidad and Tobago.
Government of Trinidad and Tobago. (1948). "Annual Administrative Report." Ministry of Energy and Energy Affairs Trinidad and Tobago.
Government of Trinidad and Tobago. (1963). "The Budget Speech." Ministry of Finance Trinidad and Tobago.
Government of Trinidad and Tobago. (1970). "The Budget Speech." Ministry of Finance Trinidad and Tobago.
Government of Trinidad and Tobago. (1972a). "The Budget Speech." Ministry of Finance Trinidad and Tobago.
Government of Trinidad and Tobago. (1972b). "The Budget Speech." Ministry of Finance Trinidad and Tobago.
Government of Trinidad and Tobago. (1972c). "The Budget Speech." Ministry of Finance Trinidad and Tobago.
Government of Trinidad and Tobago. (1972d). Budget Speech, Ministry of Finance, Port of Spain Government of T&T.
Government of Trinidad and Tobago. (1973). "The Budget Speech." Ministry of Finance Trinidad and Tobago.
Government of Trinidad and Tobago. (1976). "The Budget Speech." Ministry of Finance Trinidad and Tobago.
Government of Trinidad and Tobago. (1979). "The Budget Speech." Ministry of Finance Trinidad and Tobago.

Government of Trinidad and Tobago. (1979). Budget Speech, Ministry of Finance, Port of Spain, Government of T&T.

Government of Trinidad and Tobago. (1991). "The Budget Speech." Ministry of Finance Trinidad and Tobago.

Government of Trinidad and Tobago. (1998). Ministry of Energy, 1998.

Government of Trinidad and Tobago. (2007). "Seafood Industry Development Company (SIDC) of Trinidad and Tobago."

Government of Trinidad and Tobago. (2008). "Review of the Economy." Ministry of Finance Trinidad and Tobago.

Government of Trinidad and Tobago. (2010). "Review of the Economy." Ministry of Finance Trinidad and Tobago.

Government of Trinidad and Tobago. (2011a). "Environmental Management Authority of Trinidad and Tobago."

Government of Trinidad and Tobago. (2011b). "Review of the Economy." Ministry of Finance Trinidad and Tobago.

Government of Trinidad and Tobago. (2014a). "Review of the Economy." Ministry of Finance Trinidad and Tobago.

Government of Trinidad and Tobago. (2014b). "Economic Development Board." Ministry of Planning Trinidad and Tobago.

Grau-Perejoan, M., and Gea-Monera, M. (2018). "El Español en Trinidad y Tobago".

Gunton, I. Thomas. (2003). "Natural Resources and Regional Development: An Assessment of Advantage Paradigms." Economic Geography 79 (1): 67–94.

Gylfason, Thorvaldur. (2002). "Natural Resources and Economic Growth: What Is the Connection?" Fostering Sustainable Growth in Ukraine, 48–66.

Gylfason, Thorvaldur. (2011). "Natural Resources Endowment: A Mixed Blessing?" CESifo Working Paper No. 3353.

Haglund, Dan. (2010). "From Boom to Bust: Diversity and Regulation in Zambia's Privatized Copper Sector." In M. LARMER, and A. FRASER (Eds.), Zambia, Mining and Neo-Liberalism. Palgrave.

Hamilton, Kirk, and Hartwick, M. John. (2006). "Investigating Exhaustible Resources Rents and the Path of Consumption." Canadian Journal of Economics 38 (2): 615–621.

Handegard, O. Nils, Tronstad, V. Tron, and Hovem, M. Jens. (2013). "Evaluating the Effect of Seismic Surveys on Fish—The Efficacy of Different Exposure Metrics to Explain Disturbance." Canadian Journal of Fisheries and Aquatic Sciences 70: 1271–1277.

Hartley, Peter, Medlock, B. Kenneth, and Rosthal, E. Jennifer. (2006). "An Econometric Evaluation of the Demand for Natural Gas in the Power Generation and Industrial Sectors." The James A. Baker III Institute for Policy, Rice University.

Hartwick, M. John. (1977). "Intergenerational Equity and the Investing of Rents from Exhaustible Resources." The American Economic Review 67 (5): 972–974.

Heal, Geoffrey. (2005). "Corporate Social Responsibility: An Economic and Financial Framework." The Geneva Papers on Risk and Insurance—Issues and Practice 30: 387–409.

Hediger, Werner. (2010). "From Multifunctionality and Sustainability of Agriculture to the Social Responsibility of the Agri-Food System." YSA: 59–80.

Heike, Fabig, and Boele, Richard. (1999). "The Changing Nature of NGO Activity in a Globalising World: Pushing the Corporate Responsibility Agenda." Institute of Development Studies (IDS) Bulletin 30 (3): 58–67, July 1999.

Herciu, Michela. (2013). "Measuring International Competitiveness of Romania by Using Porter's Diamond and Revealed Comparative Advantage." Procedia Economics and Finance 6: 273–279.

Hezemans, Marijke, and Ritzen, Magda. (2004). Communities of Practice in Higher Education. International Federation for Information Processing Digital Library; Information and Communication Technologies and Real-Life Learning.

Hidalgo, C.A., Klinger, B., Barabasi, A.L., and Hausmann, R. (2007). "The Product Space Conditions the Development of Nations." Science 317 (5837): 482.

Higgins, E. George. (1996). "A History of Trinidad Oil." Trinidad Express Limited (Port of Spain). Express Production House.

Hill, M.A., and King, E.M. (1993). "Women's Education in Developing Countries: An Overview." In E.M. King and M.A. Hill (Eds.), Women's Education in Developing Countries: Barriers, Benefits, and Policies. Baltimore, MD: John Hopkins University Press.

Hinloopen, Jeroen, and Marrewijk, Charles van. (2001). "On the Empirical Distribution of the Balassa Index." Review of World Economics/Weltwirtschaftliches Archiv 137: 1–35.

Hirschman, O. Albert. (1958). "The Strategy of Economic Development." New Haven, CT: Yale University Press.

Hirschman, O. Albert. (1961). "The Strategy of Economic Development." Melville H. Watkin, The Canadian Journal of Economics and Political Science/Revue canadienne d'Economique et de Science politique 27 (1): 110–112.

Holme, Richard, and Watts, Phil. (2000). "Corporate Social Responsibility: Making good Business Sense." World Business Council for Sustainable Development.

Hosein, R., and Tewarie, B. (2004). "Dutch Disease and Deja Vu: Policy Advice for the Trinidad and Tobago Economy in the Wake of a Second Oil Boom." West Indian Journal of Engineering 26 (2).

Hotelling, Harold. (1931). "The Economics of Exhaustible Resources." The Journal of Political Economy 39 (2): 137–175.

Humphreys, M., Sachs, J., and Stiglitz, J. (2007). "Escaping the Resource Curse." NY: Initiative for Policy Dialogue, Columbia University Press.

Idemudia, Uwafiokun. (2007). "Corporate Partnerships and Community Development in the Nigerian Oil Industry: Strengths and Limitations." United Nations Research Institute for Social Development.

Ifad. (2004). Poverty Reduction—A Little Credit Goes a Long Way. Bankok Post: Interview with Phrang Roy, Assistant President, External Affairs Department.

Innis, A. Harrold. (1950). "Empire and Communications." Clarendon, Oxford.

International Centre for Research on Women. (2010). "Women's Economic Empowerment."

International Monetary Fund. (2012). "Trinidad and Tobago 2012 Article IV Consultation—Staff Report." IMF Country Report No. 12/127.

International Monetary Fund. (2014). "Trinidad and Tobago 2014 Article IV Consultation—Staff Report." IMF Country Report No. 14/271.

Jarrett, Uchechukwu, Mohaddes, Kamiar, and Mohtadi, Hamid. (2019). "Oil Price Volatility, Financial Institutions and Economic Growth." Energy Policy, Elsevier 126 (C): 131–144.

Jobity, Richard, and Pantor, Robert. (1995). "The Natural Gas Industry in Trinidad and Tobago." Central Bank of Trinidad and Tobago.

Julien, S. Kenneth. (2005). "Eric Williams and the Emergence of the National Energy Sector." Nineteenth Dr. Eric Williams Memorial Lecture. Central Bank of Trinidad and Tobago.

Karl, T.L. (2007). "Oil-Led Development: Social, Political, and Economic Consequences." CDDRL Working Papers, 80, 36 p.

Kemp, Murray C., and Ngo Van Long. "How to eat a cake of unknown size: The case of a growing cake." Economics Letters 17.1–2 (1985): 67–69.

Kemp, Murray C., and Van[1] Long, Ngo. "On Two Folk Theorems Concerning the Extraction of Exhaustible Resources." Econometrica: Journal of the Econometric Society (1980): 663–673.

Kemp, Murray C., and Van Long, Ngo. "The Role of Natural Resources in Trade Models." Handbook of International Economics 1 (1984): 367–417.

Khan, H. Mushtaq, and Sundaram, K. Jomo. (2000). "Rents, Rent-Seeking and Economic Development: Theory and Evidence in Asia." Cambridge University Press.

Kima, Jongwook, and Mahoney, T. Joseph. (2005). "Property Rights Theory, Transaction Costs Theory, and Agency Theory: An Organizational Economics

Approach to Strategic Management." Managerial and Decision Economics 26: 223–242.

Kishore, Rosemarie, and Ramsundar, Himawatee. (2007). "Community-Based Fisheries Management: A Case Study of Fishing Communities from Ortoire to Guayaguayare, Trinidad." 59th Proceedings of the Gulf and Caribbean Fisheries Institute, Belize City: Belize 59: 99–110.

Kishore, Rosemarie, Chin, X., and Ramsundar, R. (2003). Potential Impacts of Industrial Development on Coastal Fisheries in the Gulf of Paria, Trinidad. Proceedings of the 54th Annual Gulf and Caribbean Fisheries Institute, 13–27.

Klapper, L., and Love, I. (2010). "The Impact of Business Environment Reforms on New Firm Registration." World Bank Policy Research Working Paper 5493.

Kline, M. John. (2006). "MNCs and Surrogate Sovereignty." The Brown Journal of World Affairs XIII.I (2006): 123–133.

Krueger, O. Anne. (1974). "The Political Economy of the Rent-Seeking Society." American Economic Review 64 (3): 291–303.

Krugman, Paul. (1991). "Geography and Trade." Gaston Eyskens Lecture Series, MIT Press Cambridge, MA and London, Louvain University, Belgium, xi, 142.

Kurucz, Elizabeth, Colbert, A. Barry, and Wheeler, David. (2008). "The Business Case for Corporate Social Responsibility." The Oxford Handbook on Corporate Social Responsibility (pp. 83–112). Oxford: Oxford University Press.

Kuznets, Simon. (1971). "Economic Growth of Nations: Total Output and Production Structure." Cambridge: Cambridge University Press.

Kuznets, Simon. (1989). "Economic Development, the Family and Income Distribution." The American Economic Review XLV (1).

Lal, Deepak, and Myint, H. (1996). "The Political Economy of Poverty, Equity, and Growth." Oxford: Clarendon Press.

Lall, S. (1996). "Learning from the Asian Tigers: Studies in Technology and Industrial Policy." New York: Palgrave.

Lalla, H. (2001). "National Report of Trinidad and Tobago." In National Reports and Technical Papers Presented at the First Meeting of the WECAFC Ad Hoc Working Group on the Development of Sustainable Moored Fish Aggregating Device Fishing in the Lesser Antilles. FAO Fisheries Report No. 683, Supplement. ISSN 0429–9337. Le Robert, Martinique, 8–11 October 2001.

Lam, Ricky, and Wantchekon, Leonard. (2002). "Political Dutch Disease." Northwestern University.

Landow, P. George. (2013). "The British East India Company—The Company that Owned a Nation (or Two)."

Leamer, E. Edward, Maul, Hugo, Rodriguez, Sergio, and Schott, K. Peter. (1999). "Does Natural Resource Abundance Increase Latin American Income Inequality?" Journal of Development Economics 59: 3–42.

Leamer, Edward E. 1984. "Sources of International Comparative Advantage: Theory and Evidence." Cambridge, MA: MIT Press.

Leikem, Kirsten. (2012). "Microfinance: A Tool for Poverty Reduction." Senior Honors Projects. Paper 300. http://digitalcommons.uri.edu/srhonorsprog/300.

Lewis, S.K., Jaipaulsingh, F., and Singh, D. (2000). "Entrepreneurial Success of Local Oil Operators." Journal of Petroleum Technology, December 2000.

Lewis, W. Arthur. (1950). "Industrial Development in the Caribbean." Port of Spain.

Lewis, W. Arthur. (1954). "Economic Development with Unlimited Supplies of Labor." Manchester School of Economic and Social Studies 22: 139–191.

Lipsey, R.G. (1960). "The Relation Between Unemployment and the Rate of Change of Money Wage Rates in the United Kingdom, 1862–1957: A Further Analysis." Economica 27: 1–31; reprinted in AEA Series (1966) Reading in Business Cycles, 456–487.

Liu, Z.Y. Karen. (2010). "The Relationship Between American MNCs and US Government." Haworth and Lexon.

Loasby, B.J. (1991). "Equilibrium and Evolution." Manchester: Manchester University Press.

Loayza, Norman, Mier y Teran, Alfredo, and Rigolini, Jamele. (2013). "Poverty, Inequality, and the Local Natural Resource Curse." Policy Research Working Paper; No. 6366. Washington, DC: World Bank. © World Bank. https://openknowledge.worldbank.org/handle/10986/13169 License: CC BY 3.0 IGO.

Løkkeborg, Svein, Ona, Egil, Vold, Aud, and Salthaug, Are. (1996). "Effects of Sounds from Seismic Air Guns on Fish Behavior and Catch Rates." A.N. Popper and A. Hawkins (Eds.), The Effects of Noise on Aquatic Life, Advances in Experimental Medicine and Biology 730.

Loungani, Prakash, and Matsumoto, Akito. (2012). "Oil and Natural Gas Prices Together Again?" http://www.usaee.org.

Mackenzie, K. (2012). Finacial Times. Retrieved from We'll Settle This Internal Devaluation Question Quicker Than We Thought. https://www.ft.com/content/7c326fa4-9d07-3327-a0df-8c5e070479eb.

McKnight, S. (2004). "Thugs Destroy Arima URP Office Over Non-Payment of 'Ghost Gang' Cheques." Newsday Newspapers Trinidad and Tobago.

McCauley, D. Robert, Fewtrell, Jane, and Popper, N. Arthur. (2003). "High Intensity Anthropogenic Sound Damages Fish Ears." Journal of the Acoustical Society of America 113: 638–642.

McCauley, D. Robert, Fewtrell, Jane, Duncan, J. Alec, Jenner, Curt, Jenner, Micheline-Nicole, Penrose, D. John, Prince, I.T. Robert, Adhitya, Anita

,Murdoch, Julie, and McCabe, Kathryn. (2000). "Marine Seismic Surveys—A Study of Environmental Implications." APPEA Journal 40: 692–708.
Metcalfe, J. Stanley. (1998). "Evolutionary Economics and Creative Destruction." The Economic Journal 109 (453): F256–F258.
Michaely, Roni, Vila, Jean-Luc, and Wang, Jian. (1996). "A Model of Trading Volume with Tax-Induced Heterogeneous Valuation and Transaction Costs." Journal of Financial Intermediation 5: 340–371.
Ministry of Science, Technology and Tertiary Level Education. (2003). "Dollar for Dollar: Government of Trinidad and Tobago."
Mironov, V., and Petronevich, A. (2015). "Discovering the Signs of Dutch Disease in Russia." Resources Policy 46: 100–110.
Mohammed, E., Ferreira, L., Soomai, S., Martin, L., Chan, A., and Shing, C. (2011). Coastal Fisheries of Trinidad and Tobago. Government of Trinidad and Tobago.
Mohammed, Elizabeth, and Lindop, Alasdair. (2015). "Trinidad and Tobago: Reconstructed Fisheries Catches, 1950–2010." Fisheries Centre, Working Paper #55.
Mottley, W. (2008). "Trinidad and Tobago Industrial Policy 1959–2008—A Historical and Contemporary Analysis." Jamaica: Ian Randle Publishers.
Mpofu, John, Chimhenga, Sylod, and Mafa, Onias. (2013). "Funding Higher Education in Zimbabwe: Experience, Challenges and Opportunities of the Cadetship Scheme." https://doi.org/10.1057/9781137345783_13.
Murphy, Kevin M., Andrei Shleifer, and Robert, W. Vishny. (1991). "The Allocation of Talent: Implications for Growth," Quarterly Journal of Economics, Vol. 106, pp. 503–30.
Mustapha, Ishaq Muhammad, and Masih, Mansur. (2016). "Dutch Disease or Nigerian Disease: A Prima Facie? New Evidence from ARDL Bound Test Analysis." MPRA Paper 69767. Germany: University Library of Munich.
Myint, Hila. (1958). "The Classical Theory of International Trade and the Under-Developed Nations." Economic Journal 68: 317–337.
Myint, Hila. (1965). "Economic Theory and the Underdeveloped Countries." Journal of Political Economy 73 (10): 477–491.
Myrdal, G. (1968). "Asian Drama: An Inquiry into the Poverty of Nations." The Swedish Journal of Economics 70 (4): 242–245.
Newell, Peter. (2005). "Citizenship, Accountability and Community: The Limits of the CSR Agenda." International Affairs 81 (3): 541–557.
Norsk Hydro, A.S.A. (2008). "Annual Report Norwegian West Coast." Fisheries Research 67: 143–150.
Nottingham University. (2012). "Women Mean Business: Empowerment in Developing Markets." Business School and Corporate Citizenship.
Nurkse, Ragnar. (1953). "Problems of Capital Formation in Underdeveloped Regions." Oxford: Oxford University Press.

Nurkse, R. (1958). "Contribution to 'the Discussion of Professor Viner's Paper:' Stability and Progress in the World Economy." In D. Hague (Ed.), The First Congress of the International Economic Association (pp. 69–77). London: Macmillan.

Ohlin, Bertil. (1933). "Interregional and International Trade" (p. xvii). Cambridge: Harvard University Press.

Oomes, N., and Kalcheva, K. (2007). "Diagnosing Dutch Disease: Does Russia Have the Symptoms?" IMF Working Paper, 16–22.

Organisation for Economic Co-operation and Development (OECD). (2011). "Fostering Innovation to Address Social Challenges: WORKSHOP PROCEEDINGS."

Osmundsen, P. (2010). "Time Consistency in Petroleum Taxation: Lessons from Norway." In P. Daniel, M. Keen, and C. McPherson (Eds.), The Taxation of Petroleum and Minerals (pp. 425–444). Oxford, UK: Routledge.

Osmundsen, Peter, Emhjellen, Magne, Johnsen, Thore, Kemp, Alexander, and Riis, Christian. (2014). "Petroleum Taxation and Investment Behaviour." CESIFO Working Paper No. 5046.

Oyekunle, Seun. (2010). "Effect of Petroleum on Agricultural Development in Nigeria."

Page, J. (1994). "The East Asian Miracle: Four Lessons for Development Policy." National Bureau of Economic Research 9: 219–282.

Panagiotidis, Theodore, and Rutledge, Emile. (2007). "Oil and Gas Markets in the UK: Evidence from a Co-Integrating Approach." Energy Economics 29 (2007): 329–347.

Pantin, A. Dennis. (n.d.). "Wither Point Lisa: Lessons for the Future."

Pearson, H. Walter, Skalski, R. John, and Malme, I. Charles. (1992). "Effects of Sounds from a Geophysical Survey Device on Behaviour of Captive Rockfish (Sebates spp.)." Canadian Journal of Aquatic Science 49: 1343–1356.

Peneder, R. Michael. (2002). "Special Issue: Intangible Investment and Human Resources." Journal of Evolutionary Economics, Springer 12 (1): 107–134.

Penny, W.F., and Lonsdale-Harris, J. (1955). "A History of Trinidad Oil."

Perejoan, M.G., and Manera, M.P.G. (2006). "El español en Trinidad y Tobago. In Enciclopedia del español en el mundo: anuario del Instituto Cervantes 2006–2007" (pp. 209–211). Círculo de Lectores.

Pesaran, M.H., Shin, Y., and Smith, R.J. (2001). "Bounds Testing Approaches to the Analysis of Level Relationships." Journal of Applied Econometrics 16 (3): 289–326.

Peterson, L. David. (2004). "Seismic Survey Operations: Impact on Fish, Fisheries, Fishers and Aquaculture." British Columbia Seafood Alliance.

Petroleum Association of Trinidad. (1952). Trinidad's Oil an Illustrated Survey of the Oil Industry in Trinidad.

Petrotrin. (2013). "Down Memoy Lane: The Evolution of Petrotrin." Corporate Communications Department.

Pettinger, Tejvan. (2019). "Inflation and Exchange Rates." Economics Help. Accessed April 14, 2019. https://www.economicshelp.org/blog/1605/economics/higher-inflation-andexchange-rates/.

Potts, Arthur, Rocke, Judy, Maharaj, Ben, Ramnath, Shanta, and Doodnath, Lester. (2009). "Evaluating the Needs of the Fishing and Associated Livelihoods in the Coastal Fishing Sector of Trinidad and Tobago." Sciences 53: 2238–2249.

Prebisch, Raul. (1950). "The Economic Development of Latin America and Its Principal Problems." New York, USA: United Nation.

Radhu, G.M. (1970). "Transfer of Technical Know-How Through Multinational Corporation in Pakistan." Pakistan Development Review 12: 361–374.

Ramsaran, F. Ramesh. (1993). "Growth and Adjustment in a Petroleum Based Economy: Some Aspect of the Trinidad and Tobago Experience Since the 1970's." Social and Economic Studies 42 (4): 217–240.

Ratner, Michael, Parfomak, W. Paul, Luther, Linda, and Ferguson, Ian. (2015). "US Natural Gas Exports: New Opportunities, Uncertain Outcomes." Congressional Research Service, 42074.

Renwick, David. (2013). "What's Wrong with Petrotrin's Refinery Economics?" http://www.trinidadexpress.com/business-magazine.

Rocco, Matthew. (2013). "U.S. Shale Boom Drives Record Oil-Related Exports." Fox Business.

Rodrik, D. (2015). "Premature Deindustrialization." NBER Working Paper Series.

Roemer, Michael. (1977). "Resource-Based Industrialization in the Developing Countries: A Survey of the Literature." Development Discussion Paper No. 21, Harvard Institute of International Development, Cambridge.

Rose, S. (2014). "U.S. DOE Weekly Petroleum Status Report for Nov. 14." Bloomberg Business News.

Rosenstein-Rodan, Paul. (1943). "Problem Off Industrialization of Eastern and South-Eastern Europe." The Economic Journal 53 (210/211): 202–211.

Rosser, Andrew. (2006). "The Political Economy of the Resource Curse: A Literature Survey." Institute of Development Studies (IDS), Working Paper 268.

Rowthorn, E. Robert, and Wells, R. John. (1987). "De-Industrialisation and Foreign Trade." Cambridge: Cambridge University Press.

Rowthorn, Robert, and Ramaswamy, Ramana. (1999). "Growth, Trade, and Deindustrialization." IMF Staff Papers 46 (1): 18–41.

Rudnick, Hugh. (2008). "LNG in South America: The Markets, the Prices and the Security of Supply." 2008 IEEE Power and Energy Society General Meeting—Conversion and Delivery of Electrical Energy in the 21st Century.

Rudnick, Hugh, Barroso, Luiz, Cunha, G., and Mocarquer, Sebastian. (2014). "A Natural Fit: Electricity-Gas Integration Challenges in South America." IEEE Power and Energy Magazine 12 (6): 29–39.

Ryan, Selwyn. (2015). "Black Entrepreneurship in Post-Independence Trinidad and Tobago: The Eric Williams Legacy."

Rybczynski, T.M. (1955). "Factor Endowments and Relative Commodity Prices." Economica, New Series 22 (88): 336–341.

Sachs, Jeffery D., and Warner, Andrew M. (1995). "Natural Resource Abundance and Economic Growth." Cambridge, MA: NBER Working Paper Series, No. 5398.

Sachs, Jeffery D., and Warner, Andrew M. (1997). "Sources of Slow Growth in African Economies." Journal of African Economies 6 (3): 335–376.

Saeed, K.P., and Somaye, S. (2012). "Relationship Between Government Spending and Revenue: Evidence from Oil Exporting Countries." International Journal of Economics and Management Engineering (IJEME) 2 (2): 33–35.

Saeger, S. Steven. (1997). "Globalization and Deindustrialization: Myth and Reality in the OECD." Weltwirtschaftliches Archiv 133 (4): 579–608.

Sarel, M. (1996). "Growth in East Asia: What We Can and Cannot Infer." Economic Issues 1. International Monetary Fund.

Sargeant, Kelvin, and Forde, Penelope. (1992). "The State Sector and Divestment in Trinidad and Tobago: Some Preliminary Findings." Social and Economic Studies 41 (4): 173–204.

Schiff, Maurice. (2001). "Will the Real 'Natural Trading Partner' Please Stand Up?" Journal of Economic Integration 16 (2): 245–261.

Schultz, T. Paul. (2002). "Why Governments Should Invest More to Educate Girls." World Development 30 (2): 207–225.

Schumpeter, A. Joseph. (1911). "Theorie der wirtschaftlichen Entwicklung." Translated (1934). American Journal of Economics and Sociology 61 (2): 405–437, April 2002.

Schumpeter, A. Joseph. (1934). "The Theory of Economic Development: An Inquiry into Profits, Capital, Credit, Interest, and the Business Cycle." Harvard Economic Studies 46.

Schumpeter, A. Joseph. (1965). Economic Theory and Entrepreneurial History. In: Aitken HG (ed) Explorations in enterprise. Harvard University Press, Cambridge, MA.

Scottish Engineering Hall of Fame. Org, 2014.

Sears, Alexandra, and Ruta, Giovanni. (2007). "Adjusted Net Savings (ANS) as a Percentage of GNI." Contribution to Beyond GOP: Measuring Progress True Wealth and the Wellbeing of Nations. Washington, DC: World Bank.

Seers, Dudley. (1963). "The Limitations of the Special Case." Bulletin of the Institute of Economics and Statistics, May, 77–98.

Seers, Dudley. (1964). "The Economic and Social Revolution." Chapel Hill: University of North Carolina Press.

Sergeant, Kelvin, Racha, Sandra, and John, Michael. (2003). "The Petroleum Sector: The Case of Trinidad and Tobago: Trends, Policies and Impact 1985–2000." Santiago de Chile: Comisi6n Econ6mica para America Latina y el Caribe (CEPAL).

Sharma, Parmendra, and Gounder, Neeleesh. (2012). "Obstacles to Bank Financing of Micro and Small Enterprises: Emperical Evidence from the Pacific with Some Policy Implications." Asia-Pacific Development Journal 19 (2): 49–75.

Shepherd, R., and Ball, J. (2004). "Liquefied Natural Gas from Trinidad and Tobago: The Atlantic LNG Project." Geopolitics of Gas Working Paper Series.

Silvaa, Jill Marcelle-De, and Dawe, Richard, A. (2010). "The Challenge of Producing Thin Oil Rims in Trinidad." The West Indian Journal of Engineering 32 (1&2): 36–41.

Singer, H. (1950). "The Distribution of Gains Between Investing and Borrowing Countries." American Economic Review, Papers and Proceedings 40: 473–485.

Slotte, Aril, Hansen, Kaare, Dalen, John, and Ona, Egil. (2004). "Acoustic Mapping of Pelagic Fish Distribution and Abundance in Relation to a Seismic Shooting Area Off the Norwegian West Coast." Fisheries Research 67 (2004): 143–150.

Smith, Adam. (1776). "An Inquiry into the Nature and Causes of the Wealth of Nations." London: Methuen & Co Ltd.

Solow, M. Robert. (1974). "International Equity and Exhaustible Resources." Rev. Econ. Stud. Symposium, 29–46.

Spitzer, Marc. (2014). "Shale Revolution—Making US History." http://www.oilgasmonitor.com.

Stevens, Paul. (2012). "The Shale Gas Revolution: Developments and Changes." Energy, Environment and Resources, ERG BP 2012/04.

Stevens, Paul. (2013). "Shale Gas in the United Kingdom." Chatham House.

Stopford, John. (1998). "Multinational Corporations: Foreign Policy." London Business School, Foreign Policy, Winter 1998 i113 p12 (1).

Strauss, John, and Thomas, Duncan. (1995). "Human Resources: Empirical Modeling of Household and Family Decisions." Handbook of Development Economics.

Syrquin, Moises. (1994). "Structural Transformation and the New Growth Theory." In L. Pasinetti and R.M. Solow (Eds.), Economic Growth and the Structure of Long-Term Development. St. Martin Press.

T&T Chamber of Industry and Commerce. (2006). "Randolph Rust a Man of Unfaltering Faith." Trinidad Guardian Newspaper.

Tewarie, B., and Hosein, R. (2007). "Trade Investment and Development in the Contemporary Caribbean." Ian Randle.

Treaster, Joseph B. (1985). "Trinidad to Keep the Refinery Going." www.nytimes.com.

The Energy Chamber of Trinidad and Tobago. (2019). Retrieved from https://energynow.tt/blog/a-future-for-oil-in-tampt.

The Ministry of Energy and Energy Affairs Trinidad and Tobago. (2010). "The Experience of Trinidad and Tobago in LNG." Regional Integration Forum.

The Ministry of Energy and Energy Affairs Trinidad and Tobago. (1992). The Draft Energy Policy August Volume 2.

The New York Times. (1971, January 28). Desulphurization Unit Set.

The Political Economy of Natural Resource Rich Rentier States: The Case of Oil and Gas Rich Trinidad and Tobago. In S. Lalta and M. Freckleton (Eds.), Caribbean Economics: The First Generation. ISER, UWI (pp. 245–261), 1993.

The World Bank. (2014). "Microfinance, and Financial Inclusion." The World Bank.

Thomas, C.Y. (1965). "Monetary and Financial Arrangements in a Dependent Monetary Economy." Mona: ISER.

Throupe, Ron, Simons, Robert, and Mao, Xue. (2013). "A Review of Hydro 'Fracking' and Its Potential Effects on Real Estate." Journal of Real Estate Literature 21 (2): 205–232.

Timmer, P. Marcel, and Adam, Szirmar. (1997). "Growth and Divergence in Manufacturing Performance in South and East Asia." Papers 37, Groningen State, Institute of Economic Research.

Toal, Robin. (2013). "An Introduction to Micro-Finance." http://www.fundsforngos.org.

Toda, H.Y., and Yamamoto, T. (1995). "Statistical Inference in Vector Autoregressions with Possibly Integrated Processes." Journal of Econometrics 66: 225–250.

Torvik, R. (2002). "Natural Resources, Rent Seeking and Welfare." Journal of Development Economics 67 (2): 455–470.

Trinidad and Tobago Extractive Industries Transparency Initiative (TTEITI). (2013). Report 2011. http://www.tteiti.org.tt/.

Trinidad Express. (2013). "Fuad: We Need More Health-Care Specialists, T&T Signs Memorandum of Understanding with UK." http://www.trinidadexpress.com.

Trinidad Guardian Newspaper. (2006). Scouting, Cadets and Boys Brigade.

Turnpenny, W.H. Andrew, and Nedwell, R. Jeremy. (1994). "The Effects on Marine Fish, Diving Mammals and Birds of Underwater Sounds Generated by Seismic Surveys." Fawley Aquatic Research Laboratories Ltd.

United Nations Conference on Trade and Development (UNCTAD). (2012a). "Trade Income Distribution and Poverty in Developing Countries: A Survey." United Nations, Discussion Paper, No. 207.

United Nations Conference on Trade and Development (UNCTAD). (2012b). "Trade, Income Distribution and Poverty in Developing Countries: A Survey." Discussion Papers, No. 27.

United Nations Development Programme (UNDP). (2012a). "2012 Democratic Governance Group Annual Report." New York.

United Nations Development Programme (UNDP). (2012b). "The Caribbean Human Development Report." New York.

United Nations Population Fund (UNFPA). (2010). "Empowering Women." New York: UNFPA.

US Energy Information Administration (EIA). (2013). "Annual Energy Outlook with Projections for 2040." DOE/EIA-0383(2013).

Vakfi, Sabancı. (2009). "Sabanci Foundation Grant Program Projects Share Success Stories." Sabanci Foundation Grant Program Projects.

Van der Ploeg, Frederick, and Poelhekke, Steven. (2009). "Volatility and the Natural Resource Curse." Oxford Economic Papers 61: 727–760. https://doi.org/10.1093/oep/gpp027.

Van der Ploeg, Jan Douwe. (2008). "The New Peasantries: Struggles for Autonomy and Sustainability in an Era of Empire and Globalization." London, Sterling, Earthscan.

Vernon, Raymond. (1966). "International Investment and International Trade in the Product Cycle." Copyright, 1966, by the President and Fellows of Harvard College.

Villar, A. Jose, and Joutz, L. Frederick. (2007). "The Relationship Between Crude Oil and Natural Gas Prices." Energy Information Administration, Office of Oil and Gas.

Walker, J., and Howard, S. (2002). "Voluntary Codes of Conduct in the Mining Industry." Mining, Minerals and Sustainable Development Project (MMSD), IIED.

Wang, Zhongmin, and Krupnick, Alan. (2013). "A Retrospective Review of Shale Gas Development in the United States." Resources for the Future, Discussion Papers: RFF DP, 13–12.

Ward, Bernie, and Strongman, John. (2011). "Gender-Sensitive Approaches for the Extractive Industry in Peru: Improving the Impact on Women in Poverty and Their Families." Washington, DC: The World Bank.

Watkins, H. Melville. (1963). "A Staple Theory of Economic Growth." Canadian Journal of Economics and Political Science 29: 141–158.

Wiig, Arne, and Ramalho, Madalena. (2015). "Corporate Social Responsibility in the Angolan Oil Industry." CMI Working Paper.

Williams, Elizabeth. (2015). "BHP Responds to Fisherfolk." http://www.thetobagonews.com/.

Wilson, S.-A., and Mclean, E. (2014), "Understanding the Impact of exchange rate adjustment on the trade balance of selected Caribbean countries", (Working Paper Series).

Woodward, Katie. (2014). "Brazil Seeks More LNG During Drought." EIA Natural Gas Weekly Update.

World Bank. (1997). "Gender Issues in Participation." Michael Bamberger and Mark Blackden, 1997.

World Bank. (2001). "Engendering Development: Through Gender Equality in Rights, Resources, and Voice." New York: Oxford University Press.

World Bank. (2005). "Azerbaijan Issues and Options Associated with Energy Sector Reform." Washington, DC.

Wright, Gavin, and Czelusta, Jesse. (2004). "The Myth of the Resource Curse." Challenge 47 (2): 6–38.

Wright, G., and Czelusta, J. (2004). "Why Economies Slow: The Myth of the Resource Curse." Challenge 47 (2): 6–38.

Young, Allyn. (1928). "Increasing Returns and Economic Progress." The Economic Journal 38: 527–542.

Index

R. Hosein, *Oil and Gas in Trinidad and Tobago*,
https://doi.org/10.1007/978-3-030-77669-5